P9-AAY-785

UNDER CONSTRUCTION

THE ROLE OF
THE ARTS AND
HUMANITIES IN
POSTMODERN
SCHOOLING

edited by
Donovan R. Walling

Phi Delta Kappa Educational Foundation
Bloomington, Indiana
U.S.A.

Cover design by
Victoria Voelker

Cover photograph by
Vladimir Bektesh

Phi Delta Kappa Educational Foundation
408 North Union Street
Post Office Box 789
Bloomington, Indiana 47402-0789
U.S.A.

Printed in the United States of America

Library of Congress Catalog Card Number 97-67351
ISBN 0-87367-498-7

TABLE OF CONTENTS

PART I:
Laying the Foundation

PART II:
Raising the Roof Beams

INTRODUCTION

Perhaps not since the Renaissance in Italy in the 14th century has there been more interest in renewing a society's general acquaintance with and appreciation of the arts and humanities as vital to life, education, and the conduct of human affairs. But the impetus for renewal is not unchallenged.

While the National Education Goals, contained in the Goals 2000 legislation of 1994, include the arts, and national standards for the arts have been promulgated by various representative organizations, there still is resistance to placing the arts and humanities at the instructional core of general education. In the months prior to publication of this volume, for example, various state legislatures — among them Indiana and Kansas — were wrestling with whether to include the arts in basic funding formulas for the public schools. The initial resolution before the Kansas legislature specified that certain subjects (such as language arts, science, and history) are "essential to a quality basic education" but referred to the arts as "extracurricular and not necessary to a quality basic education" (Manzo 1997, p. 17). Strong protest from arts educators resulted in this language being changed, but the battle to set the arts rightfully at the core of basic education is far from over.

That education reform which omits the arts is fundamentally wrong-headed seems obvious. Maxine Greene, professor emeritus of philosophy and education at Teachers College, Columbia University, recently wrote:

> Personal agency, passion, imagination, and a making of meaning: All of these must be part of full engagement with the arts; and it is difficult to accept a call for excellent teaching and "teaching for America's future" that pays no heed to the awakenings the arts make possible, the breaking of what Virginia Woolf called the "cotton wool of daily life." (1997, p. 33)

1

The writers of the 12 essays in this volume take up Greene's notion of "awakenings the arts make possible" in a variety of critical looks at the arts and humanities and their role in postmodern schooling — that is, the education of children and adolescents in a world in which postmodernist assumptions of variety, diversity, and multiplicity have superseded the modernist assumptions of unity, universality, and homogeneity.

In Part I, Laying the Foundation, David Elkind writes that in "the postmodern world we have come to appreciate difference as well as progress, particularity as well as universality, and irregularity as well as regularity." These concepts undergird much of the writing in this volume. However, Michael Schmoker tackles some of the problems of vagueness and contradiction in the definition of postmodernism, suggesting that postmodernism may be more accurately characterized by a continuum of definitions that holds both benefits and dangers for education, not only in the arts and humanities but in schooling generally.

Eric Oddleifson addresses himself to the role of the arts in educating all students and suggests that finding creative power within themselves allows individuals to control their lives and shape their destinies. Furthermore, business and education alike can benefit from an arts education renaissance in which perceptive reason is informed by the aesthetic.

Julia Balaisis views arts education as a means of helping students to discover the magical in the mundane. Arts education reconnects us to our world and connects individuals in the collective human endeavors of living. In a similar vein, but expressed quite differently, D.C. Bradburd focuses on the idea of humanity and the discovery of the unexpected through art that transcends deconstruction and critique. And, in the last essay of this section, Russell Osguthorpe writes of the power of the arts to edify, which he defines as "to build up the soul."

Part II, Raising the Roof Beams, enlarges the theme of this volume by moving toward more particular experiences and frames of reference. Stephanie Perrin bases her essay on observing her students at Walnut Hill School and notes that education for all students must mirror the characteristics of a solid arts education, wherein young artists are kept in motion by respect, love, high expectations, safe boundaries, and faith in the future. She speaks of students' passion for learning that "keeps them up at night hanging lights in the trees and dancing in the dark."

George Demetrion approaches a specific of postmodernist experience in developing adult literacy. He addresses adult literacy issues by critiquing Forrest Chrisman's structural-functional vision and Paulo Freire's radical, critical pedagogy to arrive at a Deweyan middle ground, in which the growth of literacy is, in itself, *art* — or to use John Dewey's word, the "consummation" of lived experience.

Christine Morris and Iris Striedieck take a case-study look at elementary teacher education from the vantage point of postmodern feminist theory. Their mingled and separate voices convey the case for cultural pedagogy in "creating a holistic perspective of knowing in the context of an elementary arts methods course." Morris and Striedieck's pedagogical stance is followed by my own essay, in which I explore how humanities teaching might be reshaped to better address the contexts, needs, and interests of students who come to school from postmodern, "permeable" families.

In separate essays Raymond Pettit and Todd Siler bring this collection to a close. Pettit addresses the paradox of finding the aesthetic through the utilitarian and the practical through the artistic, thereby creating an arts and humanities curricular approach capable "of meeting the complex, multifaceted demands of the postmodern society." Siler goes a step further and suggests that postmodern education "must help us learn to see and understand ourselves. This involves seeing our knowledge from many perspectives, using it in many contexts, and sharing what we have learned." Siler shares an exercise from his ArtScience workshop that encourages readers to design the ideal learning environment by giving visual form to their ideas.

My hope in drawing together this diverse collection of essays is, first, to shed light on emerging issues in the education dialogue on

3

the arts and humanities and their place in schooling and, second, to stimulate further thought about the contexts and characteristics of postmodernism and how they may be understood in the shaping of basic school curricula. In so doing, I would echo Maxine Greene's argument with school reformers and their "all-too-familiar dismissal of the arts, as if they are frills, as if they do not matter, as if they were not central to our understanding of the culture and of ourselves." Indeed, the arts and humanities *are* central to our culture, to our society, to our democracy, and to ourselves. The writers of these essays demonstrate this understanding.

References

Greene, Maxine. "Why Ignore the Forms of Art?" *Education Week*, 19 February 1997, p. 33.

Manzo, Kathleen Kennedy. "Art Educators' Protest Prompts Rewrite of Kan. Measure," *Education Week*, 26 March 1997, p. 17.

PART I

Laying the Foundation

The Arts and Humanities in Postmodern Education

BY DAVID ELKIND

David Elkind is a professor of child development at Tufts University in Medford, Massachusetts.

Since the founding of the Republic, instruction in the arts and humanities has been a matter of ongoing controversy. Disagreements about the value of such instruction have centered on political, moral, and economic issues. The substance of these debates did not change, in any significant way, for more than a century and a half. However, during the last five decades we have been moving into a new, *postmodern* era that has transformed, or greatly modified, these three debates regarding the place of the arts and humanities in American education. Moreover, the arts and humanities have themselves undergone a comparable transmutation.

It seems timely, therefore, to revisit these controversies to arrive at a current version of the opposing arguments. Otherwise, we may continue to fight battles that already have been won or lost or that are no longer relevant. Accordingly, in this essay I will provide a brief historical review of the three conflicts over the arts and humanities that continued until about mid-century and then detail some of the postmodern changes that have significantly altered the bases of contention. Finally, I will offer an assessment of the place of the arts and humanities in the postmodern curriculum.

Modernist Controversies
Over the Arts and the Humanities

The Political Controversy. One point of contention regarding the value of a classical education was between those who professed aristocratic values and those who held to democratic political values. Americans who retained an aristocratic orientation argued for the elevating value of a classical education. Those of a democratic bent, in contrast, regarded such an education as elitist. A classical education was undemocratic in that it was a form of "high culture" available only to the children of wealthy families. Thus many Americans saw instruction in the arts and humanities as a nefarious way of perpetuating distinctions of birth and wealth that were ingrained in European societies.

Indeed, Europeans believed that the leisure enjoyed by the upper classes was essential for humankind to attain, and to maintain, the highest levels of intellectual and artistic potential. In his description of America in 1840 de Tocqueville, for example, attributed the lack of artistic and scientific creativity in America to its egalitarian ethos:

> It must be acknowledged that in few of the civilized nations of our time have the higher sciences made less progress than in the United States and in few, have great artists, distinguished poets or celebrated writers been more rare. Many Europeans struck by this fact, have looked upon it as a natural and inevitable result of equality and they have thought that if democratic institutions were ever to prevail over the whole earth, the human mind would gradually find its beacon light grows dim, and men would relapse into a period of darkness. (de Tocqueville 1840/1972, p. 30)

Nonetheless, while America had no explicit class structure, the distinction between "high" culture for the few and "low" culture for the many existed in the United States as it did in Europe. Before the Revolution, children of wealthy plantation owners in the South were sent to England for schooling, where they were given the classical, high-culture education. In the New England colonies, on the other hand, common schools were set up to teach the basics to the children of the community. Ironically, Harvard College, established in 1635, eventually was reserved for the children of the wealthy, though it was funded by John Harvard, a butcher by trade.

After the Revolution and the installation of a democratic government, classical education continued to be available for the offspring of wealthy families. However, not all children of wealth were able to acquire an acquaintance with the arts and humanities. A classical education was regarded as unnecessary and wasteful for young women. It was thought to be of value only for boys and young men. This situation persisted well into the 19th century. The wife of President John Adams, who was born in 1744 and who came from a family of solid social standing and reasonable wealth, wrote in 1817:

> My early education did not partake of the abundant opportunities which the present day afford. I never was sent to any school. I was always sick. Female education, in the best families, went no further than writing and arithmetic; in some few rare instances, music and dancing. (Earle 1993, pp. 91-92)

For children whose parents were of only modest means (the vast majority), education was limited to the Three R's and some practical training.

When universal free public education for the entire nation was instituted in the fourth decade of the 19th century, the *de facto* class distinction between classical and practical education was maintained. Public education was established primarily to attain democratic goals. As Thomas Jefferson wrote, "If a nation expects to be ignorant and free, in a state of civilization, it expects what never was and never will be" (Quoted in Cremin 1988, p. 154). But the aristocratic tradition persisted, as indicated by the following contrast between the home-grown, and variously supported, academies as opposed to the traditional Latin grammar schools:

In keeping with our developing democracy and expanding industrial and commercial life, the academy offered instruction in such a variety of subjects that there were few, if any, whose interests and needs it did not serve. In the variety of its offerings, the academy stands in marked contrast with the Latin Grammar school, which catered to the aristocratic few who were preparing themselves for college rather than for life. (Horace Mann, quoted in Mulhern 1946, p. 240)

Ironically, the academies themselves became increasingly accused of being reserved for the privileged few. By the end of the 19th century the public school had all but replaced this educational forerunner of many of today's charter schools.

During the 19th century, public elementary schools and the academies had a practical orientation and did not emphasize the arts and humanities. Parents committed to the latter type of instruction sent their children either to private schools or for private music, painting, or dance lessons. This perpetuated the *de facto* class division and the restriction of exposure to "high culture" to the relatively small proportion of young people whose parents could afford it.

However, such parents often were ridiculed by those who had little use for the liberal arts. The following satirical poem gives evidence of the attitude of many Americans to those parents who had aristocratic aspirations for their children:

I Have Brought My Daughter to You to Be Taught Everything

Dear Madam, I've called for the purpose
    Of placing my daughter at school
She's only thirteen, I assure you
    and remarkably easy to rule.
I'd have her learn painting and music,
    gymnastics and dancing pray do,
Philosophy, grammar and logic,
    You'll teach her to read of course too.

I wish her to learn every study
    Mathematics are down on my plan,
But of figures she scarce has an inkling
    Please instruct her in those if you can
I'd have her taught Spanish and Latin,
    Including the language of France;
Never mind her very bad English
    Teach her that when you find a good chance.
On the harp she must be proficient
    And play the guitar pretty soon
And sing the last opera music
    Even though she can't turn a right tune.
You must see that her manners are finished,
    That she moves with a svelte-like grace,
For though she is lame and one sided,
    That's nothing to do with the case.
Now to you I resign this young jewel,
    And my words I would have you obey
In six months return her, dear Madam
    Shining bright as an unclouded day,
She's no aptness, I grant you for learning
    And her memory oft seems to halt
But remember if she's not accomplished
    It will certainly be your fault.
            (*Godey's Lady's Book*, 1853, p. 457)

This poem highlights the ongoing desire of some parents to have their children display the symbols of "high culture" long associated with the European aristocratic life style.

The Moral Controversy. The second dispute over the arts and humanities in the public schools can be traced to the separation of church and state set forth in the U.S. Constitution. In a democracy, with many different religions, it was essential that no particular group exercise political power over the others. When it was decided to enact legislation for universal, free public schooling, similar arguments pertained. Our early political leaders were intent both on avoiding theological arguments and on promoting unity among the American people. Horace Mann, regarded as the father of free public education in the United States, was against having the matter settled at the local level. He wrote:

> This year the fires of everlasting hell will burn to terrify the impenitent; next year and without any repentance, its eternal flames will be extinguished, to be rekindled forever, or to be quenched forever as it may be decided at town meetings. (quoted in Mulhern 1946, p. 480)

After much public debate, a free public school system was established in the 1830s that was, for most practical purposes, secular.

For many religious groups, this was not a happy outcome. In response, a variety of private, parochial school networks were established that offered, and continue to offer, parents the option of religious education for their children — if the parents can afford it. There was and continues to be considerable unhappiness with how this school system is funded. To many parents it seems unfair to be required to pay taxes to support the public schools for other children while, at the same time, bearing the cost of the private education they desire for their own children. Not surprisingly, there was and is continuing pressure for the state to help support parochial schools.

The moral conflict surrounding the curriculum, however, centers not on government's efforts to keep religion outside the schools, but rather on the efforts of religious groups to regulate what is taught within the curriculum. While such groups' efforts have been a perpetual undercurrent, they were redoubled after the Darwinian revolution. Darwin's demotion of humankind to but another animal species challenged the biblical account of Genesis and its description of the creation of plants, animals, and humans. For many religious groups, the Bible is the revealed, literal word of God. It must be true, and Darwin therefore is just plain wrong. Some religious groups oppose the teaching of evolution in the public schools to this day.

Although there was a clear separation between church and state during the 19th and early 20th centuries, the strong religious sentiment of modern American society was nonetheless reflected in the public schools. For many young people of the 19th century, the Bible was the only book they knew. Thanks to daily Bible readings, most youngsters had been through it at least a dozen times before they reached adolescence. In communities where the religious ethos was very strong, the humanities that were taught were carefully screened, and the history books were written with moral lessons in mind:

> History sets before us striking instances of virtue, enterprise, courage, generosity, patriotism, and by a natural principle of emulation, incites us to copy such noble examples. History also presents us with the pictures of vicious, ultimately overtaken by misery and shame, and thus solemnly warns us against vice. (Goodrich 1833, p. xii)

Thus in some public schools, the humanities that were taught were not introduced for their intellectual benefits, but rather for the moral values they imparted. This reflected the ongoing argument between religious groups and educators over the contents of a liberal arts curriculum.

The Practicality Controversy. The third controversy regarding the arts and humanities centered on the issue of practicality. The Pilgrims and other early settlers arrived at a wilderness. The new Americans had to build their farms, their houses, their cities, and their towns from scratch. Unlike Europeans, they did not come into a world where they were surrounded by buildings and art erected and created centuries before they were born. Perhaps because Americans did not grow up surrounded by history, they did not immediately develop the passion for it that was, and is, true for many Europeans.

Another circumstance also made American society different from European society and created a negative attitude toward classical education. This country was established at the start of the machine age. From America's earliest beginnings, unlike European societies with roots dating back to Roman and medieval times, American modern culture was built on the basic tenets of industrialization. These were the values of efficiency and functionality. From this perspective, machine-made goods often were seen as "better" than handmade. Goods made by individual craftspersons were seen as uneconomic, and this became translated into many Americans' attitudes toward the arts.

A concrete example of how the translation of these values into the artistic domain can be seen in some of the portrait painting from New England. To facilitate the process of portraiture — in other words, to make it more efficient and less costly — the artist pre-painted the bodies of the family members. When the artist then sought out the family for a portrait sitting, all he needed to do was to paint their heads atop the pre-painted bodies. (I imagine this was not unlike posing for a photograph behind a painted clown or animal body at a fair.) Such an approach to portraiture was unheard of in Europe, where such a technique surely was looked on as artistically barbaric.

The American practical, no-nonsense attitude toward the arts and humanities was determined both by the early nation's frontier mentality and by the acceptance of the values of the machine age as a cultural norm. In the absence of a history of their own and without a childhood surrounded by the culture of antiquity, Americans of the 19th century lacked the affinity for the humanities that came naturally to Europeans. Likewise, the machine-age mentality and a national value for machine efficiency and functionality provided little basis for the appreciation of the decorative arts or for handcrafted products.

Although not all Americans shared these sentiments, these general values determined a national attitude toward a classical education. What purpose did it serve for children to learn Greek or Latin or to study the writers of antiquity. Students' time could be better spent learning the knowledge and skills they could put to use in everyday life. From a functional and practical point of view, the decorative arts seemed to have little value. So, while there were a few Latin schools in the United States and some parents continued to value European art and architecture, that cultural orientation became a minority view.

This is not to say that Americans during the modern era had no appreciation for the aesthetic. They did. But it was a different aesthetic than the European. This is where de Tocqueville made his error. He missed seeing how, in a variety of different domains, Americans were combining form and function in aesthetically pleasing ways. From the design of clipper ships and steam locomotives to the clapboard walls of buildings, a simple vernacular art form emerged that exemplified the incorporation of aesthetically pleasing forms that also were highly functional and efficient (Kouwenhoven 1948/1967). To be sure, the European influence also was very strong and appeared in many American buildings, including homes. But the American vernacular eventually dominated, and that is why American cities look so different from those seen in the British Isles or on the European continent.

This modernist American wedding of form and function is perhaps best illustrated by the work of those belonging to the religious group called Shakers. The Shakers lived, for the most part, in communes in and near New England. They hand-built all of their own buildings and furniture and designed and sewed their own clothing and grew all of their own food. Because they believed in celibacy and their communities grew only through conversion, eventually fewer and fewer converts joined the communes. Today, the Shaker communes are merely historical shells. However, the Shaker standards — products and buildings that are simple, unadorned, and completely functional — are held as exemplars, praised for their workmanship and classic beauty (Kouwenhoven 1948/1967).

In summary, the political, moral, and practical controversies surrounding the arts and humanities in modern America are the result of a unique American culture in conflict with that of its European heritage. It is because many Americans regarded a classical education as elitist, as immoral and impractical, that the arts and humanities have not enjoyed a high priority in American schools. This low priority explains why the arts and humanities have been poorly supported and why they are the first subjects to be cut when school budgets are reduced. Unfortunately, these same attitudes have also blinded many Americans — including educators — to the richness of a unique American vernacular culture.

The Arts and Humanities in the Postmodern Period

This century has been witness to events that have changed Americans' fundamental assumptions — and here I must include myself — about ourselves and our world. The modernists' reality was based on beliefs in progress, universality, and regularity. Two world wars, the Holocaust, the atomic bomb, depletion of many natural resources, and degradation of the environment have forced us to reconsider our belief in social progress. In the same way, we now recognize that there are far fewer, if any, universals in the social sciences than in the physical sciences. As Michel Foucault (1973) has so powerfully argued, we can study only individuals, not human nature. The grand (universal) theories of Carl Marx and Friedrich Engels, of Max Weber and Sigmund Freud, now are recognized as products of men working in particular cultures and within specific linguistic discourses. Finally, we recognize today that the world is not entirely lawful. Some phenomena, such as weather, are inherently irregular or chaotic.

Therefore, in the postmodern world we have come to appreciate difference as well as progress, particularity as well as universality, and irregularity as well as regularity. These new postmodern ideas have been felt in the sciences, government, industry, and the arts and architecture. Postmodern changes in the family already have significantly altered the functions of our schools (Elkind 1995) and some of bases of the modern debates over the arts and humanities in the curriculum.

The Political Controversy. In the postmodern world, the cultural landscape has changed dramatically. After two world wars — both begun in Europe — the Holocaust, and, for example, contin-

16

uing barbarism in the Balkans, the arts and humanities of Europe no longer can be held up as an educational path to helping humans achieve their highest potentials. While European culture has not been entirely discredited in this century, it now is the culture of the United States that is widely emulated by other societies. Our science is second to none. A much acclaimed art movement, abstract impressionism, originated in the United States. Our motion pictures and jazz and country-western music are popular all over the world. Alexis de Tocqueville and his aristocratic compatriots could not have been more wrong about the egalitarian ethos aborting the higher mental powers and artistic talents. If anything, American science and liberal arts have flourished because of our democratic values, not in spite of them.

The old modern argument that the arts and humanities are aristocratic can hardly be maintained against the evidence of their flowering in a democratic society. However, a new postmodern disagreement has emerged to replace the old. This controversy still is political. But it is not between those who argue for the merits of aristocracy and those who value democracy. Rather, it is between those who wish to define the arts and humanities in a narrow sense and those who wish to define them more broadly. In his book, *The Closing of the American Mind* (1987), Allan Bloom made a case for teaching the arts and humanities in the narrow sense with an emphasis on "the classics." He took the traditional view that training in the classics was a civilizing influence and that, in the absence of this training, students were descending to a lower moral plane.

On the other side of this controversy are those who argue that the arts and humanities should be expanded beyond the work of "dead white men." A postmodern classics curriculum should include the arts, literature, and scientific achievements of women and people of color from around the world. It should provide the history of ideas, as well as of wars, exploration, and conquests; and it should give honest renderings of the rights and struggles of native peoples. In our postmodern world the political issue regarding the arts and humanities in education is no longer one of democracy versus aristocracy but, rather, one of insularity versus multiculturalism.

Religious as Opposed to Scientific Values. In our postmodern world Americans have, as a society, become more secular. Daily Bible reading and regular church attendance are much less common today than they were a half-century ago. However, a strong Religious Right has emerged as a significant force today. As a consequence, the modern conflict between conservative religious values and liberal scientific ones continues unabated. Conservative religious groups today, as in the earlier modern era, object to certain literature in the curriculum. They also are opposed to curriculum movements, such as outcome-based instruction, and government-sponsored education initiatives, such as Goals 2000. Conservative religious groups also contend that some humanities curricula promote "secular humanism" (the advocacy of human rather than religious values) and should be outlawed.

In the case of the conflict between conservative religious values and liberal scientific values, the postmodern era has seen, if anything, a widening of the battlefield. The growing home-schooling movement among religious conservative families is but one sign of their unhappiness with public school curricula. Although many of the actions of the Religious Right are well-intended and reflect a genuine concern for the health and well-being of children, their attacks against the schools are misdirected. Of all the social institutions affecting children and youth, schools are, by and large, the most conservative and the least corrupting.

Unfortunately, in our postmodern world other social institutions wield much more influence over children and youth than do the schools. Advertising and messages about morals, sexuality, violence, and crime that come from television, films, compact discs, and audiotapes have a much greater effect on children than do the most "immoral" school curricula. Perhaps it is precisely because today's parents feel impotent in the face of these powerful societal influences in the popular media that they continue to rail against the schools. Perhaps they feel that at least with the schools they can have some impact. As a result, the old battles between the religious conservatives and the liberal scientific educators continue while the real moral influences on children and youth go relatively unaddressed.

The Controversy over Practicality. Americans of the postmodern era look at a world quite different from the one seen by our forefathers. There is no longer a domestic frontier, and many of our cities and towns have been inhabited continuously for more than two centuries. We now have a history as well as a culture of our own. We also have a greater appreciation of the arts and humanities than did our forefathers. Yet we also maintain the practical values acquired during the settling of the country and our emergence as a nation in concert with the machine age. This combination of emerging history and culture with national attitudes toward efficiency and functionality has altered the controversy over the practicality of the arts and humanities of which I wrote earlier.

What is sometimes ignored in the controversy over the value of a humanities education is that there are now American humanities in addition to classical ones and that these American humanities are taught primarily for utilitarian purposes. Consider, for example, the teaching of American history and American literature. Today these courses of study are part of the required curriculum. We regard them as essential not because of their civilizing effect, but rather because we believe they are necessary to create a responsible, knowledgeable citizenry. In contrast to the humanities of the traditional classics education, postmodern American humanities have a practical, utilitarian rationale.

Despite the growing recognition of American contributions to the world of the arts, American arts have not fared as well in the postmodern period as have the American humanities. In our schools today, the arts are still looked on as frills — the first to be cut if budgets get tight. We still do not see any practical value in educating our children in the arts. To a large extent, it is left for parents to see to this education on their own — and at their own expense. Postmodernism seems to have made few inroads on these entrenched values regarding the impracticality of the arts. And that is too bad.

For now we Americans are surrounded by visual arts in much the same way that the Europeans are. But these visual arts are the vernacular art of America that is present in the *design* of everyday things. Our homes, automobiles, boats, airplanes, washers and dryers, and even our pens and pencils are examples of the coordination of form and function — that is, having aesthetic value as well as a practical function. In the postmodern world, such everyday objects become art to be studied.

The Future of the Arts and Humanities in Education

The arts and humanities in the postmodern era are much different from the arts and humanities of the modern era, and yet much also remains the same. We Americans are no longer a frontier society; and we now have our own history, literature, art, and architecture. This has changed the political argument over the value of the arts and humanities. The moral arguments over the curriculum continue, though they pale in comparison to the "extracurricular" influences on children and youth, such as the popular media. Finally, while we Americans have developed our own arts that blend form and function in aesthetically pleasing ways, we still have yet to fully appreciate our own achievements. Many Americans still see the arts as impractical, a luxury.

Is there any hope that the arts might become a more integral part of our postmodern curriculum? I believe that there is, but only if we begin to look at the arts from a somewhat different perspective than we have in the past. Following the European tradition, instruction in the arts remains primarily a matter of art *appreciation*. However, the idea of appreciation suggests that we who appreciate are passive, while the artist is active. We are, in effect, spectators and must enjoy the arts much as we enjoy other spectator activities, such as sports. This conception of art as a spectator activity, engaged in only for amusement, has added to the low priority accorded the arts in education.

However, we are beginning to understand that there is no such thing as a passive spectator. Jean Piaget (1950), for example, gave us abundant evidence to the fact that a child constructs and reconstructs reality out of his or her experiences with the environment — even as a spectator. A painting, a musical performance, a novel — all are pieces of reality. From this perspective comes the belief that we never simply look at a painting or listen to a piece of music or read a novel; rather, in the process of experiencing it, we construct its meaning and its place in the contexts of our lives. My subjective experience of the painting or the piece of music or the novel is not the same as anyone else's. Indeed, Jacques Derrida (1981) argues that to read a novel is to rewrite it. Thus the postmodernist view is that art appreciation is an active process of reconstruction, not a passive process of registration.

Even if we accept the active role of the learner in the appreciation of the arts, this does not deal with the issue of the practicality of this reconstruction. However, there is another way of looking at the arts. Dewey (1938) suggested it long ago when he wrote that "learning is the reconstruction of experience" (p. 87). By this Dewey meant that experience in of itself does not teach; it is only when we represent our experience to ourselves and to others that we really know it. That is why teaching is the most powerful form of learning; it forces us to reconstruct and represent our experience in a meaningful way to others.

It seems to me that we have not employed the arts as a means of representing experience and learning. If children read a story, they also can illustrate it. This is a form of representation. Math facts and multiplication tables can be sung to a rhythm that facilitates learning. Children learning to read can use their bodies to make the shapes of letters. To be sure, this is not the usual sense in which we speak of the arts. But if we employ drawing, painting, dancing, clay modeling, and singing as ways of representing experience, students also will gain a deeper and fuller appreciation of the arts.

If children have used drawing, painting, or music to express their experiences, these acts will enable them to better appreciate how a painter or musician has used that medium to express his or her reality. True art appreciation means that the recipient has some idea of what the artist is trying to convey through the particular medium that he or she uses. If children are accustomed to representing their experiences in this way, then they also will gain a better understanding of what the artist is attempting. In the arts, therefore, appreciation can be incorporated as a mode of learning in every classroom.

In conclusion, while some of the modern controversies over the arts and humanities in the curriculum have changed as a consequence of the maturing of our society and because of the social changes that have been called *postmodernism*, others have not. The political controversy over the civilizing value of the arts and humanities has become one over the narrow and the broad conceptions of these disciplines. Religious objections to the arts and humanities curricula continue unabated but appear misdirected in view of the vulgarity and violence of the media. Finally, the arts still are considered impractical despite the unique American union of form and function, of the aesthetic with the practical.

One way of making the arts a more integral part of the curriculum is to use them as modes of learning, as tools for representing experience. If children use the arts in this way, such use not only will facilitate student learning, but it also will give students a fuller and deeper understanding of the meaning and value of the arts.

References

Bloom. A. *The Closing of the American Mind.* New York: Simon and Schuster, 1987.

Cremin, L.A. *American Education: The Metropolitan Experience.* New York: Harper & Row, 1988.

Derrida, J. *Dissemination.* Chicago: University of Chicago Press, 1981.

Dewey, J. *Experience in Education.* New York: Macmillan, 1938.

Earle, A.M. *Child Life in Colonial Days.* Stockbridge, Mass.: Berkshire House, 1993.

Elkind, D. "School and Family in the Postmodern World." *Phi Delta Kappan* 77 (September 1995): 8-14.

Foucault, M. *The Order of Things.* New York: Vintage, 1973.

Goodrich, C. *A History of the United States.* Hartford, Conn.: Monroe, 1833.

"I Have Brought My Daughter to You to Be Taught Everything." *Godey's Lady's Book* (May 1853): 457.

Kouwenhoven, J.A. *The Arts in Modern American Civilization.* 1948. Reprint. New York: Norton, 1967. Originally published as *Made in America.*

Mulhern, J. *A History of Education.* New York: Ronald Press, 1946.

Piaget, J. *Psychology of Intelligence.* London: Routledge & Kegan Paul, 1950.

de Tocqueville, A. *Democracy in America.* 1840. Reprint. New York: Alfred A. Knopf, 1972.

Contradictions and Consequences in Postmodernism

BY MICHAEL J. SCHMOKER

Michael J. Schmoker is a central office administrator for the Lake Havasu Public Schools in Lake Havasu City, Arizona, and is the co-author of Total Quality Education *(Phi Delta Kappa Educational Foundation, 1993). His latest book is* Results: The Key to Continuous School Improvement *(Association for Supervision and Curriculum Development, 1996).*

As the term *postmodern* springs up with ever greater frequency in the literature of education, we would be well-advised to consider carefully its meaning and implications. That's where the trouble begins. In this essay I will show 1) that the meaning — or meanings — of *postmodern* are problematic; 2) how, in some respects, the notions to which *postmodern* refers have some important implications for education, the arts, and the humanities; but 3) how so-called postmodernism is fraught with the potential for misunderstanding and, worse, could negatively affect professional communication, practice, and educators' attempts to improve schools.

My intent in this essay is to address the swirl of ideas that compose a postmodern continuum of definition. These ideas affect all areas of education, not just schooling in the arts and humanities.

The trouble with the word *postmodern* and the concept of post-modernity is that they are both elusive. Ambiguity muddies thought in a community (education) in which clear thinking should be the standard. Postmodernism must be examined and its essential features must be weighed carefully or we will find ourselves caught in the same web of embarrassment as the so-called deconstructionists in literature and the humanities. The "deconstructionist" movement, one of postmodernism's relatives, has become increasingly easy to ridicule (Shaw 1990).

What is postmodernism? One way to come to terms with postmodernism is to understand its different meanings along a continuum and then to determine the most reasonable place for educators along this continuum. For Pauline Rosenau, "The term post-modern is employed so broadly that it seems to apply to everything and nothing all at once" (1992, p. 17). Nonetheless, Rosenau offers a general description of postmodernism: It is primarily a reaction against scientific modernism, which has so disappointed educators and others in its attempt to "liberate humankind from ignorance and irrationality" (p. 5). She and others define postmodernism by its proponents' regard for science. As Andy Hargreaves says, postmodernism invites us to be skeptical of "scientific certainty, the certainty grounded in proven principles of generalized applicability" (1995*a*, pp. 12-13).

Mindful of the connections between science and modernity and between science and industrial efficiency, Hargreaves uses the term *post-industrial* as nearly synonymous with postmodern. His notion of postmodern is heavy with economics and references to the factory. But in this connection there arises an interesting ambiguity. For Daniel Bell, whose work also centers on "postindustrialism," science — writ large — is one of the defining features of the New Age. That is, the industrial age represents only a tepid foray into the possibilities of science. The new postindustrial age will be characterized by an intensification of science and humans' regard for it. We have moved, according to Bell, beyond the "industrial" concern with goods and into the era of "intellectual property and services." The postindustrial culture is one where the *"scientific* capacity of a country has become a determinant of its power and potential, and research and development (R&D)" (Bell's emphasis; 1973, p. 117). This is not a tempered view of science; rather, it constitutes the "major social change" that puts increasing pressure on young people to obtain the kind of education that a more technological — and scientific — future will require (p. 118). This contention is borne out by recent statistics, and college graduates with scientific backgrounds are finding employment in roughly half the time and at far higher salaries than their counterparts without scientific backgrounds.

For Bell, we have entered the scientific age; for Hargreaves, we are entering the "post-scientific" age. For both of these writers (and this is the rub), we do so under the banner of "postindustrialism." Again, what is interesting is the tautological connection implicit in Hargreaves' references to postindustrialism and postmodernism. Undeniably a shift *has* occurred, "whether the transitions we are experiencing are described in terms of postliberalism, postindustrialism or postmodernity." So the question becomes: Does postindustrialism, this close relative of postmodernism, elevate science, as Bell proclaims, or decry it, as Hargreaves seems to aver with his talk of the "post-scientific" age?

Hargreaves himself is discerning enough to acknowledge the potential confusion to be found in this discussion when he says, "This does not mean that these trends are entirely clear or consistent. Indeed their components and consequences are often ironic, paradoxical and perverse" (1994*a*, p. 47). But how much ambiguity can be tolerated in the name of postmodernism before we abet misunderstandings that impede communication and thus, as I shall attempt to show, school improvement? It is at least a little troubling when a recognized postmodern thinker such as Rosenau remarks that the term is employed "so broadly that it seems to apply to everything and nothing all at once" (1992, p. 17).

On the other hand, Rosenau's definition of modernity is robust enough to be blamed for Nazism, concentration camps, Hiroshima, the widening gap between the rich and poor, and the accumulated experience of Western civilization. Postmodernism, she writes, challenges bureaucracy, individual responsibility, liberal democracy, detached experiment, and rationality. And it distrusts modernity's moral claims. In addition, postmodernism "challenges global, all-encompassing world views, be they political, religious or social." Because postmodernists see modernism as having supplanted emotions, feeling, intuition, personal experience, religion, and mystical experience, postmodernists celebrate the importance of these. There is a "renewed respect for the subjective and increased suspicion of reason and objectivity" (1992, pp. 5-6).

The most sophisticated among the postmodernists avoid judgment of any kind. They neither advocate nor reject, instead speaking of being "concerned with" or "interested in" a thing. They offer "readings" but not "interpretations or findings," and they "never test because testing requires 'evidence,' a meaningless concept" for postmodernists. In the social sciences, postmodernism "reacts to uncritical confidence in modern science and smugness about objective knowledge" (Rosenau 1992, pp. 8-9).

As in Hargreaves, we can see the same mistrust of science and of global worldviews that reflect a level of certainty about the world or the universal, objective, or observable principles that govern it. But this rejection of anything like advocacy, evidence, or interpretation adds a radical aspect to the search for "postmodernism." As Rosenau points out, "the most extreme postmodernists urge us to be comfortable in the absence of certainty, learn to live without explanation" (p. 10). The operative phrase here is "most extreme," similar to the "most sophisticated" postmodernists that I referred to in the previous paragraph. Thus we might begin to see the continuum more clearly, one end of which embraces a level of certainty that rejects the kind of "absolute relativism," if you will, that more extreme postmodernists embrace.

A mistrust of science and any form of certainty is at the heart of this discussion. For most postmodernists, science and certainty are seen as the essence of *modernism*, defined by its misuse and abuse — for example, the way "science" has been trotted out as justification of unfair policies and various "isms." Many "scientific facts" advanced by those in power have been, in fact, only veiled preferences (Rosenau, p. 10). For Rosenau and other postmodernists, science has been smug, arrogant, manipulative.

The abuses of science help to explain the virulence of the postmodern reaction. But that does little to advance a sensible understanding of the role of science and certainty. The mind-bending paradox of an extreme postmodern worldview can be seen in Richard Rorty's criticism of Michel Foucault and Jean Francois Lyotard, both of whom attempted to write "so as to have no face." In their attempt to eschew any semblance of a "meta-narrative," or of seeming to advocate for any particular scheme or viewpoint, they tried to write with that dispassionate purity referred to above. But Rorty, himself a prominent voice in the postmodern tradition, criticizes Foucault and Lyotard for being "afraid of being caught up in. . . the culture of the generation to which they belong" (Sarup 1988, p. 140). Within the postmodern tradition, it seems, one has to advocate a position by unabashedly embracing it, while others — ostensibly — fiercely resist it. Hargreaves is more like Rorty, in that he advocates passionately for better schools and a better future, even justifying "anger at injustice" and "noble passions" in their pursuit (1994a, p. 24).

Another interesting juxtaposition can be found by comparing Barry Smart and Albert Borgmann. For Smart, postmodernity is, among other things, a "reconstitution of utopian thought" (1993, p. 13). It embraces "simultaneity and montage; an exploration of the paradoxical, ambiguous and uncertain, open-ended nature of reality" (p. 16) — all of which, alas, can mean so many different things. Of course science has been a disappointment as far its ability to help us make a better, more just, and humane world. Therefore, assertions and certainties of any kind are to be viewed skeptically.

But consider this next interesting set of remarks about postmodernism. Albert Borgmann (1992) credits Bacon, Descartes, and Locke for scientific modernism, that is, for elevating rationality as humankind's best hope. In the view of these three, we must systematically dominate nature "with the primacy of [scientific]

29

method" (p. 25). This begat what is commonly called "the Enlightenment," that "liberating dawn of reason that dispelled the darkness of medieval superstition and dogmatism, oppression and authoritarianism." Notice that Borgmann — a postmodernist, mind you — finds the scientific tendency, with some qualifications, heartening. He celebrates its influence in deposing monarchy and for advancing democracy. But he sees the Enlightenment as a project that has failed to fulfill its "social plank." We still have inequality and reversions to superstition and prejudice. He emphasizes his whole-hearted commitment to the completion of the Enlightenment revolution in its social and scientific aspects, to "equality of opportunity for women, blacks, Native Americans, homosexuals, and minorities generally, and to the promotion of pure scientific research and the acceptance of its well-confirmed results" (pp. 25-26).

Borgmann actually credits the Enlightenment — the mother of modernism — with progress, both actual and potential. Despite his passionate and elaborate case against the abuses and consequences of science, he makes a distinction between the Enlightenment's "violent campaign of conquest" against nature and its manifest benefits. Even more interesting is that for all this he anticipates advances in both the realms of *pure* science and *social* science. This does not sound very postmodern to my ear.

In summary, the concept of postmodernism is vast, vague, and multi-faceted. Thus it sometimes is difficult to understand the similarities and differences between various advocates of postmodernism. They traffic in sweeping generalities and terminology that may (or may not) depart from standard usage. Such words as *universals* can mean many things. This is not to say that postmodernism or its various understandings are meaningless, but that there is a dire need for clarity and cases. Would Hargreaves, as passionate an advocate for postmodernism as Borgmann, credit the Enlightenment with helping to end such medieval notions as monarchy or dogma? Perhaps. On the one hand, he writes that "purposive rationality and reasoned reflection . . . remain extremely important as sources of technical, moral and political deliberation" (1995*a*, p. 23). But then, in the same article, he goes on to denigrate "purposive rationality's" preeminence; it was "integral to the modern age, and its concern with control, regulation, ordering and centralization and power," as well as the "perverted realizations of science in war, weaponry or environmental disaster" (p. 25). It is not clear whether his problem is with purposive rationality or science per se, or with its abuses.

This is the central difficulty. "Purposive rationality" can produce both bad and good fruit. But instead of attacking the motives or objectives of those who employ science, the attack is on science and rationality themselves. Hence the commonalities that are present in both postmodernism and modernism threaten to cancel out the distinctions. For example, Hargreaves is able both to denigrate and to celebrate rationality simultaneously. Borgmann seems in one place to be criticizing science and all its works, then embraces science in its "pure" form where there are "well-confirmed results," as well as for its potential for helping to fulfill a more enlightened social agenda. Some might suggest that there is a certain consistency here, since paradox and "simultaneity" — as Smart points out — are regarded by many as part of the postmodern spirit. The danger in such a game is that without an elaborately nuanced treatment, the concept of postmodernism can promote the notion that anything goes, regardless of any appeal to logic or evidence or consistency.

Moreover, if "evidence" is a "meaningless concept," then what of Foucault's use of evidence throughout his *Madness and Civilization* (1965) to support his tenet that culture defines insanity? The subtitle is indicative: "A History of Insanity in the *Age of Reason*" (emphasis added). No amount of studied neutrality can conceal the irony — and advocacy — that his title reveals. He clearly is building a case, even creating a kind of grand (meta?) narrative that the postmodern mentality claims to abhor. Similarly, Hargreaves' repeated appeal to justice and caring, to the sinister and insidious impact of focusing on "technical competence" at the expense of caring and moral matters, is itself a kind of meta-narrative — especially in that he attempts to bolster his case with formal

31

research (a form of history) done by others. And we can assume that some of the researchers he cites have in fact been guilty of "testing" their hypotheses against the evidence — a notion that evidently represents a problem for many postmodernists.

The Postmodern Continuum and
Its Benefits and Dangers

In spite of differences in various definitions of postmodernism, there are common threads, and thus the notion of an intact continuum. Therefore, postmodernism holds both benefits and dangers for education. A key issue is knowledge and our regard for it and how we use, organize, and think about formal and professional expertise. These, in turn, pivot on where we situate ourselves on the postmodern continuum. One end represents a wholesome circumspection about science, rationality, and apparent certainties; the other end is outright rejection of the legitimacy of science and systematic rationality.

The closer we come to the latter end of this continuum, the more difficult it is to defend our position. How can we communicate while attempting to escape from narrative, from history in the broadest sense, and from evidence-testing, the assumption that language can be functionally referential and intelligible? How can we aver that science (rather than its abuse) is, by its very nature, sinister or misbegotten? This sort of assault on rationality constitutes a grand but flimsy meta-narrative in itself — and no less a meta-narrative than, say, Francis Fukuyama's *The End of History*, which, like postmodernism, is built on a similar fin-de-siècle. As Wittgenstein saw it: Without rules, one doesn't have a game (1953).

But there is a paradox in this. However arbitrarily we may regard the notion of game (which Wittgenstein took very seriously), we must — and in fact, we all do — play this game, which is to recognize its rules, however existentially. This game is like physics, which is fraught with paradoxes like whether "particles" or "waves" have any reality apart from each other, a theory that physicists have yet to prove conclusively. Nonetheless, there is a kind of reality in that, as in the "game," it must be reckoned with in the real world (Wheatley 1992).

In examining postmodernity in education, I would begin with a qualified case for it, or at least for its best impulses toward the opposite end of the continuum. In *The Reflective Practitioner*, Donald Schon elaborates at length on the distinctions between rigorous, scientific experimentation that reflects a belief in "technical rationality" on the one hand and, on the other, "reflective practice," which is conducted in situations that almost never allow for the same level of control found in the clinic or the laboratory. This is an important point. Schon's emphasis is on the inarticulate, extra-rational aspects of context, of the contextual factors that can make or break professional or organizational improvement. These aspects, he contends, deserve our attention, not the established, generalizable knowledge that traditionally has been the mark of the professions. Schon has a point. Practitioners do need opportunities to personally, experientially assess, evaluate, and adjust practice. A guideline or an imported "innovation," however well-established under carefully controlled conditions, cannot be precisely replicated in the real classroom. If they wish to succeed in the classroom, they will invariably need to respond to unanticipated, idiosyncratic, contextual obstacles that complicate the application of clinical techniques.

The problem of making the transition from clinical to classroom practice has important implications for postmodernity in education, with its trenchant critique of science and research and their influence on classroom practice. Hargreaves is right: For all our innovations, such as "research-based" staff development, the results have been disappointing (1995*b*, p. 56). Andrew Gitlin (1990, p. 537) remarks on the same thing. Many of the major, one-size-fits-all reforms — all supposedly "research-based" — have had virtually no discernible effect on the quality of education that most children receive. Many of these so-called movements simply have faded away — but only after wasting untold amounts of time and energy.

We might cynically conclude that modernism duped us with the factory model. The modernist fallacy was that reflection was not needed "in action," as Schon puts it. Practitioners did not need to collaborate. Only those in administrative and policymaking positions needed to do the reflecting — for the rest of us. This fallacy of modernism brings us to an important part of Hargreaves' sense of postmodernism, in which more enlightened workplaces are far more appreciative of the intellectual and reflective resources of all individuals. The postmodern man reflects the "boundless self" that Hargreaves rightly recognizes for its richness, the "self" having been previously constrained (1994a, p. 69). Hargreaves celebrates the postmodern recognition that practitioners can be far more effective than managers in solving problems if they work in a setting that encourages them and is geared to take advantage of their "reflection in action." Hargreaves' postmodernity addresses this notion, while recognizing that roles and boundaries — of individuals, groups, and classes — are changing.

Subsequently, there has been an increase in self-management in both business and schools (Hargreaves 1995a, pp. 12-13). Schools, like the best "postindustrial" work settings, are waking up to the fact that the richest resources for school improvement are the individual and collective intellectual contributions of practitioners. The measure of a good administrator, therefore, has become his or her awareness of this fact and ability to organize and to tap into this intelligence, rooted as it is in action. Administrators who impose "innovation" without so much as consulting teachers, much less making them equal partners in change, are less likely to succeed. This is perhaps the great lesson of postmodernism. School improvement is more likely to succeed when we recognize as essential the intellectual contributions, cooperation, and passion of classroom practitioners, a point that Sarason makes very effectively (1982; 1991).

People can be recklessly arrogant in the way they use and brandish "science" in defense of policies they favor, believing that, by itself and without good judgment, science can solve all of our ills.

Paul Theobald and Ed Mills' understanding of postmodernism is chiefly defined by its relationship to science and narrative (1995). The "postmodern movement," they write, "has called into question the 'grand narrative' that science is the engine of continual human betterment." Like Schon and others, they emphasize that it is "increasingly accepted that science actually creates the conditions that lead to some fundamental human problems" (1995, p. 464). Science — in the form of education research and testing — will not "inexorably lead us to the promised land." It can, on the contrary, be a force for destruction. And so the "scientifically predicted inevitability" of success in school improvement that Theobald and Mills refer to has been replaced in many schools by disillusionment.

We have spent a considerable amount of our capital and credibility in the abuse of "research," education's "science." "Research-based" practices often have been "imposed . . . multiple, contradictory, and overwhelming" (Hargreaves 1995a, p. 13). At times, practitioners have been treated as if they were empty vessels that need merely to be filled, that is, told precisely what to do, not why. Many teachers have been accorded little or no time for interaction with colleagues in order to help them deal with the problems they inevitably will encounter in implementing so-called research-based practices. In short, there has been a gross underestimation of the complexity of what is found at the ground level to even the best and most established practices and innovations *in situ*.

Thus the skepticism that postmodernity encourages is warranted. Gitlin's litany of major, failed innovations dramatically conveys the problem with scientific presumption. Hargreaves cites how Madeline Hunter's "Essential Elements of Instruction" (EEI) was mandated on a vast scale. Emphasis on such "single models of excellence," in this case one that often was interpreted in ways that proved to be prescriptive and intrusive, is fraught with dangers. Studies conducted in the last few years have revealed EEI to be restrictive and prejudiced toward a discrete-skills emphasis that may "actually inhibit the growth of effective

35

characteristics of teaching" (Hargreaves 1994*b*, p. 56). In my own battle with the "essential elements," I remember how frustrating it was for me to communicate how this approach hampered me in teaching sophisticated skills. I remember feeling constrained from conducting discussions with students that might otherwise have proved valuable, all because they seemed not to "fit" the EEI model. My requests for meaningful evidence that the EEI approach worked were met with alarm and suspicion. EEI and its supposed benefits were not to be questioned.

Moral Issues and the Postmodern Mindset

Finally, the scientific mindset does not immediately evoke a concern with the moral issues that are central to teaching and play a key role in the arts and humanities. As Fenstermacher and Soltis point out, teaching cannot help but be a profoundly moral activity (1986). Research has not concerned itself with this. Nor has it given the arts and humanities the chance they need to demonstrate their ultimate, spiritual importance. This leaves them especially vulnerable in the age of efficiency.

We are what we talk about. Schools do need to deliberate about important moral issues. The notion of moral discourse in schools is still quite foreign, both in the classroom and in the faculty meeting. What sort of graduates are we trying to create? What are our obligations — or the limits of our obligations — to students? What are the social, psychological consequences of certain kinds of testing, of long periods of enforced quiescence? Are we reflecting on the nature of what their day is like as students spend six or more hours in our charge? Are we putting ourselves in their place? Is the culture of the school one that reflects a hierarchy, descending from athletic prowess and popularity, at the very top, to caring, compassion, or love of learning at the bottom? What are we doing to change — or tacitly sustain — such a culture? These are fundamentally moral matters with which "science" does not concern itself. Postmodernity, with its wider, more vigorous appreciation for the human versus the purely "practical," can awaken educators to the full scope of teaching and the kinds of schools we are creating.

On the other hand, I am concerned by the postmodernists' seemingly headlong rush to clear the decks of modernism altogether. The postmodern impulse can be just as reckless and unnecessarily reactive as it accuses "science" of being. We need to make a distinction between the abuses of science and what is done in its name, on the one hand, and on the other hand, the outright rejection of scientific method or findings, which include the best of education's knowledge base. These matters deserve a more qualified and nuanced treatment.

The key problem for me is the failure of prominent postmodernists to fully engage the real context of schools. Hargreaves is typical of many who accuse schools of being far too concerned with the technical capability of teachers and with universal solutions to educational ills (1994*a*). But is the problem science in general or merely *bad* science? Hunters' EEI is an example of "bad" science, arguably the absence of real science. It exemplifies the tendency to overlook the importance of testing and piloting, especially *in context*, to see what results may be obtained in real classrooms.

Where Schon and others err is in their rush to discredit generalizable knowledge and research and their claim that research is overemphasized. It may be true of the non-teaching professions that an unexamined, lockstep adherence to established technical procedures has had an unfortunate impact on effectiveness. But I would contend that in education, at least, quite the opposite is true — that research, "technical rationality," and professional knowledge are far from overemphasized. In education, there is a startling and debilitating lack of emphasis on proven practice, especially the right kind of technical competence. Lortie observed a striking lack of a "viable, generalizable body of knowledge and practice" in schools. He found a lack of "commonly held, empirically derived and rigorously grounded practices and principles of pedagogy" (Lortie 1975, p. 79). This is the stuff of "science." Without what he called a "stronger technical culture," teachers cease to work confidently toward learning goals with children. This "scientific approach normally begins with the assumption that there is an underlying order in the phenomena under study" (p. 212).

This is the heart of my concern. The failure of teachers to perceive such an underlying order — the "universals" that post-modernity tends to dismiss — serves to undermine practitioner confidence and "the search for occupational knowledge" (Lortie 1975, p. 212). Both this knowledge and this search are essential to improvement.

We must make distinctions carefully. First, a good number of so-called universal solutions have been imposed on schools; but they are, like our implementation of EEI, examples of poor science, rather than of science per se. In addition, I would argue that as bad as some of these imposed innovations were, their influence has been exaggerated. For one thing, as John Goodlad and his associates found, once an innovation is introduced through conventional staff development, it exerts only a very limited and increasingly diffused influence "behind the classroom door" (1970, p. 72).

Second, there is something disingenuous about blaming hyper-rational or scientific approaches for our school's ills when, in fact, science — bad or good — never really has been given a chance. The fact is, teachers do not spend much time in staff development, and most staff development efforts lack a meaningful follow-up component. Therefore teachers are only nominally influenced by most of what they are taught or told in staff development settings. And teacher evaluation and supervision rarely ensure conformity to organizational standards for practice. This accounts for EEI's limited influence, even in its heyday, because many teachers dug it out of the closet only when they were being evaluated.

We must be careful not to overestimate the influence of rational, top-down directives on classroom instruction, whether the directives come in the form of Goals 2000 or national standards for arts education or the teaching of history. After all, the typical school district spends only about one half of one percent of its budget on training (Darling-Hammond and Goodwin 1993). For all the much-deserved abuse that staff development has taken for being typically shoddy and "one-shot," its most glaring and crippling feature is its infrequency — and thus the insignificant influence it has. Teachers suffer not from a glut of good technical knowledge and skill training but from a dismaying shortage of the right training—the kind that reflects *good* science and the best it has given us.

Consider the following areas of knowledge:

- Research says that traditional writing instruction is ineffective, retrograde, and infrequent (Rothman 1992).
- Rubrics and criteria heavily favor both higher engagement and better performance.
- Monitoring student progress in the aggregate, while looking for patterns of success or frustration, favors improvement.
- Teachers and schools work and collaborate more effectively when they have a clear, common objective (Rosenholtz 1989; Little 1990; Good, Biddle, and Brophy 1975).
- Students — even the "slowest" or lowest performing — are quite capable of doing "higher order" thinking; that such sophisticated tasks are, in fact, the best way to succeed with such students — with all students (Means, Chelemer and Knapp 1991).
- Students work more effectively when they can see the relevance of a task, when it demands that they make connections between it and things they already know.
- "Less is more" — coverage is killing our students at the expense of intellectual engagement and depth (Newmann 1992, pp. 2-4).
- Beyond learning the basics of decoding a text, reading is about the best activity for students to engage in to improve their reading skills (Krashen 1993).

Each one of these statements is a product of research, of *good* science in education. This is not empty theory; there are real schools and classrooms that serve as evidence of the effectiveness of these practices and structures. Such science represents a world of methods and frameworks that have the potential for vastly improving the quality of education we provide and enriching the professional lives and improving the morale of teachers.

Science can be a powerful force for improvement. David Berliner cites studies that reveal a strong, even "unambiguous" relationship between the implementation of recommended teaching practices and achievement, many of them grounded in the effective schools research (1984, p. 73). This does not eliminate the importance of context. If anything, the effective schools correlates that Hargreaves consigns to obsolescence (a "bygone age") affirm the importance of context by emphasizing the importance of "frequent monitoring" of progress, which Fullan and Rosenholtz see as essential. We must regularly gather data in context in order to know, in Fullan's words, "how well or poorly change is going in the classroom or school," if we wish to succeed (1991, p. 87). That is as local and context-sensitive as you can get. Grant Wiggins makes the same point when he laments our failure to be "data-driven and results-oriented" (1994, p. 18) in our tendency to "never pilot anything. We just send ideas and innovations off and wave at them from the pier, never to see them again," as he commented during an address he gave in Phoenix. This is what educators did with EEI, the Effective Schools movement, the middle school movement, and with much of what has gone on in the name of site-based management and Total Quality.

The common denominator here is what Lortie calls "general principles" and "common solutions" to presumably common problems and efforts — language that makes some postmodernists uncomfortable. But it is naive to pretend that educators do not face many of the same challenges regardless of where they teach and at what level. Many challenges have the same or very similar solutions, and we ought to know what those solutions are and disseminate them.

The tendency to inflate context — to exaggerate our differences — while playing down the similarities in the problems we

40

face as educators is especially manifest at the local level. Rosen-holtz (1991) emphasized the importance of common school and district goals versus an incoherent "jumble" of emphases. Similarly, Good, Biddle, and Brophy emphasize the importance of a limited but common set of school goals, because such focused goals mobilize behavior (1975). Thomas Donahoe avers that school improvement will not occur until we begin to work with collective focus like the combined rays of "one sun." Schools, for him, are not organizations at all, but only places where teachers, like freelancers, gather to follow their individual pursuits (1993, p. 299). Little observed an unfortunate lack of common and effective effort by teachers in the same school, that an effective autonomy needed to be tempered by collective constraints (1990).

It is this collective tendency that, although demonstrably allied to improvement, seems to make postmodernists uneasy. Perhaps this is why Hargreaves seems to be uncomfortable with even the notion of "continuous improvement." He can see that it relies on "organizational learning"; on common or "single-minded" direction, mission, or vision for schools; on rational "systematic cycles" of improvement — and he expresses grave reservations about all of these (1995*b*, pp. 15-16). Organizational learning evidently violates his sense of postmodernity, the heart of which cannot brook any intrusion on individual autonomy. "Continuous improvement," he warns, "can easily degenerate into interminable improvement," which may interfere with the teachers' right to merely be left alone to "cultivate their own gardens, making small changes with their own classes" (pp. 17-18). Collective purpose, even mission statements, are "too fixed to enable sufficient responsiveness to changes in policy mandates. . . . Planned change that follows systematic cycles of development, implementation and review is too inflexible and bureaucratic to respond to local circumstances." It appears that beyond a call for dialogue in the moral sphere, Hargreaves is not in favor of anything that puts requirements or expectations on teachers for what they or their students are to learn or do. In what sounds increasingly shrill, he avers that where collective improvement is stressed, "only incurable change addicts prosper" (1995*b*, pp. 16-18). He paints all "singular models of teaching" with the same broad brush — that they deny teachers the opportunity to "exercise proper discretionary judgments in the classroom" (1994*b*, p. 56).

For Hargreaves, "flexibility" and "local circumstances" are much more important in the hierarchy than anything like achievement or evidence of learning. There is no mention of focused, achievement-oriented collaboration or examples of it, no acknowledgment that such "freedom" helps to account for the fact that most teachers in mid-career or later are a disillusioned and extremely conservative lot whose best years of teaching are behind them, or that a kind of sad, pervasive fatalism hangs over the profession in general (Lortie 1975; Evans 1989). A passionate, orchestrated, collective attempt to improve learning does not seem to be one of Hargreaves' priorities.

I do not presume that this is characteristic of all who profess postmodernist sympathies. However, as valuable and penetrating as most of Hargreaves' work is, it does occasionally illustrate what I consider to be an excessive postmodernism, with its rejection of any means by which to ascertain or define effectiveness, with the apparent priority it places on nearly unconditional autonomy and individual experience — despite the clear connection between such autonomy and a feckless, ineffectual "conservatism" (Little 1990, p. 511), the "hesitant and uneasy" individualism Lortie observed among the ranks of teachers.

The existence of bad science and our abuses of science do not explain or erase the fact that schools are badly in need of the best that research can give us. The quality of technical, instructional, inservice training is poor; collaboration is typically more therapeutic than productive. On inspection, schools, for the most part, are not collectively focused or awash in technical training. Indeed, they are decidedly lacking in opportunities for teachers to engage in moral and philosophical dialogue, whether in the arts and humanities or in other disciplines.

Finding a New Way to Think About Postmodernism

Even Nathaniel Gage, whose reputation rests on his high regard for science, sees practice in much the same way as Schon, as having "both artistic and scientific components." He compares teaching to the tension and release between certainty and uncertainty, general and contextual knowledge, found in the medical profession. Doctors must exercise judgment in situations where innumerable factors are at work; the answer is not always in the textbook (Gage 1978, p. 17). Doctors, teachers, and other professionals need not eschew science in order to acknowledge the importance of what Polanyi calls "tacit knowing" — art, in other words — in their work (1966).

Again, words like *science*, *certainty*, and *universal* can mean many things; this in itself makes this discussion difficult. Some people see the word "empirical" as categorically distinct from "science," meaning something more personal or individual, such as Schon's "reflection in action." Others, such as Berliner, use such expressions as "empirical science," which reflects a very different cobbling of these two concepts. I find these combinations attractive and useful. For example, I like the way Nathaniel Gage qualifies his use of the word *science*. For him, "scientific knowledge" need not embrace the kind of pure, problematic definition with which Schon seems to be operating. The systematic organization and use of testing, correlation, and experimentation can be useful, without insisting that all science is as rigorous as some of the testing done in the physical sciences. For Gage, scientific investigation exists on a continuum that reflects levels of rigor (Gage 1985, p. 7). I believe this is as it should be.

To reject certainty or the legitimacy of the scientific approach does not liberate teachers. It enfeebles them. The attack on rationality incompletely addresses some of the problems of the education workplace while ignoring the need for a more technically and morally deliberative culture.

The last point I would make is one that Little already has made in the realm of effectiveness, that collective, task-oriented effort is essential to effectiveness. The other aspect of this is that teachers need collective effort to feel fulfilled, to provide what Dan Lortie calls "tangibility," a clear, discernible record that they are accomplishing something, not just with occasional or individual students, but with groups of students, which has always been their expressed ideal (1975, pp. 127-28). This is corroborated by the work of Mihalyi Csikszentmihalyi, who found that goals are in fact the stuff of fulfillment, and even that striving for them with others adds a rich, social dimension to our efforts (1990).

Science, certainty, and truth, sensibly construed, are essential to effective education in the sciences, of course, but equally so in the arts and humanities. Andrew Sullivan, raised in Britain and until recently the editor of the *New Republic*, speaks occasionally to the excesses of the postmodern influence. After a recent visit to Britain, he lamented, "It is simply not part of most English people's upbringing to consider — let alone believe — the possibility of universal truths." "Equally insidious, " he writes, is the fact that "virtually no English undergraduate reads, say, the *Nichomachean Ethics*, with a view to seeing whether Aristotle might be voicing eternal truths about human nature." Subsequently — and this is the point — "the intellectual muscles that allow serious public debate to take place atrophy young." Britain's war with the Enlightenment is promoting "cultural exhaustion" that is "ultimately corrosive of civil discourse." (1995, p. 50).

The implications for civic, personal, and professional life should be clear. Postmodernism has helped us to see that effective practice is both art and science, that its pursuit of improvement should never preclude the need for wisdom and rigor and vigilance. But postmodernism, as it is sometimes construed, also holds the dangerous potential for extinguishing the search for broad, general solutions to common education problems. Ideas have consequences. Our children and their teachers stand to be hurt most by a misguided assault on collective, concerted effort and on the general application of sound, empirically tested principles.

References

Bell, Daniel. *The Coming of Post-Industrial Society*. New York: Basic Books, 1973.

Berliner, David. "The Half-Full Glass: A Review of Research on Teaching." In *Using What We Know About Teaching*, edited by Philip Hosford. Alexandria, Va.: Association for Supervision and Curriculum Development, 1984.

Borgmann, Albert. *Crossing the Postmodern Divide*. Chicago: University of Chicago Press, 1992.

Csikszentmihalyi, Mihaly. *Flow: The Psychology of Optimal Experience*. New York: Harper Perennial, 1990.

Darling-Hammond, Linda, and Goodwin, A. Lin. "Progress Toward Professionalism in Teaching." In *Challenges and Achievements in Education*, edited by Gordon Cawelti. Alexandria, Va.: Association for Supervision and Curriculum Development, 1993.

Donahoe, Tom. "Finding the Way: Structure, Time, and Culture in School Improvement." *Phi Delta Kappan* 75 (December 1993): 298-305.

Evans, Robert. "The Faculty in Midcareer: Implications for School Improvement." *Educational Leadership* 46 (May 1989): 10-15.

Fenstermacher, G.D., and Soltis, J.F. *Approaches to Teaching*. New York: Teachers College Press, 1986.

Foucault, Michel. *Madness and Civilization: A History of Insanity in the Age of Reason*. New York: Vintage, 1965.

Fukuyama, Francis. *The End of History and the Last Man*. New York: Free Press, 1992.

Fullan, Michael G., with Stiegelbauer, Suzanne. *The New Meaning of Educational Change*. New York: Teachers College Press, 1991.

Gage, N.L. *The Scientific Basis of the Art of Teaching*. New York: Teachers College Press, 1978.

Gage, N.L. *Hard Gains in the Soft Sciences*. Bloomington Ind.: Phi Delta Kappa, 1985.

Gitlin, Andrew. "Understanding Teaching Dialogically." *Teachers College Record* 91, no. 4 (1990): 537-63.

Good, Thomas L.; Biddle, Bruce; and Brophy, Jere E. *Teachers Make a Difference*. New York: Holt, Rhinehart and Winston, 1975.

Goodlad, John; Klein, M. Frances; et al. *Behind the Classroom Door*. Worthington, Ohio: Charles A. Jones, 1970.

Hargreaves, Andy. *Changing Teachers, Changing Times*. London: Cassel, 1994. a

Hargreaves, Andy. "Restructuring Restructuring: Postmodernity and the Prospects for Educational Change." *Journal of Educational Policy* 9, no. 1 (1994): 47-65. b

Hargreaves, Andy. "Development and Desire: A Postmodern Perspective." In *Professional Development in Education*, edited by T.R. Guskey. New York: Teachers College Press, 1995. a

Hargreaves, Andy. "Renewal in the Age of Paradox." *Educational Leadership* 52 (April 1995): 14-19. b

Krashen, Stephen. *The Power of Reading.* Englewood, Colo.: Libraries Unlimited, 1993.

Little, Judith Warren. "Teachers as Colleagues." In *Educator's Handbook*, edited by V. Richardson-Koehler. White Plains, N.Y.: Longman, 1987.

Little, Judith Warren. "The Persistence of Privacy: Autonomy and Initiative in Teacher's Professional Relations." *Teachers College Record* 91, no. 4 (1990): 509-36.

Lortie, Dan C. *Schoolteacher: A Sociological Study.* Chicago: University of Chicago Press, 1975.

Means, Barbara; Chelemer, Carol; and Knapp, Michael, eds. *Teaching Advanced Skills to At-Risk Students.* San Francisco: Jossey-Bass, 1991.

Newmann, Fred M. *Student Engagement and Achievement in American Secondary Schools.* New York: Teachers College Press, 1992.

Polanyi, Michael. *The Tacit Dimension.* Garden City, N.Y.: Doubleday, 1966.

Rosenau, Pauline Marie. *Postmodernism and the Social Sciences.* Princeton, N.J.: Princeton University Press, 1992.

Rosenholtz, Susan. "Workplace Conditions that Affect Teacher Quality and Commitment: Implications for Teacher Induction Programs." *Elementary School Journal* 89 (March 1989): 421-39.

Rosenholtz, Susan J. *Teacher's Workplace: The Social Organization of Schools.* New York: Teachers College Press, 1991.

Rothman, Robert. "In a Pilot Study, Writing is Gauged." *Education Week*, 22 April 1992, p. 24.

Sarason, Seymour B. *The Culture of the School and the Problem of Change.* 2nd ed. Boston: Allyn and Bacon, 1982.

Sarason, Seymour B. *The Predictable Failure of Educational Reform.* San Francisco: Jossey-Bass, 1991.

Sarup, Madan. *Post-structuralism and Postmodernism.* New York: Harvester Wheatsheaf, 1988.

Schon, Donald A. *The Reflective Practitioner: How Professionals Think in Action.* New York: Basic Books, 1983.

Shaw, Peter. "Devastating Developments Are Hastening the Demise of Deconstruction in Academe." *Chronicle of Higher Education,* 28 November 1990, p. 1.

Smart, Barry. *Postmodernity.* London: Routledge, 1993.

Sullivan, Andrew. "London Diarist: Do I Have To?" *New Republic,* 20 November 1995, p. 50.

Theobald, Paul, and Mills, Ed. "Accountability and the Struggle over What Counts." *Phi Delta Kappan* 76 (February 1995): 462-66.

Wheatley, Margaret. *Leadership and the New Sciences.* San Francisco: Berrett, Koehler, 1992

Wiggins, Grant. *Assessing Student Performance.* San Francisco: Jossey-Bass, 1993.

Wiggins, Grant. "None of the Above." *Executive Educator* 16 (July 1994): pp. 14-18.

Wittgenstein, Ludwig. *Philosophical Investigations.* New York: Macmillan, 1953.

The Necessary Role of the Arts in Education and Society

BY ERIC ODDLEIFSON

Eric Oddleifson is managing director of GMO Renewable Resources in Boston and chairman of the Center for Arts in the Basic Curriculum.

British mathematician and philosopher Alfred North Whitehead once wrote:

> The ultimate motive power in education and life is the sense of value, the sense of importance. It takes the various forms of wonder, of curiosity, of reverence — of tumultuous desire for merging personality in something beyond itself. This sense of value, of importance, imposes on life incredible labors, and apart from it life sinks back into passivity, and apathy.
>
> The most penetrating exhibition of this force is the sense of beauty, the aesthetic sense of realized perfection. This thought leads me to ask, whether in our modern education we emphasize sufficiently the function of art.
>
> We cannot without great loss, ignore in our inner lives, in the life of the spirit, so great a factor as art! Our aesthetic emotions provide us with vivid apprehensions of value. If you maim these, you weaken the force of the whole system of inner awareness and progress and of spiritual apprehensions. (1967, p. 40)

We need to deepen our capacities for intelligent thought and action. We rely primarily on analysis and reason and seek little understanding from our perceptions, intuitions, insights, feelings, and emotions. Yet there is a power in balancing reason with perception. Capacities emerge, useful in shaping our destinies and the world we live in. Once we discover how to touch these inner strengths, we gain control over the events that influence our lives.

A number of professions seek to understand this power better. Academics, such as Harvard's Howard Gardner and David Perkins, Yale's Robert Sternberg, and Stanford's Elliot Eisner, have significantly advanced our understanding of the nature of intelligence and how knowledge is constructed. Economists now focus on human knowledge and skills as vital "factors" of production that cause economic growth. Some scientists seek a more humanistic, integrative science. Mathematicians claim aesthetics as the grounding for their discipline. Educators now understand that intelligence is multi-faceted, complex, and not easily measured — at least with existing tools. The business community, seeing the ability to construct knowledge as a competitive advantage, is attempting to understand the phenomena of organizational learning and is addressing the problem of assessing/measuring the qualitative aspects of human development.

The coming decades will see a growing interest in the relationship of the inner man to the outer world and qualities as expressions of subjective truths. Deeper capacities for intelligent thought will provide us with the tools to improve the world and our individual positions in it. The law of "intention and desire" (as described by Deepak Chopra), as well as the power of the imagination and intentionality in perception (as noted by quantum physicist Stephen Edelglass), will become the basis of a new renaissance in humanistic thought and action. As unlikely as it may seem, this renaissance likely will be led by business and fed by a merging of the arts with the sciences.

The sciences, together with their "symbol system," mathematics, will not by themselves yield ultimate, irreducible truths, despite scientists' fervent desire that they do so. Our continuing hope that science, with its focus on understanding and controlling the natural world, will save us from ourselves and bring peace, love, and harmony to the world is misplaced. We must either look beyond science or better understand its true nature in order to gain a more comprehensive understanding of the world and man's relationship to it.

Science is a continuing process of discovery. Joseph Campbell described science as the process of developing new thoughts, new things, and continuing transformation.

> For the really great and essential fact about the scientific revelation — the most wonderful and most challenging fact — is that science does not and cannot pretend to be "true" in any absolute sense. It does not and cannot pretend to be final. It is a tentative organization of mere "working hypotheses" that for the present appear to take into account all the relevant facts now known.
>
> And is there no implied intention, then, to rest satisfied with some final body or sufficient number of facts?
>
> No indeed! There is to be only a continuing search for more — as of a mind eager to grow. And that growth, as long as it lasts, will be the measure of the life of modern Western man, and of the world with all its promise that he has brought and is still bringing into being: which is to say, a world of change, new thoughts, new things, new magnitudes, and continuing transformation, not of petrifaction, rigidity, and some canonized found "truth."
>
> And so, my friends, we don't know a thing, and not even our science can tell us sooth; for it is no more than, so to say, an eagerness for truths, no matter where their allure may lead. (1972, pp. 15-16)

Business likely will become as active as science and the arts in seeking truths about man's intelligence and relation to the world. The reason? The dramatic slowing over the past 25 years of economic productivity in the Western world. There is a pressing need to fully understand the root causes of this slowdown as well as the apparent failure of technology — despite massive capital infusion — to reverse it. Business needs to broaden its understanding of the factors of production, which in neoclassic growth theory (with its law of diminishing returns) includes land, labor (as a cost), and financial capital. Historically, technology has been excluded from the model, as have the benefits of added knowledge (most likely because of the difficulties inherent in its measurement).

New economic growth theory suggests that growth can continue indefinitely, even without technological progress, if human capital (for example, the knowledge and skills embodied in the workforce) is included as a factor of production. The old law of diminishing returns on financial capital, without added technology, may not apply. Attention to human capital can yield increasing, not decreasing, returns to financial capital.

A second strand of new growth theory seeks to put technological progress explicitly in the neoclassic model as well and begins to examine the relationship between human learning — the addition of knowledge and skills — to enhanced technology. This line of inquiry suggests the need to properly measure employee learning (and research and development) within the business firm. The accounting profession, long focused on purely financial measures of performance, is responding to this need by providing tools to measure more qualitative aspects of productivity and growth, an example being "The Balanced Scorecard," devised by Robert Kaplan at the Harvard Business School.

Business also seems to be realizing that our perceptive capacities may be more important than we ever imagined. Leading business management writer, Peter Drucker, argues that mankind is in the midst of evolutionary transformation from analysis as the organizing principle of life to one where perception is at the center. Information-based societies are organized around meaning, and meaning requires at its heart common perception. He says:

> In governmental and business planning we increasingly talk of "scenarios" in which perception is the starting point. And, of course, an "ecology" is perception rather than analysis. In an ecology, the "whole" has to be seen and understood, and the "parts" exist only in contemplation of the whole.
>
> Contemporary philosophers deal with configurations —

with signs and symbols, with patterns, with myth, with language. They deal with perception. (1989, pp. 263-64)

Drucker observes that by teaching the arts as the rigorous disciplines they are, we could enhance our perceptive capacities — but we fail to do so.

> In the world view of many mathematicians and philosophers, perception was "intuition" and either spurious or mystical, elusive, mysterious.
>
> Science did not deny its existence (though a good many scientists did). It denied its validity. "Intuition" the analysts asserted, can neither be taught nor trained. Perception, the mechanical world view asserts, is not "serious" but is relegated to the "finer things of life," the things we can do without. We teach "art appreciation" in our schools as indulgence in pleasure. We do not teach art as the rigorous, demanding discipline it is for the artist.
>
> In the biological universe, however, perception is at the center. And it can — indeed it must — be trained and developed. (1989, pp. 262-63)

And what of the arts in all this? Arts advocates shout, "We have the answer," but are largely ignored. They are hampered by the three-centuries-old "mental model" of Enlightenment thinking, which denies their validity as legitimate and necessary functions of the intellect, and mind.

The arts are seen by many as pure emotion with little or no cognitive base. Yet recent research into the functioning of the brain reveals that the senses (sight, hearing, touch, smell, and taste) are forms of cognition, or understanding, as powerful as pure reason can ever be. And the emotions themselves are now seen as underpinning our capacities for constructive thought. Daniel Coleman (1995), science reporter for the *New York Times*, in his book, *Emotional Intelligence*, reveals new understandings of the emotions as another cognitive system hardwired into our brains. Coleman suggests that emotional intelligence is a master intelligence, or "meta-ability," governing how well or poorly people are able to use their other mental capabilities. How critical the arts are to these new understandings is found in one definition of the arts as "emotion, wrapped in intelligence."

Yet the arts also suffer from being narrowly viewed as music, dance, theater, and visual art, rather than as "an eagerness for truths" expressed in "symbol systems" other than those used by science (words and numbers). As expressions of an "eagerness for truths," they are identical to the scientific process of discovery and represent an equally powerful measure for exploring the relationship of man to nature. The arts awaken the "craving to comprehend" — as does scientific exploration, with its continuing revelations of interconnectedness. This craving is the motivating force behind all learning.

Because the arts deal with qualities, not quantities, science has labeled them "not real" — with growing and potentially disastrous consequences for the Western world. Needed is a new paradigm, a new mental model to encompass the discovery process of both science and art.

Schiller noted many years ago that aesthetic education is the one true preparation for rational life and the foundation of any ordered politics. A way to link the aesthetics of both science and art has been suggested by author Robert Pirsig, using his "metaphysics of quality" (found in his book, *Lila: An Inquiry into Morals*). Pirsig, author of *Zen and the Art of Motorcycle Maintenance*, suggests that we view the arts as a high-quality endeavor. Even motorcycle maintenance can be art if performed to the highest standards. He suggests that we apply our broadened understanding of what constitutes art in education by teaching all academic subjects more artistically, including the individual arts disciplines, which are academic subjects in their own right.

Douglas Sloan, professor of History and Education at Teachers College, Columbia University, argues the same point. He writes:

> Making the arts in this sense the center of education means above all summoning up the image of the whole of education itself as involving an artistic approach and sensitivity. It then becomes more accurate to describe education as an art than to speak of the arts in education. In this conception

there is no place for that separation between the arts and the
rest of the educational curriculum. (1983, p. 223)

The Mission of Education

This, then, might become schooling's new paradigm. As unlikely
as it may seem, there is a small but growing cadre that recognizes
that the arts should indeed guide all we do in school (and in our
lives as adults as well). The arts represent different ways of seeing and experiencing the reality of the world; they strengthen our
various intelligences, and they are a practical way to tap the
power of the aesthetic in support of Schiller's view of its importance. Ron Berger, a sixth-grade teacher in Shutesbury, Massachusetts, writes:

> My position has been that arts are not just important for
> the "carry-over effect" of energy and interest which occurs
> in artistic schools and which fuels academic growth, but
> because they can be at the core of a culture of high standards
> in a school. It is not a carry-over of energy, but rather an
> entire structure of creating, critiquing and sharing all acade-
> mic work within an aesthetic model. I have argued that arts
> can form the basis of school norms and standards for work
> in a manner which is incredibly powerful. Student work is
> strong not just because they have more energy for it, and not
> because there is a clear transfer of intelligences, but rather
> because academic work is embodied in projects which are
> viewed artistically at all points in their creation.

Leading educators embrace this idea. The arts, as forms of language, are at the core of the late Ernest Boyer's Basic School curriculum. An article in support of the arts appears in the May 1996
edition of *Horace*, the newsletter of the Coalition of Essential
Schools. It comments on recent research sponsored by the U.S.
Department of Education, which found that skills from the arts
can transfer to other areas — a proposition long denied by most
educators. The article goes on to say:

> But we also found that this transfer cannot occur unless
> teachers change their classroom structure — their use of

time, grouping, instructional strategies, active and participatory learning for all kids — to allow those skills and abilities to come out and be used.

For students who struggle in schools with curricula based primarily on verbal proficiency, the study found, using arts processes proved extremely powerful. We saw huge changes for those with more kinesthetic, musical, and artistic tendencies. (*Horace*, 1996)

Our challenge as business people, scientists, educators, and parents is, through policy, to allow teachers to change their classroom structure and at the same time to provide them with the tools to effectively teach within this new classroom environment. In this fashion, education itself can indeed become an art with the arts embedded at the core of the curriculum.

Educators are getting serious about professional development. It is up to community stakeholders (parents, businesses, service agencies, and taxpayers) to support them in their efforts in making education an art. There can be a big payoff — much more effective education at little if any added cost, as the townspeople in Shutesbury, Massachusetts, have discovered. Indeed, a classroom centered in the arts, as Ron Berger describes it, is the most effective way, both in pedagogy and cost, for all children to meet the internationally based academic performance standards under development by the New Standards project of the Center for Education and the Economy (and others). Berger writes:

It would be possible to attend an educational conference on High Standards in Learning and never hear the word *art* mentioned.

During times of "educational crisis," art is the first thing discarded from schools. Interestingly, in the teaching approach I embrace, art is at the core of standards.

In my classroom, I have tried to build an environment where art is more than a decoration or supplement for work, but rather a primary context in which most information is learned and shared. The infusion of arts has had, I believe, a profound effect on student understanding, investment, and standards.

This classroom approach is not an easy one. It demands of teachers a willingness to abandon textbooks as much as possible, to gather and create resources themselves, and to work together. It demands of administrators a willingness to sanction and support teachers in doing this. It demands of everyone in the school the courage to trust children with a great deal of responsibility and autonomy.

Though this approach is different, the school staff where I work has won over the hearts of a fairly conservative town community through their dedication, and through the extraordinary success this approach has had with the town's children. As a whole, students not only do well on standardized testing measures, but importantly and demonstrably do well in real-life measures of learning. They are capable and confident readers, writers, and users of math; they are strong thinkers and workers; they treat others well.

Reason and Analysis Are No Longer Sufficient

Until the Age of Enlightenment we felt ourselves to be at the mercy of the forces of nature. With the discovery of patterns in nature's behavior, combined with our ability, through mathematics, to measure and relate them, we experienced the exhilarating feeling that we were no longer at the mercy of mysterious and random forces. As indicated by *The Economist*:

> The power of Newton's great work was that it demonstrated (or appeared to demonstrate) the staggering power of science and the susceptibility of the physical world to human understanding. In that way, Newton inspired later thinkers to demand ever more of reason. If the intellect could comprehend the universe, in its seemingly limitless complexity, then surely it could also comprehend justice, authority, right and wrong.
>
> Through reason, man would master nature and himself; through reason, men everywhere, regardless of culture or tradition, would discover the universal rules by which they should live their lives. (1996, p. 85)

However, "enlightened," or rational, thinking now is under attack. *The Economist* asks, "Are these ideas mankind's finest intellectual achievement — or, as it is once again fashionable to argue, a catastrophic error?"

Is a new balance needed, as *The Economist* indicates, between the analytic part of the human mind and the instinctive part, between rationality and feeling, so that man can address the world more steadily? Have we ignored, or minimized, a whole chunk of our inherent capacity? Deepak Chopra describes "the space beyond reason," or the nonrational part of our minds, as a huge region unknown by science, because of the materialistic bias of science. Chopra writes:

> The rational part of our minds is generally quite fearful of the non rational part. But the threat has been greatly exaggerated. We spend much of our lives in the space beyond reason. If I say, "I love you," the sound waves from my voice bounce against your eardrum, setting up a vibration that the inner ear turns into an electric signal. This impulse is passed along the neurons to the brain's speech center, and you look pleased.
>
> Reason knows all about this journey, except for the last step, which is the most important. Why are you pleased that I love you? Why do those electrical impulses in the brain have a meaning? If I say a different sentence, "You have terminal cancer," the same physical impulses carry my voice to your brain's speech center, but now you are devastated. Scientifically, the signals are all but identical, yet the results they produce could hardly be more different. An EEG cannot decipher the meaningfulness of brain activity; the squiggles on the readout have nothing to say about what distinguishes love from hate, joy from sorrow, inspiration from tedium.
>
> Meaning slips through the fingers of science. The materialistic bias of science leads it to shun things that cannot be directly contacted by the senses. Yet nature has reserved a huge region set apart for things that cannot be seen, touched, or weighed. If you have ever observed a flock of swallows flying at dusk, you have seen them wheel and turn together, veering off at impossible tangents in the blink of an eye.

How does each bird know to turn at the precise instant the others do? Scientists have established that there is no bird acting as leader — the impulse is somehow shared by every bird at once. The magic lies in each one but also in between, over, and around them. It is fluid and invisible, like the air, but more so. (1991, pp. 52-53)

Ned Herrmann, both a successful sculptor and painter, as well as for many years manager of Management Education at General Electric Company, suggests we can better access the space beyond reason by developing our right-brain capabilities. He writes:

Modern Western society — the "developed" world — has increasingly demanded and reinforced left hemispheric skills. As industrialization replaced agriculture, our civilization focused its attention on behaviors that served the interests of a production oriented, business-centered, financially driven style of social organization. It rewarded the left-brain cognitive mode — orderly, replicable, and verbal — which serves these interests better than the spontaneous, less structured right modes.

Although it emerged later, the left brain's cognitive focus on fact, rationality, and verbal communication eventually earned it a position of power over the quiescent modes of the right brain. It has done so within each of us, within most of our social institutions, and in all of our business organizations. The left-brain modes have become especially entrenched in our educational system, which typically emphasizes the "three R's" and neglects — or even attacks — the cognitive capabilities of the right brain, such as art, intuition, music, and dance.

There have been unfortunate — even devastating — consequences to this rigid emphasis on the left brain. Well-meaning parents unknowingly constrict their children by failing to recognize and honor right-brain as well as left-brain gifts with respect to education and career choices. Well-intentioned teachers take their students down the wrong learning path because they don't know how to discern and use the preferred learning style of each student. Dedicated spouses and managers reduce the performance of family members or associates because they are taught to discount rather than appreciate precious differences. As a result, our right-brain capabilities remain latent at best, and often atrophy, at great cost to our personal satisfaction as well as human effectiveness as problem-solvers.

The easily dominated right brain needs all the help it can get to reclaim improved status in the Western world. Until it does, we will experience a high degree of internal conflict and a dissatisfaction in our society.

In terms of thinking style preferences, research has shown that the right and left brains are in a constant state of competition. Our two minds tend to be divided against each other.

I believe it is human destiny to move beyond this mental conflict to a more integrated wholeness, reflecting a smoother collaboration among the specialized parts of the brain. However, we will need to become far more aware of how to handle thinking preferences than we are now. We need to emphasize all the mental skills people favor, so our repertoire of potential behavioral responses can develop fully. This will give us powerful advantages in dealing with life's problems — both personal and professional. (1989, pp. 21-23)

The Individual as a Creative Power

A balanced mind, or whole brain, is vastly more powerful than even Ned Herrmann indicates. Such minds have the capacity to constructively enter the space beyond reason, and in so doing they directly alter the circumstances and events that shape lives. Through balance, not only will we be able to address the world more steadily, we will change it. James Allen, a 19th century Englishman, recognized that we ourselves are creative powers. We become, literally, what we think:

> Every man is where he is by the law of his being; the thoughts which he has built into his character have brought him there, and in the arrangement of his life there is no element of chance, but all is the result of a law which cannot err. This is just as true of those who feel "out of harmony" with their surroundings as of those who are contented with them.

Man is buffeted by circumstances so long as he believes himself to be the creature of outside conditions, but when he realizes that he is a creative power, and that he may command the hidden soil and seeds of his being out of which circumstances grow, he then becomes the rightful master of himself. (1989, pp. 21-22)

Deepak Chopra subscribes to the idea that we have complete control over ourselves and our world. According to Chopra, that control is a function of how we perceive the world, perceiving being the function of gaining knowledge, insight, or intuition through the senses. He writes:

Perception appears to be automatic, but in fact it is a learned phenomena. The world we live in, including the experience of our bodies, is completely dictated by how we learn to perceive it. If we change our perceptions, we change the experience of our bodies and our world. (1993, p. 40)

Stephen Edelglass, who teaches science at Green Meadow Waldorf School, supports Chopra's views:

An integrated art and science curriculum is a very powerful idea. Training perception is, for me, the ground of science education. A phenomenological epistemology explores the role of intentionality in the act of perceiving what we perceive and also intentionality in the quality of how we perceive.

The knowledge gained through intentionality in perception says something about the world; it is not solipsistic. At the same time inner experience can be included within what is known scientifically.

When a student is able to move from the phenomenon (percept) to the concept, she becomes filled with an experience of content — and she begins to experience herself. She becomes confident in her own thinking, in being able to comprehend, and in that comprehension, master her own life. (1993)

Related to the power of intentionality in perception is the power of the imagination. We also realize that the effort to imagine something, or make it up in one's mind, may be the root cause

61

of its happening. This is how one "commands the hidden soil and seeds of one's being out of which circumstances grow."

Successful companies have gone beyond simply making a profit to imagining the future as the path to achieving it. We also realize that it is the spirit of inquiry that drives us toward the good and that creates the future. Cultivating this power is the combined role of the arts and humanistic sciences. As processes of discovery, they embody the spirit of inquiry and spark the "craving to comprehend," which can animate us all. And putting this power to work for the good of mankind is the newly emerging role of business.

The inelegant expression, "what goes 'round, comes 'round," succinctly summarizes the point — experience in the world is directly related to how we view it. This is the law of our being. The thoughts we have directly shape our experience. As James Allen observed, "To desire is to obtain; to aspire is to achieve." He goes on to write:

> And you, too, youthful reader, will realize the Vision (not the idle wish) of your heart, be it base or beautiful, or a mixture of both, for you will always gravitate toward that which you, secretly, most love. Into your hands will be placed the exact results of your own thoughts; you will receive that which you earn; no more, no less. Whatever your present environment may be, you will fall, remain, or rise with your thoughts, your Vision, your Ideal. You will become as small as your controlling desire; as great as your dominant aspiration. (1989, pp. 78-79)

Changing How Business Thinks and Interacts

The MIT Center for Organizational Learning, sponsored by 18 of the nation's largest corporations, is exploring the power of individual transformation, encouraged and supported by corporate learning infrastructures. Learning organizations view their people as assets (rather than as costs), and self-knowledge and personal growth are formally recognized as vitally important to the success of the organization.

Peter Senge (1991) indicates that individual transformation requires dissolving frozen patterns of thought. He writes:

> We have drifted into a culture that fragments our thoughts, that detaches the world from the self and the self from its community. We have gained control of our environment but have lost our artistic edge. We are so focused on our security that we don't see the price we pay: living in bureaucratic organizations where the wonder and joy of learning have no place. Thus we are losing the spaces to dance with the ever-changing patterns of life. We are losing ourselves as fields of dreams.
>
> We argue that the main dysfunctions in our institutions — fragmentation, competition, and reactiveness — are actually byproducts of our success over thousands of years in conquering the physical world and developing our scientific, industrial culture. These dysfunctions are not problems to be solved — they are frozen patterns of thought to be dissolved.

Senge takes a humanist view of organizational change. He describes the disciplines to be practiced by individuals interested in effecting change — systems thinking, personal mastery, mental models, building shared visions, and team learning — as more like artistic disciplines than traditional management disciplines.

After decades of focus on "the bottom line" or increasing owner/shareholder value at all costs, is liberal capitalism beginning to move beyond its narrow focus, toward an interest in human development? This move proceeds less from a sudden interest in social responsibility than from a search for higher quality performance. Managers now understand that attention to individual and organizational learning increases productivity and ultimately enhances profits.

Harvard Business School's Gerald Zaltman encourages individual growth, organizational learning, and better managerial performance by drawing on recent work about the nature of mind, knowledge, and intelligence. Describing his premises he writes:

> *Most social communication is nonverbal.* Eighty percent of all communication is nonverbal. This is consistent with

the finding that two-thirds of all stimuli reaching the brain are visual, with the balance being conveyed through sound, taste, smell, and touch. Nonverbal communication includes paralanguage, or the tone, pitch, and other speech qualities that determine whether we literally mean what we say.

Thoughts occur as images. Having thoughts and expressing them can be quite different. This raises the question, "What is it we have when we have a thought?" Thoughts are images, and only infrequently verbal images. (Zaltman and Schuck 1995, p. 5)

The point that language is *not* required for human conceptual thinking but is only one of several "symbol systems" used to express intelligence is beautifully made in *Post Captain* by Patrick O'Brian. In describing the thoughts of Dr. Stephen Maturin while listening to a concert in London in the year 1803, he writes:

A foolish German has said that man thought in words. It was totally false; a pernicious doctrine; the thought flashed into being in a hundred simultaneous forms, with a thousand associations, and the speaking mind selected one, forming it grossly into the inadequate symbols of words, inadequate because common to disparate situations — admitted to be inadequate for vast regions of expression, since for them there were the parallel languages of music and painting. Words were not called for in many or indeed most forms of thought: Mozart certainly thought in terms of music. He himself at this moment was thinking in terms of scent. (1990, p. 470)

Zaltman continues:

Metaphors are central to cognition. A consensus has emerged across many disciplines in the past two decades that metaphors, the representation of one thing in terms of another, is fundamental to thinking and knowing.

Metaphors actively create and shape thought; we cannot know anything unless it is perceived as an instance of one thing and not another. Thought is more inherently figurative than it is literal.

Cognition is grounded in embodied experience. This premise, although supported by research in many fields, is less widely known. It states that abstract thought is shaped by perceptual and motor experiences. Perceptual experience includes all sensory systems, not just vision. Basically, metaphorical understanding and associated mental models are grounded in everyday bodily experience.

Thus, viewing the body as a multi-media system which shapes our thinking suggests that the various subsystems such as the visual subsystem are important technologies to use in "getting the inside out."

Reason, emotion, and experience co-mingle. Human thought involves both reasoning and emotion; effective decision making, whether by customers or managers, requires both. Therefore, it is necessary to consider emotion, logical inference, and embodied experience as mutually dependent and inseparable dynamics. (Zaltman and Schuck 1995, pp. 6-8)

Organizational learning, which is now capturing the attention of the best business managers, must be grounded in these new understandings about how we think and communicate. Many managers also understand that the entire "ecology" of the business organization is changing. The former CEO of Hanover Insurance, Bill O'Brien, describes his view of these changes:

Work is viewed as a platform on which people mature and achieve happiness by developing their competencies as well as contributing to the Gross World Product. As an employee, a person is first a human being and second an instrument of production. When workers sense this fundamental order in a company, they will devote considerable energy to achieving the company's business goals.

Corporate ecologies based on values and visions (aspirations) will generally outperform command-and-control corporations.

Learning exclusively through the mechanical, reductionistic model has served business well up to now. But it must be augmented by systemic understanding of the enormous inter-connectedness in our world.

Leadership in a vision-driven, value-guided organization has a high component of service, learning, and love. It is about building character and advancing learning throughout the organization. (*Systems Thinker*, 1996)

As business continues to explore the need for imaginative, perceptive thinking — not only in its leaders but throughout the organization — a greater appreciation for training in the arts and an aesthetic approach to education will follow.

Changing the Meaning of Science

As Peter Senge has described it, our current societal dysfunction is the result of our scientific success. Physicist David Bohm, who died in 1992, would agree. He wrote:

> The prevailing attitude in science has been to put the major emphasis on analysis and on splitting off the key factors of each situation. Scientists hope that this will enable them to extend their powers indefinitely to predict and control things. In fact, this spirit is now spreading beyond science, not only into technology, but also into our general approach to life as a whole. Understanding is now valued as the means to predict, control, and manipulate things.
>
> We're beginning to realize that the cost of progress is more and more specialization and fragmentation to the point where the whole activity is losing its meaning.
>
> I think we need to change what we mean by "science." (Bohm and Peat 1987, pp. 10-11)

Robert Root-Bernstein (1989), associate professor of physiology at Michigan State University and a MacArthur Fellow, sees many similarities between science and art. He views science as a process of discovery and believes that creative thought, or transformational thinking, is the ability to conceive an object or idea interchangeably or concurrently in visual, verbal, mathematical, kinesthetic, or musical ways. He suggests that we use what he terms "tools of thought" to give meaning to facts and to facilitate transformational thinking. These tools, most of which are embodied in the arts, include analogizing, forming and recognizing patterns, visual and kinesthetic thinking, modeling, play-acting, manual manipulation, and aesthetics. He believes that the mind and senses alike must be trained equally and in tandem to perceive and to imagine, and he points out that few, if any, of these tools of thought are in our standard science curricula.

David Bohm and F. David Peat, in their book, *Science, Order, and Creativity*, broaden the idea of imagination, finding in it the beginnings of a new, more comprehensive science:

> Literally *imagination* means "the ability to make mental images," which imitate the forms of real things. However, the powers of imagination actually go far beyond this, to include the creative inception of new forms, hitherto unknown. These are experienced not only as visual images, but also through all sorts of feelings, tactile sensations, and kinesthetic sensations and in other ways that defy description. The ability of Mozart and Bach to sense whole musical works all at once could be regarded as a kind of musical imagination. The activity of the imagination does not therefore resemble a static-picture but rather it is closer to a kind of "play" that includes a subtle orchestration of feelings, as well as a sense of intention and will. (1987, pp. 261-62)

What Bohm and Peat describe is the aesthetic impulse itself. It also seems to be another way of describing Deepak Chopra's law of intention and desire, as well as the workings of Stephen Edelglass' intentionality in perception. Certainly, the exercise of the imagination lies at the heart of the creative process and carries with it transcendent power. The process of imagining the future has much to do with bringing it into being.

Craig Holdrege (1993), a science teacher, observes:

> Humankind needs a science in which the scientists consciously include the active human being as a part of the reality they strive to understand. This means taking concrete inner and outer experiences much more seriously. It means overcoming the habits of mind which lead us to treat consciousness as a mere epiphenomenon of underlying neural processes, and

sense experience as a subjective, (i.e., inaccurate) picture of an underlying "real" world of matter and forces.

The Metaphysics of Quality:
A More Inclusive Mental Model

Robert Pirsig (1991) proposes the "metaphysics of quality" as a way to reunite man and nature. He writes that the scientific mental model is based on the assumption that the universe is composed only of subjects and objects, and anything that cannot be classified as a subject or object is not real.

While introducing readers to the "metaphysics of quality" in *Lila: An Inquiry into Morals*, he suggests that there is no empirical evidence for this assumption at all. He believes, instead, that there are many sets of intellectual reality in existence, with varying degrees of quality. His "metaphysics of quality" supports and encompasses David Bohm's belief that different kinds of thought and different kinds of abstraction may together give a better reflection of reality:

> The Metaphysics of Quality subscribes to what is called empiricism. It claims that all legitimate human knowledge arises from the senses or by thinking about what the senses provide. Most empiricists, however, deny the validity of any knowledge gained through imagination, authority, tradition, or purely theoretical reasoning. They regard fields such as art, morality, religion, and metaphysics as unverifiable.
>
> The Metaphysics of Quality varies from this by saying that the values of art and morality and even religious mysticism are verifiable, and that in the past they have been excluded for metaphysical reasons, not empirical reasons. They have been excluded because of the metaphysical assumption that all the universe is composed of subjects and objects and anything that cannot be classified as a subject or an object is not real. There is no empirical evidence for this assumption at all. It is just an assumption.
>
> It is an assumption that flies outrageously in the face of common experience.

This may sound as though a purpose of the Metaphysics of Quality is to trash all subject-object thought, but that is not true. Unlike subject-object metaphysics, the Metaphysics of Quality does not insist on a single exclusive truth. If subjects and objects are held to be the ultimate reality, then we are permitted only one construction of things — that which corresponds to the "objective" world — and all other constructions are unreal. But if Quality or excellence is seen as the ultimate reality, then it becomes possible for more than one set of truths to exist. Then one does not seek the absolute "Truth." One seeks instead the highest quality intellectual explanation of things with the knowledge that if the past is any guide to the future, this explanation must be taken provisionally; as useful until something better comes along. One can then examine intellectual realities the same way he examines paintings in an art gallery, not with an effort to find out which one is the "real" painting, but simply to enjoy and keep those that are of value. There are many sets of intellectual reality in existence, and we can perceive some to have more quality than others, but that we do so is, in part, the result of our history and current patterns of values.

The Metaphysics of Quality provides a better set of coordinates with which to interpret the world than does subject-object metaphysics because it is more inclusive. It explains more of the world, and it explains it better. (Pirsig 1991, pp. 113-16)

Awakening the Craving to Comprehend

If the values of art and morality are experienced (and therefore verified) through aesthetics, it would suggest that beauty is the basic law or principle from which all others are derived. Kant described aesthetics as the branch of metaphysics concerned with the laws of perception. What is it about aesthetics that awakens "the craving to comprehend," as Herman Hesse describes it in *The Glass Bead Game*?

It draws together our analytic, perceptive, and emotional capacities to deepen our understanding, building the only true

69

and lasting foundation for rational life, as Schiller suggests. Perhaps the best definition was provided by Keats, when he wrote, "Beauty is truth, truth beauty."

Robert Scruton provides some insights in his new book, *Modern Philosophy*. He believes that it is through aesthetics that we can reconnect with the world, and others — the connection that has been denied us in the exercise of pure "rational" thought uninformed by our senses or emotions, as Plato would have it. Kindergartners offer us a glimpse of early aesthetic behavior, as they are not yet disconnected from the world, Ron Berger points out. Scruton writes:

> Disinterested contemplation of the world means contemplation of the world in relation to the self, and contemplation of the self as *part* of the world. Such a view would explain why aesthetic experience is so gripping: we are seeking for our home in the world: not the home of the body and its appetites, but the home of the self. The endlessness of aesthetic interest reflects the fact that we can never find that home: the self is not *in* the empirical world but lies at its limit.
>
> In the "Aesthetic Attitude," we seem to have discovered a special kind of rational interest; interest in something for its own sake, and without reference to our empirical desires. What is the value of such an interest, and what does it tell us about our condition?
>
> It is an interest in the *phenomenal* world, as Kant would put it: that is, the world as it appears. The object of aesthetic interest is perceived through the senses, and the element of experience seems to be essential. You respond to the *look* of the landscape, the *sound* of the birdsong, and the *feel* of the wind against your face. The term "aesthetic" derives from the Greek word for perception.
>
> Aesthetic judgment is a part of practical reason, and our truest guide to the environment. It is by aesthetic judgment that we adapt the world to ourselves and ourselves to the world. Schiller argued that the "aesthetic education" of man is his one true preparation for rational life, and the foundation of any ordered politics. (1995, pp. 443-44, 449)

Stephanie Perrin, the head of Walnut Hill, a private school for artistically inclined students, describes the school's educational principle as supporting a process of integration, not only of the arts and humanities with the sciences and math but, more importantly, spirit and matter, soul and body.

> The aims of both systems of education at Walnut Hill are to produce young people who, in addition to being knowledgeable and well-trained in the specifics of both the arts and the liberal arts, are also able to think critically; to make judgments; to be self-aware both in terms of their feelings and their ethical and moral stance; to be aware of others and able to work with them; to gather and assess information; to have a sense of agency and control in the world; and to be able to generalize and adapt a variety of skills and attitudes to meet whatever challenges life presents. The aims are simply to be able to keep on learning.
>
> These higher order skills and attitudes can be developed in either of the systems. They can be taught through the study of music or the study of biology. It is at this level of functioning that the systems can be said to share an outcome: the creation of the educated young person.
>
> We try to support that process of integration, that rich understanding that incorporates spirit and matter — soul and body — that will allow our students to move toward their future with the tools to engage in this world with full intellectual, emotional and moral understanding and the courage to act on that understanding. (Perrin 1991)

This passage describes precisely the "balance" we need to deal with the world more effectively, as called for by *The Economist*. It is a balance between head, heart, and hand. It develops "perceptive reason, informed by aesthetics," which is a mental model in response to — and in contrast to — Enlightenment thinking, with its adulation of rational thought, uninformed (and thus limited) by the absence of trained perceptions and controlled emotion.

The Power of the Imagination

Elliot Eisner observes that educators' indifference to the refinement of perception and inattention to the development of imagination have limited children's cognitive growth. Conversely, those trained in the arts have educated imaginations and developed cognitive capabilities.

The arts community has much to teach us about educating the imagination, or developing the spirit of inquiry that guides and informs the creative process. Robert Fritz believes that the secret of the creative process is understood intuitively by artists but that the idea is so simple artists have never made it explicit. In his book, *The Path of Least Resistance: Learning to Become the Creative Force in Your Own Life*, he writes:

> A common mistake people make when first entering the orientation of the creative is to seek to "find out" what they want as if it were a deeply hidden treasure to be discovered and revealed.
>
> They are looking in the wrong direction. Creating what you want is not a revelatory process, nor is what you want something to be discovered.
>
> If not by revelation or discovery, then how do you derive the *what* in the question What do I want? The answer to this question is known, either rationally or intuitively, by those who are actively involved in creating.
>
> The answer to this question permeates all creative acts, from creating your life the way you want it to be, to designing the latest technological advances in computer science.
>
> Our educational tradition unfortunately has had a tendency to belittle the power and significance of this answer. And yet, once you begin to use it, new creative power and flexibility are available to you.
>
> How do you create the *what* in "What do I want?"
>
> YOU MAKE IT UP!
>
> Please do not miss the point. This is truly a remarkable insight into the deeper nature of the creative orientation. If not by need, and not by the demands of the circumstances, and not by revelation, then how do you conceive of what you want? Simply by "making up" the results. (1989, p. 66)

Business is beginning to understand that the ability to imagine the future can actually bring it about. In *Competing for the Future*, by Gary Hamel and C.K. Prahalad, the authors observe:

> The goal of this book is to help managers imagine (or make up) the future and, having imagined it, create it. There is not one future but hundreds. There is no law that says most companies must be followers. Getting to the future first is not just about outrunning competitors bent on reaching the same prize. It is also about having one's own view of what the prize is. There can be as many prizes as runners; imagination is the only limiting factor. Renoir, Picasso, Calder, Serat, and Chagall were all enormously successful artists, but each had an original and distinctive style. In no way did the success of one preordain the failure of another. Yet each artist spawned a host of imitators. In business, as in art, what distinguishes leaders from laggards, and greatness from mediocrity, is the ability to uniquely imagine what could be. (1994, p. 25)

James Allen writes that developing an independent point of view — or vision — indeed brings it into being.

> He who cherishes a beautiful vision, a lofty ideal in his heart, will one day realize it. Columbus cherished a vision of another world, and he discovered it; Copernicus fostered the vision of a multiplicity of worlds, and a wider universe, and he revealed it; Buddha beheld the vision of a spiritual world of stainless beauty and perfect peace, and he entered into it.
>
> Cherish your visions; cherish your ideals; cherish the music that stirs in your heart, the beauty that forms in your mind, the loveliness that drapes your purest thoughts, for out of them will grow all delightful conditions, all heavenly environment; of these, if you but remain true to them, your world will at last be built. To desire is to obtain; to aspire is to achieve. (1989, pp. 74-75)

This is, perhaps, the reason Albert Einstein observed that imagination is more important than knowledge. Imagining something, or creating something, is so obvious to artists, whose stock in

trade is the creative, that they do not see their own capacities —
just as the fish do not see the water.

The late James Rouse, real estate developer and community
builder, understood the power of a vision. He wrote:

> Visions describe what best should be, could be — if and
> when mankind has the will to make them real. . . . I don't
> think people understand the power of visions. That erecting
> a vision of what ought to be under a given circumstance, and
> then believing that it can be accomplished because it ought
> to be, generates power; generates action by people; gener-
> ates energy; generates the capacity to fulfill it, because it is
> held up. I believe that whatever ought to be done, can be
> done. (1996)

What motivates a creator? Why bother to imagine a picture, a
dance, or the future of business? Robert Fritz observes:

> The desire for the creation to exist — not for a return on
> investment, not for what it may say about you, but for the
> love of the thing, the creation, itself. One creates music
> because we love it enough to make it happen. The reason
> you would create anything is because you love it enough to
> see it exist. (1989, pp. 58-59)

The Better Alternative:
Perceptive Reason Informed by the Aesthetic

This brings us back to the power of the aesthetic impulse — a
blend of reason, emotion, and the senses, which is "a special kind
of rational interest, interest in something for its own sake —
which could lead to clues about the meaning of life itself," as
Robert Scruton observes.

The ultimate energizing power of the aesthetic is putting purpose
and meaning into a world that appears to have none. The aesthetic delivers a sense of purposefulness — of Mind, as Herman
Hesse describes it. It provides a balance between the rational and
the emotional/intuitive parts of our being. It allows us to view and
experience the world more steadily, and as a participant. Guided

by the aesthetic impulse, we begin to understand what it means to be a part of the world, and not an enemy of it. It underlies a more humanistic science and resolves the dilemma of man's place in the world ("inside-out" versus "outside-in").

It provides purpose to liberal capitalism, where investment in the personal growth and development of the employee while providing needed goods and services leads to financial profit. It is the shore on which Elliot Eisner stands, calling to those of us in the rowboat, lost offshore in the fog. It is the force which moves mathematicians. It is "the structure within which to create, critique, and share all academic work, forming the basis of school norms and standards for work in a manner which is incredibly powerful" (Berger 1990).

Creating, critiquing, and sharing all academic work within an aesthetic model deepens our intelligence. It is the educational response to the need for a better alternative — called for by *The Economist* — to the philosophy of the Enlightenment that has shaped Western thinking over the last three centuries. It supports David Perkins' (1992) contention that intelligence is not fixed but can be taught.

Great teachers, such as Ron Berger, Stephen Edelglass — and Karen Gallas, a first- and second-grade teacher in the Brookline, Massachusetts, school system — teach perceptive reason. We must find ways to help others emulate them. In this way our young people can better adapt themselves to the world, and each other. As Robert Scruton observes:

> By recognizing, through aesthetics, the sublime purposefulness that flows through all things, even though as free beings who are compelled at every moment to see themselves as apart from nature — we can find our home in the natural order. (1995, p. 455)

Developing a culture of high standards through an aesthetic model leads to an order of magnitude increase in school effectiveness. This can be done at little, if any, extra cost — but only when parents and taxpayers recognize the power inherent in the practice of education within an aesthetic model and demand the arts in both curriculum and pedagogical practice.

As our awareness of our inner strengths and our connectedness to the world and to each other increase, a great renaissance will occur in both the practice and the teaching of the arts in schools. There is a power here that, while difficult to measure, nevertheless exists. As we develop better assessment tools and as our understanding of the nature of intelligence continues to grow, our appreciation of this power will increase, leading to the positioning of the arts at the core of the curriculum.

References

Allen, James. *As a Man Thinketh*. Philadelphia: Running Press, 1989.

Berger, Ron. "Building a School Culture of High Standards." Manuscript. May 1990. Available from the author at Pratt Corner Road, Amherst, MA 01002.

Bohm, David, and Peat, F. David. *Science, Order, and Creativity*. New York: Bantam, 1987.

Campbell, Joseph. *Myths to Live By*. New York: Bantam, 1972.

Chopra, Deepak. *Unconditional Life*. New York: Bantam, 1991.

Chopra, Deepak. *Ageless Body, Timeless Mind*. New York: Crown, 1993.

Coleman, Daniel. *Emotional Intelligence*. New York: Bantam, 1995.

"Crimes of Reason." *The Economist*, 16-22 March 1996, p. 85.

Drucker, Peter. *The New Realities*. New York: Harper & Row, 1989.

Edelglass, Stephen. Personal communication, December 1993.

Fritz, Robert. *The Path of Least Resistance: Learning to Become the Creative Force in Your Own Life*. New York: Ballantine, 1989.

Hamel, Gary, and Prahalad, C.K. *Competing for the Future*. Boston: Harvard Business School Press, 1994.

Herrmann, Ned. *The Creative Brain*. Lake Lure, N.C.: Brain Books, 1989).

Holdrege, Craig. "Book Review of *Matter and Mind* by Stephen Edelglass, Georg Maier, Hans Gebert, and John Davy." 1993.

Horace, Newsletter of the Coalition of Essential Schools 12, no. 5 (May 1996), quoted in Oreck, Barry. "The Arts and Other Languages: From Elective to Essential," *ArtsConnection*.

O'Brian, Patrick. *Post Captain*. New York: W.W. Norton, 1990.

Perkins, David. *Smart Schools*. New York: Free Press, 1992.

Perrin, Stephanie. "The Aims of Education at Walnut Hill: The Art of Learning." Working paper for the Klingenstein Fellowship, January 1991.

Pirsig, Robert M. *Zen and the Art of Motorcycle Maintenance*. New York: Morrow, 1974.

Pirsig, Robert M. *Lila: An Inquiry into Morals*. New York: Bantam, 1991.

Root-Bernstein, Robert. *Discovering*. Cambridge, Mass.: Harvard University Press, 1989.

Rouse, James. *Prism*, newsletter of the Business Enterprise Trust (Spring 1996): 3.

Scruton, Robert. *Modern Philosophy*. New York: Penguin, 1995.

Senge, Peter. "Transforming the Practice of Management." Paper presented at the Systems Thinking in Action Conference, November 1991.

Sloan, Douglas. *Insight-Imagination: The Emancipation of Thought and the Modern World*. Westport, Conn.: Greenwood, 1983.

The Systems Thinker, newsletter published by Pegasus Communications, Cambridge, Mass., March 1996, p. 3.

Whitehead, Alfred North. *The Aims of Education and Other Essays*. New York: Free Press, 1967.

Zaltman, Gerald, and Schuck, Linda. "Sensing the Voice of the Customer." Paper presented at the Harvard Business School Colloquium, Multimedia and the Boundaryless World, November 1995.

Generating Hope Through Arts Education

BY JULIA BALAISIS

Julia Balaisis is a drama educator and cooperative education coordinator at Cardinal Carter Catholic High School with the York Region Separate School Board in Ontario and a doctoral student in the Ontario Institute for Studies in Education, University of Toronto.

We recognize a growing hopelessness and desperation in society today, an anxiety naturally concentrated in those with most at stake — our youth. There is fear for the future, including the future of work itself, with the knowledge that jobs, as we have come to know them, are becoming increasingly scarce. Employment has been the means to sustain an economic standard that we, in the First World, have not only become accustomed to, but for which we have cultivated our appetites. As such, employment has been the means through which we have maintained our place and status in society, our empowerment and the means by which we have defined our worth.

Various agents within society have solutions to deal with the current economic downturn, diminishment of resources, and subsequent societal disequilibrium. Business and industry recommend a change in mind-set concerning the very concept of jobs, encouraging "multi-skilling" and increasing flexibility of the workforce to deal with the growing outsourcing of jobs. Employability skills profiles are developed to list and encourage that which is demanded by the new workplace. Current government practice advocates constraint, urging self-sufficiency and a "get tough" business agenda for everything, including health care, social services, and education.

Education sees its current mandate to engage in job training by employing service learning and seamless school-to-work transitions as part of the new pedagogy and to move away from "soft" ways of knowing into the hard disciplines, *the basics*. This focus on training for the job market places trust squarely on the belief that a continuation of our consumer industrial worldview will bring renewal. Measurable outcomes in education call for obvious and tangible indicators of success and mirror the way profits witness *superficially* to the health of a society. There is a serious misplacement of worth when that which truly brings quality to life is regularly and systematically undervalued. Our experiences, relationships, and the ongoing nurturing and caretaking that these require are difficult to measure by our society's assessment tools (profits!), because that which is most meaningful and worthwhile in life traditionally has been and continues to be work that, for the most part, does not garner wages at all.

While education needs to maintain its relevancy to current social, cultural, and economic practice — and it needs to take active responsibility for making students better prepared for jobs — education must seriously allow for the critiquing of society itself and assist students to unearth that which is unconscious and dangerous within systems in order to create shifts in thinking and new possibilities. A critical view developed by James Hillman sees that "business as defined by the ideas of Western Capitalism, has become the fundamental force in human society, and in the manner of monotheism, promulgates a fundamentalist faith in its basic tenets" (1995, p. 3). This is a warning to education insofar as education is fundamentally adaptive. In today's terms, when education focuses solely on the support of existing structures, it secures faith in capitalism and consumerism. The underpinning of this faith reveals an assumption that I believe is intrinsically faulty: If business and the economy continue to grow, we will all prosper, by a trickle-down effect. While struggling to succeed in the system, it is easy to underestimate the extent of the damage that has been perpetrated by the profit motive — injuries that require for their repair and healing a depth and breadth of solution that goes beyond economic re-stabilization. Dewey challenged education early in the industrial era, and the challenge must be sustained.

The kind of vocational education in which I am interested is not one that will "adapt" workers to the existing regime; I am not sufficiently in love with the regime for that. It seems to me that the business of all who would not be education time-servers is to resist every move in this direction and to strive for a kind of vocational education that will alter the existing industrial system and ultimately transform it.

We require a transformation in our way of doing business. Believing and functioning in a free-market economy too often goes unchallenged and needs further analysis. John Raulston Saul looks with this critical eye:

> The marketplace has been constantly evoked over the last quarter-century as the source of freedom and democracy as well as the only possible force to lead us back to growth. But after two decades of having their way, the exponents of this theory have no results to show us . . . they have been in charge, they have held and continue to hold the levers of power, and they have not produced . . . this experiment in market leadership has not reinforced democracy or individualism, nor has it brought growth . . . in citizen-based democracy. (1995a, p. 133)

The slow but sure dismantling of true democracy, a democracy that embraces empowerment and participation, has repercussions that reach to a spiritual plane and subsequently distorts our relationships with ourselves, others, and our world. The threat of disempowerment creates anxiety and frustration and is manifested as a spiritual need in young people today. The seeking of other-world experiences reveals a spiritual vacuum at the base of the needs of youth. Drug and alcohol abuse is alarmingly on the increase, as are other ways of dropping out of the mainstream. Many find their need for belonging and initiation rites through gang and cult association. Some find substitutions for direct human interaction through an addiction to "surfing the net." As the promises of consumerism become increasingly empty, it is insufficient to urge young people to continually adapt to change in order to survive. They need to be activated as instruments of change to make sustainability possible on a wider scale.

For those who would shy away from spiritual understandings or solutions, assuming that it calls for more religion, I call attention to Charlene Spretnak's understanding that:

> spirituality is an intrinsic dimension of human consciousness and is not separate from the body. . . . From one perspective, we realize that we need food, shelter, and clothing; from another that some sort of relationship among people, animals, and the Earth is necessary; from another that we must determine our identity as creatures not only of our immediate habitat but of the world and the universe; from another that the subtle, suprarational reaches of mind can reveal true nature of being. (1982, p. xv)

It is here that I believe the arts have something special to contribute. In time of scarcity and fear, we need our personal resources more than ever, serving in other ways besides training us to compete in a global marketplace. Students are, more than ever, in need of being motivated and satisfied from things other than consumer goods. They need that which satisfies at a deeper level. Without acknowledging these other realities, young people could well be impeded in developing their human "being" skills that are essential in improving their own survival rate, emotionally, mentally, and physically. This is not a spirituality that sedates, but instead nurtures us to create meaning at both personal and collective levels in order to energize for action.

The arts are perhaps the only way we have left to address a spiritual need in the multicultural, pluralistic society that we are evolving. In our struggle to deal with the inclusion of multiplicity within our school systems, we are reluctant and awkward with respect to spirituality; thus we largely practice avoidance. The hybrid of new-age spirituality indicates a hunger among young and old alike and points to how traditional religions are not fully meeting current needs. I am proposing a place and inclusion into the curriculum for this fuller dimension of knowing and being that is activated through an arts focus, one that is a means by which we nurture and create a vision for action. I am advocating a bias for an arts curriculum that today is under increasing threat by the current business/education agenda.

I will elaborate how these broad and urgent needs can be fulfilled by the arts in three significant ways. First of all, the arts democratize as they allow for participation through the acknowledgment and expression of our individual "voices." Second, the arts and their processes powerfully unite people, meaningfully linking humans together. Third, the arts improve the basic quality of life in its most mundane and daily forms, thus reintegrating ourselves with our cosmos and life itself. These essentials work to strengthen our sense of identity, belonging, and self-esteem and are prerequisites for any creation of vision, alternatives for the future, and transformation of complacency into action.

Art as a Means of Voicing and Empowerment

The arts allow us to find and activate our inner voice — our personal way of knowing. While all arts encourage expression of the individual, my experience primarily as a drama teacher leads me to illustrate this through discussing the unique possibilities in drama education. Voicing is about caring for our soul in reactivating and trusting our expression and yearning. While inner knowing or operating intuitively has been our birthright, it is one that we have largely lost. The mythic structures of the scientific era, propelled by a Cartesian and Newtonian mechanistic model of the universe, necessitated the mediation, verification, and technological endorsement of natural processes that led to their greater discreditation. What emanated from spiritual and soul realms suffered scientific scrutiny that disabled much of this lifeblood in the human spirit. As moderns we are more distant and disconnected from innate wisdom by the continued silencing of our inner voices, the intermittent or perfunctory attention paid to it, and the regular threat of its co-optation. In breaking down our self-trust in this manner, our ability to act is subsequently inhibited. Yet spiritual needs cannot be easily suppressed, and reawakened interest is ubiquitous, as evidenced in the host of bestsellers that call attention to the urgency to care for soul needs.

Youth are particularly vulnerable in both their need for spiritual nurturance and their susceptibility to censorship. As children, they are easily silenced when they know or see, and they often learn to internalize the censor and remain quiet. This also happens easily in school, especially as increasing demands for concrete results train students to further trust the rational ways of knowing. Our path to success, as society defines it, often is strewn with many little deaths along the way. The greatest tragedy is to find oneself at the end of life, never having heeded the promptings of the soul or inner nature.

Clarissa Pinkola Estes in her book, *Women Who Run with the Wolves,* points out the necessity of accessing the inner realm that she knows as the wildness within, this being our animal, intuitive self. While her book addresses women, it applies to us all as she speaks of the gifts available in accessing our wild self:

> When women reassert their relationship with the wildish nature, they are gifted with a permanent and internal watcher, a knower, a visionary, an oracle, an inspiratrice, an intuitive, a maker, a creator, an inventor, and a listener who guide, suggest, and urge vibrant life in the inner and outer worlds. When women are close to this nature, the fact of that relationship glows through them. This wild teacher, wild mother, wild mentor supports their inner and outer lives, no matter what. (1995, p. 6)

In speaking of intuition, I am defining it as knowing with *all* the senses, "seeing," in the broadest sense of that word, things as they really are. Benefits of intuition include the ability to comfort, caution, nurture, affirm, reassure, give right direction, free from worry, guide in accomplishing tasks, call to action, curtail unsafe behavior. Intuition provides the knowledge of when to act, move, get out, escape, provide encouragement to continue; it ultimately leads you into the life you need to live. This is no less than the gift of discernment — an essential commodity in an ever increasingly complex, treacherous world. This is not a knowledge gained by thinking as we commonly understand it, but by finding the wisdom that is at the heart of intuitive knowing. We certainly want our children to be safe in the world, yet one marvels at the limitations of the present common admonishment to children "not to talk to strangers" — a gross over-simplification and clumsy labeling that can be a precursor to disaster instead of safety. Again, it acknowledges only rational knowing.

Yet how do we get children to use their intuition and exercise personal power when this knowing is one that we have by and large lost? Drama becomes a key tool in this process. I will cite and use a traditional folk tale, one that is explicated at length by Estes for the intent purpose of enabling intuition. This story is not only a revelation of the value and the qualities of intuition — and points us to its access — but in activating this story in dramatic form, students can actually engage the tools of intuition in our classrooms.

Estes retells a story about a young girl who is without her voice in a variation of the familiar Cinderella story. Vasalisa is silent to the cruelties heaped upon her by her new guardians. She obediently does what she is told, even when sent to what will be her probable death in the journey to get fire from the fearsome Baba Yaga. She is silent in obedience and out of touch with her own pain — or at least incapable of doing anything about it, even complaining.

Yet her mother, while on her deathbed, had given her the most valuable of gifts: the way to Vasalisa's own knowing that will be the activation of her own voice. It is in the gift of a doll that resembles Vasalisa herself, which the mother says will befriend her and guide her in her life. The mother tells Vasalisa to feed the doll and take care of it, and it will always advise her well, no matter what trouble she may be in. The doll will always know how to help. With this gift, the mother gives Vasalisa more than the good counsel to trust herself or an exhortation to listen to her own inner workings. The mother knows how difficult a task this would be for someone unfamiliar with this way of trusting and especially without having the support of a loving mentor to help point her to herself. Instead, the mother gives a gift that Vasalisa is truly capable of accessing, in projecting the young girl's own wisdom onto something outside of herself, yet readily accessible — the doll. This is the gift of projected play, make believe, and taking on a role. *This is the gift of drama.*

By listening for the doll to speak to her, Vasalisa can relax and wait, instead of busily generating thought. Little by little, in trusting this interaction, Vasalisa will eventually claim the doll's wisdom as her own. But for the time being, it needs to be "out there," where it can more easily be seen.

As the story proceeds, Vasalisa is given many nearly insurmountable tasks that she must accomplish to save herself from certain death. All of the tasks are miraculously accomplished through the reassurance and assistance of the doll, to the point where Vasalisa earns safe leave and finally returns home with the required glowing ember, a symbol for her much greater self-empowerment.

This is the tool available to help us open to ourselves, which is available in drama. Here I am not referring to drama as oriented toward theatrical production but the art form of learning by going deeper with aesthetic sensibility to where we find ourselves reacting and creating honestly in the imaginary circumstances. It is important for drama educators to trust participants as the artists, relying on their evolving inner knowing so that the work becomes a genuine exploration, not issuing from preconceived goals or, in this case, just playing the story. Using this approach, participants easily and emotionally hook into the creating, projecting themselves into roles that distance them from their usual personal constraints; and the story takes on its own direction, maintaining truth to its spirit. This amounts to nothing short of liberation.

The qualities that are unique to this type of drama work are those same tools by which intuition and self-empowerment are actualized:

- Drama firmly hinges on imagination and creativity, as does intuition, which is not accessible through conventional mental cognitive processes. Using the metaphor of the story, Vasalisa waits and listens to the doll without busily generating solutions.

- Drama works in its capacity to give the comfort of apparent distancing in the function of role-playing. In the same way that a puppet can free the expression of a young child and a mask can liberate and enrich, both in theater and in ritual, use of role can protect while accessing the new frontiers of inner realities. There is a safety in role as there is greater safety for the young girl to more easily listen to her doll than to directly generate inner thinking or to muse on inner workings.

- There is a physicality and an embodiment in drama work, just as the doll embodies the wisdom of the girl. While visualization and meditation are excellent tools for accessing and developing intuition, drama has the added feature by which one can integrate the physical self, both body and voice. Acting assists in processing new information at the cellular level where new memory incarnates. This embodiment allows for the eventual natural and spontaneous functioning out of reflex.

- There is a collective element in drama whereby a safe container or holding space is provided by a supportive community. Since drama mostly happens in groups, this allows for further support of others and a synergistic potential for greater validation within the holding of a human container. Isolation is obviated, though the individual is the starting and ending point. Vasalisa is not alone with her doll.

- And finally, as drama educator Dorothy Heathcote puts it, "True gut-level drama has to do with what you at your deepest level want to know about what it is to be human . . . [and]

acquires significance as it reverberates in the chambers of the universal" (Wagner 1979, p. 76). While each of the arts contributes to enhancing the quality of life in its own way, the way of drama is through the human experience — to understand and experience human behavior in its intricacies.

In actual classroom practice, we inventively play and explore the story, calling on the doll advisors (played by class members) at every dilemma. We finally play the end of the story, which is not revealed beforehand, in order to fully work the final "test." Whereas the set-out tasks have been accomplished, we, as Vasalisa, always return to the circumstances and situations that are the constant dilemmas in our lives. The teacher works in role with the students to further engage them, encourage reflection, and go deeper in the drama. The teacher continually maneuvers in role herself to further deepen the drama and help students maintain their own roles.

At the end of the story, students explore the results of their empowerment and how Vasalisa will return to her home, now to negotiate with confidence, claim her rights, and assert conditions by which she will remain. Further application can extend these dramatic techniques to deal with situations at personal life cross-roads. One student submitted this reflection after the work that I have described:

> This work opened me. It made me realize that I haven't thought of everything, nor can I, nor should I only rely solely upon the way I previously understood thinking. This lesson re-awakened me to myself — We must continue to learn from this.

Each and every art form has its own point of entry into ways of knowing by accessing both subjective and objective realities, but drama squarely positions us simultaneously in both worlds.

Arts as a Means of Creating Meaningful Community

When the term "global perspective" appears in the news media, as it does regularly in newspaper articles, the term does not concern the welfare of the planet as an ecosystem nor the people who inhabit the world. The term most often concerns global competitiveness and how we are to go about maintaining our "edge" in the marketplace and the world economy.

Education, in its adaptive aspect, supports the consumer industrial worldview and trains students to function in this competitive environment. This encourages the type of individualism in which students need to get an advantage over others in order to secure for themselves the limited opportunities perceived to be available, particularly in the job market. This has been the selfish and egotistical understanding of individualism that, in many cases, has driven people to work at furthering their own wealth and fueling capitalism. While the development of the individual is important in order to protect personal rights, expression, privacy, and ways of being, as I argued earlier, there is a troubling anticollectivist focus in education — and in our global perspective in general — when what we really need is a sense of social responsibility for one another. Saul defines individualism as inseparable from the collective, containing social concern and biased for responsibility: "the exercise through public participation of our obligations to the body of the citizenry" (1995*b*, p. 172).

The alienating consequences of an education that mentors the individual without reference to social responsibility result in the distancing of ourselves from one another in ever more dangerous ways, where we increasingly fear "the other" as one who is capable of taking away the little that is left to us. The outcomes for students that foster independence and self-reliance must be balanced with the ones that teach interdependence and mutual support. Gregory Smith warns that:

> our children could well lack the social skills and dispositions needed to foster their own survival. . . . Only as children come to see that their well-being depends on the well-being of others will they begin to reclaim and reshape the patterns of mutual support that have sustained human communities throughout millennia. (1992, p. 3)

I know that the arts contribute greatly to the building of the community of citizens that we need. Recently I attended a graduation ceremony for students completing a four-year secondary school education in a program that, in addition to regular studies, allowed them to major in either visual arts, music, dance, or drama. I listened carefully to valedictory addresses from representatives in each program. It was remarkable, and incredibly moving, how each valedictory address focused not on the specifics of the art form that they studied, but on the bonding and closeness that was established among students and teachers through the program. It was not what they learned but what they received through the work that was important. Of course, all transferable life skills are learned through the process of working and studying; but none is more important than the qualities of long-lasting friendship, belonging, understanding, and love. Certainly these qualities are important to every human being and especially to young people, because they offer a much-needed affirmation of their humanity. But the emotion and clarity of focus with which these young students expressed their sense of valuing one another and bonding as a community made me think that these students had indeed experienced this at a very deep level. Finally, these students reflected the precious commodity of hope. They were still capable of dreaming, somehow trusting that dreaming was still worthwhile. Being a teacher in a high school and having heard many valedictory addresses, I was stimulated to new reflection by the experience.

Although any type of collaborative project (such as a political campaign, a community project, a school trip) likely engenders feelings of camaraderie and fellowship, and nostalgia after it is over, it seems that involvement in an artistic endeavor requires and receives more investment of an extremely personal nature. Besides giving energy, time, thought, and effort when one creates a work of art (either working collectively in the production of a play or, in parallel fashion, by creating a painting), there is something of depth and personal content that goes into the work as well. Who you are becomes part of the work. When the task is completed and, whether of perfect standard or not, is validated by one's group, one has the sense that one's self is affirmed in the process. Therefore the potential for accomplishment reaches to more intense levels of reality.

In 1995 I had the pleasure of being part of creating a production of Benjamin Britten's opera, *Noye's Fludde*, which was Canada's way of contributing to the 50th anniversary of the United Nations. Approximately a hundred people were involved: 60 young children from elementary schools, a dozen teenagers and young adult semi-professionals, a few featured noteworthy artists, technical personnel, and a team of directors and designers. It was a long project of at least eight months duration, especially involving lengthy work with the young people in training them to sing and act. We traveled with this production to major cities, culminating in performances in San Francisco as part of the United Nations 50th Anniversary Gala. Throughout rehearsal and the dozen performances, the bonding of the group was astounding: young and old, professional and amateur, privileged and struggling, of all races, creeds, colors, and talents — we were one. This was not an elite program by any means, as children who were in the Scarborough Board's Children's Choir, pooled from a vastly diverse city, were eligible to participate.

For us, it brought a similar hope to that which the founders of the United Nations must have felt. We were one; and though eventually we would disband and this project would be completed, it was imprinted on our hearts forever. And we were assured that this possibility for bonding could be repeated, both for us personally and for many more people. We, so touched by it, would continue to seek comparable community bonding experiences. The continuance of this project was inconsequential compared to the fact that we lived the experience of harmony and closeness and have it in our repertoire for life. The investment of each and every one of the group — far beyond the large degree of personal time and commitment, included the investment of self — as each character was portrayed uniquely for that special yet limited amount of time. There would be other productions at other times by other people, but this production was ours and we belonged in it with one another.

While the process of creating art is itself capable of performing magic, there is equal power in the celebratory and elevating qualities in the artistic product. There is power in the metaphor that is the work of art, which has the ability to strongly counteract the infectious numbing in our society of workaholism, techno-communication, and fractured and fragmentary relationships.

Whether it be in the daily workings of an arts classroom or in the international production of a showpiece, the high-quality investment of body, mind, emotion, and spirit that art demands makes the artistic endeavor exceptional in its ability to bring people together meaningfully, where everyone works simultaneously in two worlds, the personal and the collective, and where the increase of one works toward the betterment of the other. We create a circle with the people involved in our art — a circle of equality, bonding, and respect — and all good art ultimately cries out for the completion of a larger circle, including the audience, where its evolution continues in the sharing.

Art as a Means of Improving Quality of Life

In studying both student and teacher responses with regard to the value of the arts in the curriculum, time and again the recognizable benefits that come to the fore are those that include the development of interpersonal skills and creative thinking. This has been the long-standing rationale for the inclusion of the arts in the curriculum and even officially warrants their inclusion in the current business-education agenda. Perhaps this can be seen as a throwback to the old focus of drama education for the purpose of teaching speech and elocution skills, as having a place in day-to-day relating, whether personal or professional.

We also have valued arts education as a means of improving our quality of life, which is seen as touching us primarily in our leisure time, as in art appreciation. Following this line of thought, it is understood that if one studies visual arts, for example, one will be able to experience and enjoy artistic masterpieces both in books and galleries, thereby taking pleasure in experiencing them as well as becoming a more "cultured" individual. It also follows that this may inspire our leisure time by opening us up to artistic hobbies, such as painting or participating in community theater. The same applies to the study of music: learning to appreciate a wider variety of musical styles or perhaps learning to play an instrument. In dance and drama, we gain poise, grace, and confidence to better carry ourselves in public. All this is true insofar as it improves our quality of life.

But what is most valuable in the study of the arts in this respect is the way they can affect our ability to see and experience the most mundane events and circumstances in order to transform the experience of the ordinary with more fully awakened senses and consciousness.

In the growing chaos of our postmodern times, nature is less accessible, values shift, and much meaning is seriously under threat. With almost universally growing frustration and fear, created in a scarcity mentality, we need to find renewed sources of contentment and happiness, most likely to derive from bonding with others and with the cosmos itself. Although our busy-ness or despair makes us increasingly incapable of seeing this, the arts can reawaken us and open our eyes.

Recently, at the urging of one of my students who was placed at the Art Gallery of Ontario for her cooperative education placement, I embarked on learning how to draw. Like many other adults, my drawing ability had been stuck at the level of an 8-year-old. While learning to draw not only gives one newfound ability and appreciation in visual art, I found that I came to shift and improve my ability to see, which struck me as more important. The drawing instruction trained all of us to draw what we saw and not what we assumed we were seeing. I left the art class as though seeing for the first time: lines of nature, shades of color, play of light and shadow, texture and tone. For my classmates and me, our scope of vision increased to where we could find fascination in the simplest and smallest corners of our lives.

93

In a parallel experience, while most people greatly appreciate music, its study not only pushes back the boundaries but also increases awareness of sound itself, absence of sound in a world of noise, and music in the most unlikely times and spaces. Opening to dance helps us understand the communication of the body and its effect on space and time. Drama study opens us to our humanness and its complexity, levels of meaning issuing from tension, constraint, rituals, or the breaking of rituals that exist in everyday life, and relationships. Drama study builds tolerance and compassion for our own and one another's humanity.

This is the new, improved quality of life that art can give us — a way to experience life with all senses, moving us from self-absorption and fear to awe, appreciation, and compassion. Now more than ever, life in the postmodern age demands that we need to instill in our youth a capacity for self-reliance and self-satisfaction that does not separate us from each other or from our planetary home. Thomas Berry calls for a new functional cosmology that connects us to our planet by means of a personal and responsible relationship:

> Most of all we need to alter our commitment from an industrial wonder world achieved by plundering processes to an integral earth community based on a mutually enhancing human-earth relationship. . . . We need only to listen to what the earth is telling us. (1988, pp. 30, 35)

I return to my classroom with renewed inspiration to invite my students to look and see. "We only see what we look at. To look is an act of choice. As a result of this act, what we see is brought within our reach" (Berger 1972, p. 8). Seeing anew releases us from limiting ways of seeing, not only increasing potential for joy but also opening us up to new ways of recognizing our universe. We begin by seeing things as they really are, as in the drawing class, and then from this freeing we can widen our lenses of perception to perceive in fresh ways for our own sake and for the sake of our planet. This does not further pacify at a time when lethargy is epidemic and action dormant, but rather increases our bonding with and understanding of creation that unearths the necessary passion to preserve and replenish. Every act of art is a sign of hope that creation, in its many forms, is not forgotten. Art invites us to play in the territory of possibilities and to envision our future in new ways.

Conclusion

The arts become exceptionally important and powerful in transitional times, when we need more than ever to find and hold fast to meaning. Above all, we need hope in a time when it is easy to despair. With the carpet pulled out from under us in so many ways during the transition from the modern to the postmodern age, we need connection to the basic elements of life — earth's grounding, fires of passion, deep waters of emotion, and air's flight of inspiration. For students, arts experiences mean opportunities to deal constructively within a spiritual context that holistically addresses all the aspects of humanity. We need more than the ability to minimally function in the present system; we need to use the arts as tools for coping and adapting. We need to find more than jobs in the changing and elusive world of work; we need to find our vocations in a complex and often precarious life. We need to find ways of doing the tremendous amount of work that needs to be done on this planet.

Hillman and Ventura (1992) say that, in this age, the work to be done is the work of the soul. We must not adjust to the dysfunction we see around us, which in turn makes us increasingly dysfunctional. Rather, we must create cells of revolution to find, keep, and build on that which is the best of our human heritage. We must offer this job opportunity to youth: "If you want to volunteer for fascinating, dangerous, necessary work, this would be a great job to volunteer for — trying to be a wide-awake human during a Dark Age and keeping alive what you think is beautiful and important" (p. 237).

Education in the arts begins calling our names individually to awaken us, nurturing us through the assurance of value and

95

belonging, then guiding us to live in the full vista of life's experience. The results are far-reaching, for when the individual is secure and healthy, our society will be as well. The repercussions are planetary where "the growth toward inner realization of any individual results in a modified global field" (Pike and Selby 1995, p. 19). I believe education is still the best and perhaps the only venue to reach nearly everyone, arts education being the best way to touch in order to heal and transform and, ultimately, to re-instill hope in a turbulent time.

References

Berger, John. *Ways of Seeing*. London: British Broadcasting Corporation, 1972.

Berry, Thomas. *Dream of the Earth*. San Francisco: Sierra Club Books, 1988.

Estes, C.P. *Women Who Run with the Wolves*. New York: Ballantine, 1995.

Hillman, James. *Kinds of Power*. New York: Doubleday, 1995.

Hillman, James, and Ventura, Michael. *We've Had a Hundred Years of Psychotherapy — And the World's Getting Worse*. New York: HarperCollins, 1992.

Pike, Graham, and Selby, David. *Reconnecting*. Surrey, U.K.: World Wide Fund for Nature, 1995.

Saul, John Raulston. *Unconscious Civilization*. Concord, Ontario: Anansi Press, 1995. a

Saul, John Raulston. *The Doubter's Companion*. Toronto: Penguin, 1995. b

Smith, Gregory. *Education and the Environment*. Albany: State University of New York Press, 1992.

Spretnak, Charlene, ed. *The Politics of Women's Spirituality*. New York: Anchor Press, 1982.

Wagner, Betty Jane. *Dorothy Heathcote: Drama as a Learning Medium*. London: Stanley Thornes, 1979

Postmodernity, Humanity, and Art

BY D.C. BRADBURD

D.C. Bradburd teaches English and theater arts at Monument Mountain Regional High School in Great Barrington, Massachusetts.

Fragmentation. Flexible ethics. The destruction of myth by myth itself. The clear, striking view that the icons of the past crumble on human frailty; that the modern world has failed; that the icons of the present are temporal, fading, gone; that icons of the future are virtual, both figuratively and cybernetically. There is no coherent myth, global or national, perhaps not even local; and its absence is healthy because people are not susceptible to demagogues who seek power through its subtle espousal and repetition. There is no coherent myth, global or national, perhaps not even local; and its absence is unhealthy because, without a unifying core, society has no center. The world becomes a series of chaotically related events posted in 15-minute notorieties, 30-second sound bites, and deletable Internet "flames" — all of which are culled for us by experts at manipulating *de facto* mythets and giving them the gloss of culture and the glue of relativity.

Postmodern deconstruction has made its proponents more aware, while it has performed autopsies on the body of which it inquires. There is much rightness in exposing the injustice of manipulation and the failure of institutions and ideas to accommodate the range of humanity that has been marginalized. But in the absence of traditional community such deconstruction obliges, many more people have become marginalized, living as voyeurs of experience or as electronic auditors of their own lives.

The traditional role of education in general is to provide literate, functional citizens of the world in which they live. Postmodernists would emphatically disagree, maintaining that "literate" or "functional" are constructs of veiled political agendas and that these agendas are passed down from the knowledgeable "haves" to the submissive, unintelligent "have-nots" in a system that perpetuates — indeed, deifies — the social order, all of which is deterministic and stultifying (Ranciére 1991, p. 7) Ultimately, it is about repression and control. As educators, we are compelled to consider such claims and act upon their veracity.

Postmodernists would say that "literate" and "functional" can be extended to refer to self-possessed, unique citizens who can deconstruct, interrogate, make decisions based on wide, tolerant perspectives. Such citizens can measure their self-worth against their own potential and find individuated purpose. It is the task of the arts and humanities in particular to function in this amended context and, in spite of the postmodern concept of *de-centering* — the "absence of anything at the center or any overriding truth" (Rosenau 1992, p. xi) — to allow for some amount of the universal, even the marginal, de-centered universal. The artistic spirit coupled with the intellect's postmodern critique provides the opportunity to build community driven by humanness and commonality.

Of course, there first must be agreement as to what postmodernism is and of the need to raise its specter before school boards and budget committees. Educators are representatives of a system driven by strong, vocal, and respected advocates of conservatism. There exists a codified, if not always applied, canon of expected knowledge and accomplishment (consider Hirsch, Bloom, State-wide Boards of Regents and reform, school boards elected by the resident majority, and so on) whose determination clearly would be challenged by postmodern inquiry or deconstruction. Is the challenge to the status quo worth it? Should educators — particularly public educators who are hired, in fact, by a political body — be willing to consider postmodernity as a viable education concern? Within the autonomy of the classroom will such a challenge even matter when there is difficulty enough in providing books, keeping teacher-to-student ratios manageable, and dealing with discipline and accountability? Won't teachers educated in the modern way simply continue to teach as they were taught?

Actually, such questions are moot. Now, or soon, unless postmodernity phases into calcification, there will be high school graduates who take postmodern angst and disenfranchisement to colleges where they will be taught by postmodern teachers to be postmodern teachers themselves. They will be hired because schools will find turnover necessary, youthfulness desirable, and the paying of entry-level salaries attractive. In some cases, these new teachers will be appropriately subversive, raise issues of postmodern complexity, and probably be censured the first hundred times they do so — except by some older teachers who are aware and supportive of their intent and who themselves, perhaps, have been quietly subversive for years. But sooner or later these "radicals" will become chairpersons, administrators, and even school board members and community parents. Some, perhaps, already are. They are students of bell hooks and Paulo Freire, readers of Derrida and Lyotard and their adherents and revisionists; and many of them will come from marginalized segments of society (including adolescence) and have much to gain by being outspoken. Because it is signified by its proponents and because it has the popularity to have numerous and vocal signifiers, postmodernity, with or without the nominative imprimatur of a scholastic design, will be (or already is) an educational factor, whether it is recognized as such or not. Too often education seizes on the already rationalized as innovative. It might be wise to engage in the postmodern presence while its presence is timely.

Unfortunately, that presence is elusive, controversial, and veiled by self-ambiguity.

The first logical ambiguity is the very idea of a coherent post-modern presence or style, because postmodernity considers institutions and constructs as suspect, even the construct of post-modernism. "The post-modernists conclude there is reason to distrust modernity's moral claims, traditional institutions and 'deep interpretations'" (Ashley, quoted in Rosenau 1992, p. 6). "Post-modernism challenges global, all encompassing world views, be they political, religious or social" (Rosenau 1992, p. 6). As an outgrowth of the modern age and as a potential worldview, post-modernism negates itself, remaining in self-critiquing confusion.

Even in its own context, postmodernism is elusive, eclectic, undefined — a summary of fragments. French philosopher Jean François Lyotard, in "Answering the Question: What Is Post-modernism?" maintains: "Eclecticism is the degree zero of contemporary general culture: one listens to reggae, watches a western, eats McDonald's food for lunch and local cuisine for dinner, wears Paris perfume in Tokyo and 'retro' clothes in Hong Kong; knowledge is a matter for TV games" (Lyotard 1982). British historian Robert Hewison notes in *The Heritage Industry*: "Postmodernism is modernism with the optimism taken out" (Hewison 1987). Journalist Elizabeth Wilson states: "Post-modernism refuses to privilege any one perspective, and recognizes only difference, never inequality, only fragments, never conflict" (Wilson 1988). Charles Jenks, an architect and architectural writer, said: "To this day [I] would define Post-Modernism . . . as double-coding: the combination of modern techniques with something else . . . in order to communicate with the public and a concerned minority" (Jenks, quoted in Cahoone 1996, p. 472). Professor Nicholas Burbules, in his essay on "Postmodern Doubt and Philosophy of Education," cites Lyotard as the author of "the most quoted characterization of postmodernism," quoting the latter's statement: "Simplifying to the extreme, I define post-modernism as incredulity toward meta-narratives" (Burbules 1996, p. 2). Rosenau (1992, p. xii) says that such "meta-narratives" are "modern and assume the validity of their own truth claims" and are akin to "global world views, [and] mastercodes." Rosenau goes further to classify the narrative concept by mentioning that "mini-narratives, micro-narratives, local narratives, traditional narratives are just stories that make no truth claims and are therefore more acceptable to post-modernists."

Even the word itself, *postmodern* or *post-modern*, is structurally controversial, with the hyphen indicating a posture of criticism and its absence indicative of an acceptance of postmodernism's legitimacy (Rosenau 1992, p. 18). Furthermore, there is a difference between *skeptical* postmodernists and *affirmative* ones. Citing Baudrillard and Scherpe, Rosenau describes the former as "offer[ing] a pessimistic, negative, gloomy assessment . . . that the post-modern age is one of fragmentation, disintegration, malaise, meaninglessness, a vagueness or even absence of moral parameters and societal chaos." She describes the latter as those who, while agreeing with the skeptics' "critique of modernity . . . have a more hopeful, optimistic view of the post-modern age . . . . They are either open to positive political action (struggle and resistance) or content with the recognition of visionary, celebratory personal non-dogmatic projects that range from new age religion to New Wave lifestyles and include a whole spectrum of post-modern social movements" (p. 16). Delightfully, she subsequently concludes: "Based on the foregoing [arguments in Chapter 1] it should be clear that the term post-modern is employed so broadly that it seems to apply to everything and nothing all at once" (p. 17).

Nevertheless, it is possible to glean some central thrusts in the postmodern world, and these center on a disenchantment with the products of the modern age and, causally, with the philosophies that engendered that disenchantment. Disenfranchisement, perverted ideologies from the political to the commercial, shifting realities, and the real horrors of multiple wars, weapons, diseases, and disillusionments have led to a doubting of modern ideals, simultaneously looking back to older ideals that preceded modern thinking and to a new discourse that questions everything in order to defend against being co-opted by another metanarrative of subtle, controlling design. Postmodernism demands that everything be questioned and that everything be suspect. Nowhere is this disenchantment with "truth" more noticeable to educators than in the often centerless conformity or rebellious anarchy of the adolescents that they teach.

Youth and Crisis

Contemporary society often thinks of youth as a transitional period during which individuals search for a viable adult identity, a moment of initiation. Against this commonsense view, Erik Erikson argued that youth searches for "fidelity," for something worth believing in and trusting (Grossberg 1992, p. 176).

A look at the sayings emblazoned on the notebooks that students carry or on the graffiti left on desks or, even more obviously, on the T-shirts and pins they wear brings postmodernity openly into the classroom. "Life's a bitch and then you die," "I'm with stupid," "Sex, drugs and Rock n Roll," are more than iconoclastic. They are desperate, self-demeaning in their extension, and pervaded with aimless worthlessness. Even "successful" students, the ones who buy into the system, who are purposeful in their studies and vested in the mythic legacy that academic success equals societal fulfillment, are at risk. Because most schools accept the left-brained, concrete approach to academic success as desirable, these students succeed for the short term. In their polarity, however, they, too, are marginalized; and the world of college or work or static mobility is waiting to shock them from their rigid path. Besides, some fragment of postmodern outcry reaches them in their music, in the nihilism of Beavis and Butthead, or in Hollywood's graphic sense of the world's malaise that they, as intelligent students, must somehow see. Perhaps they keep their discontent clandestine because schools and societal rules are targets, not forums for such commentary. Perhaps they cannot articulate such a schism. The crisis of postmodernity even pervades students in schools that are safe and descriptively progressive. The fortunate districts talk about the readiness level of their Crisis Response Teams and their contingency plans for in-school violence. The grittier veterans of such events put them to use.

Grossberg claims that the "anchoring crisis" compounded of "structures of global terror and local boredom" is unavoidable and that, indeed, "the global and the local are increasingly indistinguishable" (1992, p. 210). He goes on to say that terror, which he defines as "the uncontrollability of affect," has become "boring," while boredom, "the absence of affect," has become terrifying. "The postmodern sensibility articulates the uncertainties that many students feel," says Grossberg, "the fact that life *does* feel different" (p. 210)

> After all, presumably every age has had its own terrors. It is more that such emotional terrorism has become part of the infrastructure of everyday existence. The commonplace has become dangerous, and this edifice of terror defines the only collective sense of direction. Whatever you are doing, you would be scared (or cynical) if you knew the truth. (Grossberg 1992, p. 210)

One response to this dilemma has been to dull reality by blending it electronically. We are entertained as real police execute raids and arrests during prime time. The President of the United States is a televised performer at his own inauguration and a personality on MTV, while the Vice-President, appropriately discreet, journeys into cyberspace in an intimate gesture of populism. The time from news event to best seller shrinks in the microburst of a satellite dish. News is a montage of artfully selected and edited impersonal, personal experiences. It presents at a safe emotional distance the immediate faces of tragedy in full 27" color and the pictures of destruction replayed again and again into diminishment, while the reporters who are our surrogate emotional vampires lean in to ask, "How did you feel when . . . ?"

I am at my daughter's high school graduation. We are in a large concert hall — no stuffy gym for us — the home of an internationally famous orchestra. Her high school orchestra is on stage in their stead, and around them are administrators and distinguished guests. The teachers who attend have come as observers, not participants; and the graduates sit in a cluster, looking up at the stage, their status as "the processed" once again confirmed.

They wait to cross the elevated platform in a brief, truncated rite of passage. Before that quick dispatch, they listen to a few final adult salvos and hear their peers talk about commencement and departure. Underneath their rented robes they are wearing T-shirts and shorts, and, if they have not been admonished on behalf of adult expectations, they will launch beach balls, spray string, and confetti at various unprescribed moments. Later, outside the hall, amid hugs and farewells, they will realize that a structure has been removed from their lives, and all that has institutionally encapsulated them has (at least for the summer until they go on to college) been removed.

Actually, I am speculating on these events because I was unable to see them. From where I sat, midway in this large venue, my view of the stage was totally obscured by the phalanx of video cameras set up across the center aisle. Grandparents watched the ceremony, but parents recorded it, too busy in their technology to applaud, occupied as directors and crew at an event postponed for a later, more individual time and space. Even the argument that such an event should be recorded as a family heirloom is specious, because the local cable company (with professional equipment and an unobstructed perch) is recording the event and will replay it numerous times, suitable for taping at home. Instead of celebrated, this event was distanced, fragmented, and frozen by parents who saw their children through the tearless eye of the viewfinder, rendering the actual into the electronically "virtual," distanced reality that is both numbing and safe. It is as if what can be replayed and scrutinized can be controlled, altered (and electronically, at least, it can), and kept external, even when the event might not be tragic.

From opening bell to commencement, the crisis is here.

Addressing the Problem

Can schools and teachers of the arts and humanities have an effect on this postmodern malaise? Is there hope to be offered? Is a concordance possible between the institutionalized value system that represents education and this student generation of cybernauts who live and gather bodiless on threads of the World Wide Web? Is there a compromise that will bring them and us into a dynamic, less fearful, and more interactive (without the media) relationship with the present? The answer is, "Perhaps." But such a compromise (a concept unacceptable to many postmodern hard-liners but necessary given the entrenched reality of the system and the efficacy of change from within) will require the courage to rethink and re-execute the classroom dynamic and to allow students an equality of intelligence neither they nor their teachers may be prepared to accept — that is, to replace surety with skepticism.

Professor Burbules maintains that "postmodernism should be viewed as, at heart, a kind of doubt . . . not a set of theses or positions, but a common mood or attitude . . . of a wholly different nature from Cartesian doubt" (Burbules 1996, p. 4). Burbules goes on to speculate on three ways of dealing with the ensuing phenomenon of "coping with the paradox of doubting the very things one can hardly do without. . . ." He suggests, first, the use of irony, because it "denies our certainty by unmasking the world as an ambiguity." He continues with the trope of tragedy that:

> arises from a pained awareness that the contraries we embrace are often equally valuable. . . . To view education from the standpoint of tragedy is to abandon foundationalism and to believe that doubt and uncertainty make us better educators — in part because they re-emphasize our dependence on each other, including our students, and in part because they insulate us somewhat from the false claims for the value of what we have to offer. (p. 4)

Burbules presents parody as the third trope:

> thriv[ing] on paradox and treating it with . . . a wink and a shrug, enacting a perspective while simultaneously lampooning it; or provisionally embracing multiple perspectives without actually advocating any of them. (p. 5)

Realistically, however, Burbules acknowledges, "Education seems to be an endeavor of an entirely different spirit with an implicit faith in progress and betterment." Admitting that some key tenets of education today are "profoundly challenged by the postmodern critique," he nonetheless maintains that it would be "unacceptable, and self-defeating, to abandon all educational efforts, or continue them only in bad faith" (p. 6). The solution, he proposes, is to:

> question our authority, and invite others to question it, even within contexts that arrogate authority to us whether we wish it or not. [note] At a deeper level, we can adopt methods of inquiry and interrogation but also turn these methods upon themselves, exploring their usefulness. Such a stance allows for both a respect and appreciation for approaches that broaden our understandings, but also a wary suspicion of the tendency for teachers, texts and methods to become hypostatized, entrenched. (p. 7)

Importantly, Burbules also proposes that educators "remain open to the unexpected, the tangential, even the countervailing moment that disrupts one educational purpose for the sake of another" (p. 7).

To what end should educators promote the disruption of order and singular direction? This is the key question, particularly for those who teach the arts and humanities, the presumably expansive aspects of curriculum. The alternative, the refusal to contemplate such issues of change, is a silent denial of all that postmodernism raises as a doubting inquiry into the state of the world, its margins, and the students who are paradoxically being prepared to enter that of which they are already a subdued part.

Speculating on Change

In *The Ignorant Schoolmaster,* Jacques Ranciére uses the experiences of Restoration schoolteacher Joseph Jacotot as a platform from which to discuss the roles of student and teacher. Jacotot succeeded, Ranciére relates, in finding a method by which, among other things, illiterate parents could teach their children to read. At the core of such a de-centered "classroom" is the concept of

106

"a confidence in the intellectual capacity of any human being" (Ranciére 1991, p. 14). "The pedagogical myth," Kristin Ross, the book's translator, asserts, "divides the world into two: the knowing and the ignorant, the mature and the unformed, the capable and the incapable" (p. xx), promoting what Ranciére considers as a division of intelligence into "inferior and superior" (p. 7). It is unlikely that teachers assume the inferior posture in the teacher-centered classroom; and so, by example, the classroom becomes a place where students are immediately limited by their assumed ineptitude.

Yet if the postmodern malaise is to be affected, educators need to find a way of:

> providing students with the opportunity to develop the critical capacity to challenge and to transform existing social and political forms, rather than simply adapt to them. It also means providing students with the skills they will need to locate themselves in history, to find their own voices, and to provide the convictions and compassion necessary for exercising civic courage, taking risks, and furthering the habits, customs and social relations that are essential to democratic public forms. (Giroux 1996, p. 690)

To return the classroom and its students to an equilibrium in which there is a regained "sense of alternatives [by] combining a language of critique and possibility" (Giroux 1996, p. 693), prevalent methods of pedagogy must be the first area of speculative doubt and change. Professor Katherine Cummings, surveying some pervasive education theory, focuses attention on "an obsessional pedagogy" that (in paraphrase) includes a central core that is white, middle-class male; a teacher-centered classroom in which the teacher re-centers by authority a knowledge that has previously been intentionally dispersed; a tendency to reserve information to ensure the teacher's continued mastery; the urge to get back to the basics; and the thrust that directs students to communicate with force and precision within certain narratives that are logocentric — that is, presumed correct in and of themselves (Cummings 1991, p. 101).

However, educators who wish to liberate must:

> reject the banking concept [of education] in its entirety, adopting instead a concept of women and men as conscious beings, . . . They must abandon the educational goal of deposit-making and replace it with the posing of problems of human beings in their relations with the world. . . . The teacher is no longer merely the-one-who-teaches, but one who is himself taught in dialogue with the students, who in turn while being taught also teach. They become jointly responsible for a process in which all grow. (Freire 1993, pp. 60-61)

This replacement of the teacher as "midwife of truth" (Zavarzadeh and Morton 1991, p. 11) with an equality of dynamic and expression is in many ways contrary to the "dissemination of appropriate knowledge" by which much education is governed. However, changing the dynamic of students in the classroom allows the possibility that their role as citizens in the world also will change. The same is true of the role of the teacher-citizen.

Nor does such a scenario imply anarchy. Instead, it requires that the teacher use methods that are inclusive of doubt and the concepts of inquiry instead of expected result.

"First," Giroux believes, "educators need to be skeptical regarding any notion of reason that purports to reveal the truth by denying its own historical construction and ideological principles" (p. 692). To this educators might add what Freire calls the problem-posing method, which "does not dichotomize the activity of the teacher-student" who is not "cognitive" at one point and "narrative" at another, but rather is in continual dialogue with students who "no longer docile listeners — are now critical co-investigators in dialogue with the teacher," allowing the affirmation of "men and women as beings in the process of becoming" (pp. 61-65). If teachers teach not "what they are taught" but "as they are taught," then perhaps students will interact in the world as they are taught to interact in the classroom. Perhaps, too, teachers are deluding themselves by relying on "obssesional curricula" to bring change into the world by content instead of process.

Writing

Beyond curricula, there are certain tools whose use also must be re-evaluated. For the humanities teacher in a non-arts classroom, writing and discourse are primary. Not surprisingly, postmodernity requires a reconsideration of these devices as well.

Zavarzadeh and Morton approach the humanities in part by declaring:

> Consequently, what is seen in the humanities curriculum as the transcendental human essence is unveiled as a collectivity of conventions. In the (post)modern view, man emerges not as the instigator of meaning but as the effect of intersections of meaning-generating signs. (1991, p. 5)

They further argue that "analysis in the dominant [prescribed] curriculum is essentially an anti-intellectual activity taught in order to divert attention from a genuine interrogation of textuality. Analysis is aimed at extracting meaning from the text, which means that it accepts the existence of an already formulated meaning in the text" (p. 8). If they are correct, then true investigation in the classroom requires a different approach, especially when "text" is taken in the postmodern sense to mean any construct to which a student might be asked to submit a reply. Such an insistence on analysis actually is deceptive because it "allow[s] individual variation, but insist[s] on the central truth of the text" (p. 6). These authors suggest instead that educators turn the "interpretive essay" into a critique that investigates the conditions of the text and demystifies the stance of the author and those whose words the author supports (p. 7). In other words, the student, rather than searching for the "truth," explores the basis on which such "truth" is constructed.

Orality

Writing is not the full extent of discourse and, though we have entered electronically into a world of "secondary orality" dependent on print for its existence (Ong 1989, p. 3), the roots of the power of oral language still remain and are available for educators to use. "Writing," says Ong, "fosters abstractions that disengage knowledge from the arena where human beings struggle with one another. It separates the knower from the known. By keeping knowledge embedded in the human lifeworld, orality situates knowledge within a context of struggle" (p. 44).

And orality is innate. "What all human children learn best," Ranciére says, "is what no master can explain: the mother tongue" (p. 5).

Poet and essayist Martha Heyneman writes in *Parabola* magazine's issue on "The Oral Tradition":

> What did I really transmit orally? I ask my son, my youngest child, by now a grown man. . . . I have just come from a storytelling festival. The conversation revolves around the oral tradition and whether it can continue without artificial help, because, to be honest, what comes naturally to us today is not oral but electronic transmission — TV, camcorders, computer mailboxes. . . .
>
> I am feeling the universal remorse of parents of grown children. When it is too late, all the things we failed to do pursue us like Eumenides. I never taught my son to say his prayers, as my father taught me. I never told him a story such as my father [did]. . . . I had no stock of gentle moral saws as my mother had. . . .
>
> Our son . . . has always been — even from birth — the quiet one, the ponderer. By the time his answer comes . . . I have almost forgotten the question.
>
> "The language," he says.
>
> "What?"
>
> "The language."
>
> . . . The magnitude of what he is saying gradually dawns upon me.
>
> The most important thing I have transmitted to him orally is the language itself.
>
> Whoever thinks of that? It happens unconsciously. It flows as naturally as mother's milk, and indeed begins to flow before it. The newborn is slung, still wet, across your belly. "Hello," you say, and something quite material springs

into existence between you — a second umbilicus, as real as the first, and far more commodious, for the father has access to it also. . . .

Through this second, invisible, umbilical cord there immediately begins to flow, not blood, but language. . . .

What if no one ever looked at you or spoke to you in the first crucial months of your life? (1992, pp. 4-5)

What if no one ever looked at you or spoke to you in the critical time of your adolescence?

At least two primary oral concepts can be installed in the classroom, dialogue and narrative. Ong sees writing as technology (p. 81), noting that literate human beings structure even their oral discourse around the technical structure of writing. But, citing Hirsch and Olson, he also notes, "Writing establishes what has been called 'context-free' language or 'autonomous' discourse which cannot be directly questioned or contested as oral speech can be because written discourse has been detached from its author" (p. 78). Thus oral discourse in and of itself moves naturally toward the place of critique, replacing an unresponsive text with a living, accountable speaker (p. 79). In the critical classroom, both teacher and student are accountable and interchangeable.

Furthermore, Ong refers to the 1977 work of Julian Jaynes, asserting that a verifiable shift from orality to literacy around the time of the invention of the alphabet in 1500 B.C. led to breakdown of a "primitive stage of consciousness in which the brain was strongly 'bicameral'" (p. 29). While we probably do not need the primitive, right hemispheric "voices" Jaynes suggests were translated into speech by the left brain, the concept of whole-brain learning is a recent, valid education concern. Given the assault on our senses and our logic that postmodern life presents, the ability to see both sign (the specific) and design (the greater, often undetected pattern — as Rico and others relate) is broadening in its possibilities and certainly relevant to detecting the greater patterns that postmodern critique demands be seen.

There are, of course, cautions as to how orality might be employed.

Because dialogue is an encounter among women and men who name the world, it must not be a situation where some name on behalf of others. It is an act of creation; it must not serve as a crafty instrument for the domination of one person by another. . . .

Founding itself upon love, humility, and faith, dialogue becomes a horizontal relationship of which mutual trust between the dialoguers is the logical consequence. . . .

Only dialogue, which requires critical thinking, is also capable of generating critical thinking. Without dialogue there is no communication, and without communication there can be no true education. (Freire 1993, p. 70-74)

The Socratic method, on one hand, requires an unequal center of locus in the teacher. On the other hand, as verbal anarchy it is neither fair nor safe. Thus those who desire such dialogue in their classrooms must be cognizant of that fine balance between equality and control. They must be cautious of teacher-centricity and of predicting and controlling the process and outcome by "artful" selection of the bright speaker, the class intellect, the squeakiest wheel. This neutrality of selection is not a new teaching skill, but its lack of teacher-center may be new. The unpredictable direction of its outcome is even more outside the concept of behavioral objectives and discreet lesson plans. Perhaps one thing that Burbules meant when he referred to the "countervailing moment" was the opportunity for such surprises.

Narrative, because of its potential to become pronouncement, also is tricky to employ. To some students, anything the teacher or a dominant classmate says takes on the aura of meta-narrative and may be received as unquestioned truth. Alternatively, sometimes such a moment of "truth" draws a snicker or a why-bother-to-argue response of silence. Yet Jacotot, according to Kristen Ross, believed, "Storytelling then, in and of itself, or *recounting* — [is] one of the two basic operations of intelligence . . . [and] emerges as one of the concrete acts or practices that verifies equality" (Ranciére 1991, p. xxii). The postmodern idea of discourse demands that even such personal narrative, such compelling accounts of difference and human experience, be tested against constructs of truth. Giroux recounts:

> To focus on voice is not meant to simply affirm the stories that students tell; it is not meant to simply glorify the possibility for narration. Such a position often degenerates into a form of narcissism. . . . For [educator and author bell] hooks, the telling of tales of victimization, or the expression of one's voice is not enough; it is equally imperative that such experiences be the object of theoretical and critical analysis so they can be connected rather than severed from broader notions of solidarity, struggle and politics. (1996, p. 696)

Critical pedagogy and oral and written methods that refute the idea that knowledge is passed down rather than investigated create, in Giroux's words, "new spaces where knowledge can be produced" and provide "the knowledge, skills, and habits for students and others to read history in ways that enable them to reclaim their identities in the interests of constructing forms of life that are more democratic and more just" (p. 692). Within a "pedagogy of difference," there is the possibility of exploring the self as a "primary site of politicization," in which it is necessary and desirable to "engage issues regarding the construction of the self [that address] questions of history, culture, community, language, gender, race and class" (p. 691). Most important, Giroux sees critical pedagogy as important in creating "a language of possibility that is capable of thinking risky thoughts, that engages a project of hope, and points to the horizon of the not yet" (p. 696).

The ability to risk, to hope, and to exercise the potential of the future indeed may be the most desirable outcome of postmodernity's doubt and education's self-critique. To tap this ability, postmodern schools need to increase voice and discourse, hire faculty of conflicting viewpoints, fund diverse materials, foster doubt and inquiry, instill hope in the intelligence and worth of every individual, employ play as a function of hope, and grow a sense of community by using the arts to explore and express.

The Arts

There is in the power of this postmodern discourse both risk and hope and, in spite of critical assertions to the contrary, the potential to find a center. There also is the opportunity to return humanness to the humanities and to celebrate the existence of art without ascribing to it an implied transcendence that returns the viewer to the role of critic. In all the narrative, in all the expressions of clay, paint, articulated body, raised note, group harmony, or cacophony, image, or impression, there exists not just contextual substance and not only respect for and illustration of difference. The arts in the postmodern school should certainly be a basis for both textual critique and tolerant understanding in the real, not patronizing sense. But the arts also can build community.

I once was told that if I wanted to understand my humanness, I should walk the streets of a city, New York in my case, and truly look at the faces of the people I passed (carefully, of course, for it is an unspoken rule of New York City life not to violate such illusory privacy). I was told that I should study those faces for their pain, of which I saw much, and their joy, which was spectacular by its rarity. What I saw and what I felt had nothing to do with race or age or gender, nothing to do with "special needs" or economic difference, though it clearly came in a diversity of bodies and costumes. I did not deconstruct; rather, I reacted. I cannot articulate all that I saw except perhaps in poetry, though I might have photographed it or carried the image to a painter's studio if I had those talents. I know that what I saw is being danced, painted, played symphonically, beaten on tin drums, sprayed on subway cars, and chalked on pavement by children, because I feel its resurgence in those presences. I know that I saw through the eyes of my own bias and into the maw of persona and captive demographics, but I also know that, deconstructed or not, I was moved by something that was in me as much as it was in the faces I experienced. And I know that when a student discovers that breath and movement and poetry are linked; that poets, despite their acculturation, touch human chords beyond deconstruction (though certainly subject to its scrutiny); that when fifty students raise voices together and move their audience and themselves to tears, then something that celebrates commonality in the midst of difference has arisen.

We can question art, kill it with analysis, and revive it with critique. We can react to it, question our reactions, compare them, and measure the results against those of other social cohorts. Ultimately, because humanity knows loss, domination, and frustration and longs for peace or contentment or release from rage and oppression, whatever those concepts might mean locally, the arts have the potential to portray what I saw on those faces in New York. Art displays no metaphysical soul to taunt the postmodern declamation, but an interior reflection that is lonely for common acknowledgment. When the gallery opens, the curtain goes up, the street musician passes her hat, the magician performs in the dry fountain of Washington Square Park, an audience is drawn; and they do not assemble only to be influenced by the propaganda potential of what they see. Like any tool of expression, art can be misused, and caution is best applied in such places of subtle persuasion. But the arts, I believe, go even further than the spoken word in stripping discourse of its artifice.

I will, in the postmodern way, question the gallery I am in or the street corner I am on: its shape, its financial foundation, its crowd, its prejudice. I will seek out venues that allow difference to speak. I will search for a "plurality of readings" (Olkowski-Laetz 1990, p. 103). I will present these cautions to the students with whom I work and allow them to educate me to my narrowness and my inexperience. But I will do these things because I am driven to find underneath the text the look in the eyes of a photograph, the tension in a dancer's back, the single word in a darkened theater, the note of wisdom in a jazz phrase, the anxiety and protest in a metallic guitar, the painted sky that I have slept under, and the teeth-gritting malice in a punk T-shirt. All of these expressions of the arts say, "You are like me and I am like you." I will join in that community that lies under the paint and under the eyes. I will present the possibility of its existence to the students

115

I encounter, so that they can critique my assertion and perhaps find self-expression in some humanly transient and imperfect art form; for art, like sound, is as transient as its beholder (Ong 1989, p. 71).

I will present it to you from *author* to *reader* and invite your discourse.

I will assert here that there is indeed a community to join and a center that all postmodernity cannot deny and, in fact, uses as some of its keystones: the unsettled human condition, the need for understanding, and the common hurt that engenders suffering and fear and presents, in opposition, the potential for joy. I would enjoin postmodern education to do the same and to recognize that the arts can provide the unexpected blow that breaks the stasis of educational prescription.

References

Burbules, Nicholas. "Postmodern Doubt and Philosophy of Education." In *Philosophy of Education 1995*, edited by Alven Neiman. Urbana, Ill.: Philosophy of Education Society, 1996. Pages 39-48. Online: http://www.eduiuc.edu/coe/eps/papers/

Cahoone, Lawrence, ed. *From Modernism to Postmodernism: An Anthology*. Cambridge, Mass.: Blackwell, 1996.

Cummings, Katherine. "Principled Pleasures: Obsessional Pedagogies or (Ac)counting from Irving Babbitt to Allan Bloom." In *Texts for Change: Theory/Pedagogy/Politics*, edited by Donald Morton and Mas'ud Zavarzadeh. Chicago: University of Illinois Press, 1991.

Freire, Paulo. *Pedagogy of the Oppressed*. New York: Continuum, 1993.

Giroux, Henry A. "Towards a Postmodern Pedagogy." In *From Modernism to Postmodernism: An Anthology*, edited by Lawrence Cahoone. Cambridge, Mass.: Blackwell, 1996.

Grossberg, Lawrence. *We Gotta Get Out of This Place*. New York: Routledge, 1992.

Hewison, Robert. *The Heritage Industry*. London: Metheun, 1987.

Heyneman, Martha. "The Mother Tongue." *Parabola* 17 (Fall 1992): 4-12.

Jenks, Charles. "The Death of Modern Architecture" and "What is Post-Modernism?" In *From Modernism to Postmodernism: An Anthology*, edited by Lawrence Cahoone. Cambridge, Mass.: Blackwell, 1996.

Lyotard, Jean François. "Answering the Question: What is Postmodernism?" In *Critique*, no. 419 (Paris, April 1982). Reprinted from *The Postmodern Condition: A Report on Knowledge*, 1979; revised, 1986.

Morton, Donald, and Zavarzadeh, Mas'ud. *Texts for Change: Theory/Pedagogy/Politics*. Chicago: University of Illinois Press, 1991.

Olkowski-Laetz, Dorothea. "A Postmodern Language in Art." In *Postmodern: Philosophy and the Arts*, edited by Hugh Silverman. New York: Routledge, 1990.

Ong, Walter J. *Orality and Literacy: The Technologizing of the Word*. London: Routledge, 1989.

Ranciére, Jacques. *The Ignorant Schoolmaster: Five Lessons in Intellectual Emancipation*. Translated by Kristin Ross. Stanford, Calif.: Stanford University Press, 1991.

Rico, Gabrielle. *Writing the Natural Way*. Los Angeles: Tarcher, 1983.

Rosenau, Pauline Marie. *Post-Modernism and the Social Sciences: Insights, Inroads and Intrusions*. Princeton, N.J.: Princeton University Press, 1992.

Wilson, Elizabeth. *Hallucinations: Life in the Postmodern City*. London: Hutchinson Radius, 1988.

Zavarzadeh, Mas'ud, and Morton, Donald. "Theory Pedagogy Politics: The Crisis of 'The Subject' in the Humanities." In *Texts for Change: Theory/Pedagogy/Politics*, edited by Donald Morton and Mas'ud Zavarzadeh. Chicago: University of Illinois Press, 1991.

The Power of the Arts to Edify

BY RUSSELL T. OSGUTHORPE

Russell T. Osguthorpe is associate director of the Faculty Center and a professor of pedagogy in the Center for the Improvement of Teacher Education and Schooling at Brigham Young University in Provo, Utah.

While in Washington, D.C., to visit a group of student teachers, I asked the taxi driver to take me to the hotel on Dupont Circle, to wait while I checked in, and then to take me directly to a high school in Anacostia.

"I don't drive in that part of the city," he said without hesitating.

"We'll make it," I assured him. "I've been there before; it's a nice school."

Reluctantly, he asked me to retrieve his maps in a side pocket behind the back seat. I gave him the maps, checked in at the front desk, and got back into the cab. Thirty minutes later we arrived at the school, a multi-story structure the students called "the tower of power." I paid the taxi driver, entered the school, passing through the usual metal detectors, and signed in with the guard, who greeted me as if he knew me. On the way to the principal's office I paused for a moment at the open door to the music room, where the school's a cappella choir was practicing an African-American revival song.

119

When I arrived at the principal's office, she greeted me warmly but with the usual urban formality, "Nice to have you with us today, professor. Let's go up to the sixth floor, and I'll introduce you to Mrs. Rockland, the English teacher who's been supervising one of your student teachers." Mrs. Rockland (a pseudonym) welcomed us but explained that I would not be able to see our student teacher "in action" until later, because "right now the students are listening to a local fiction writer talk about his latest book."

"But you are certainly welcome to stay and hear Mr. Jones," she said.

I accepted her invitation and went into the classroom, where the students were gathered around Edward P. Jones, the author of *Lost in the City*, a collection of short stories about the African-American experience in our nation's capital (see Jones 1993). A young woman raised her hand and said, "I don't read much, but this book was interesting. I thought sometimes I was reading about myself. How did you make your stories sound so real?"

"I guess I just rely on my own experience," Jones responded. "I grew up in the city, and I've always lived here."

"But how do you write stories about girls my age? Seems like you know so much about girls," another student asked.

"I never really thought about it. When I write, I get into the character, and it doesn't matter whether it's male or female, I just let the character lead me."

Rather than addressing Mr. Jones, the next student asked if Mrs. Rockland would read her own short story so that Mr. Jones could hear it. "Maybe he can help you get it published," the student said. Only after repeated coaxing did Mrs. Rockland agree to read her story about a girl in D.C. who finally resisted the pressure to become sexually active at a young age. At the conclusion of the story, everyone applauded, including Mr. Jones, who expressed genuine praise for Mrs. Rockland's story.

As an outside observer, I was convinced that the foundation funds that supported Mr. Jones' visit had been well spent — not that students had necessarily learned something that would help them on their next exam, but that we all had been changed in some way by our participation in the session. I believe that the author benefited from students' questions, that students learned something about their own experience by reading the fictional accounts of others' lives, and that the teacher felt rewarded for her efforts to write stories that would cause her students to reconsider the pressures of the culture around them. By engaging in communal discourse with literature as the focal point, we became "alive" to new ideas and "possessed the living through enjoyment" (see Dewey 1934, p. 27). In one sense, we had all been *edified.*

The Meaning of Edify

The first meaning of the word *edify* is "to build or construct." The French verb *edifier* is used much like the verb *erect* in English — "to construct a building." But the second meaning of the word focuses more on the function of spiritual strengthening, drawing a person closer to "virtue." Briefly stated, *edify* means "to build up the soul" (Simpson and Weinere 1989, p. 71).

When we teach in our schools or in our homes, we often believe we must "gain attention" and "motivate" and "energize," but we seldom think about what it means to edify. In fact, as I was reading through a teacher's remarks on a manuscript for a book I recently completed, I found the following comment penciled in the margin next to a paragraph on edification: "[Edification] is not legal in the schools" (see Osguthorpe 1996). I assume that she interpreted *edification* to be a strictly religious term and that religion should not be taught in the schools.

But her definition was, in my opinion, far too narrow. Yes, *to edify* means to draw a person closer to virtue, but the term is not tied to a single religious or cultural tradition; it is universally applicable to all humans. The teacher who wrote the short story on teenage pregnancy was not afraid to teach her students the difference between right and wrong. Her example reminded me of my wife's mother, who once taught English in what would now be called an "alternative high school" — a school for students who did not survive in the regular system. Decades later she still enjoyed explaining how she taught some of her students to read when they were 17 years old and how she had them correct their own tests. "They always gave themselves two marks on each test," she recounts. "One was for the percentage of items they got right, and the other was for honesty. I always taught them that it was much more important to get an 'A' in honesty than it was to get a 100% correct on the test."

Edification not only draws us closer to virtue, it helps us face daily challenges with more strength and faith. The short story author strengthened the students and teacher twice: first, by the stories he shared with them and, second, by the encouragement he gave them to use their imagination to create similar tales. When someone recognizes another's success, as the author acknowledged the teacher's writing skill, both are fortified. Edification thus builds faith in both the "speaker" and the "listener." It helps bind us to one another, expanding our capacity to learn what is needed so that we can attack unfamiliar problems.

The Arts and Edification

It is not only through the arts that one is edified, but the arts are uniquely suited to edify the learner — even though few have used the term to define the purposes of arts or humanities education. I believe that such education can edify learners in four distinct ways: 1) the message(s) conveyed by the art object, 2) the artist's approach to the creative act, 3) the pedagogy associated with teaching others about the art object or about the creative act, and 4) the creative act itself — the process of producing an art object.

The message. Every art object — a poem, a painting, a musical score, a dance — carries a message to the observer. Referring to these products as "expressive objects," Dewey (1934) taught that artists have intent, otherwise they would not be motivated to create new images or compose new melodies.

Comparing literal representations with artistic productions, he explained that it is the intent of the artist that separates the two:

The poem or painting does not operate in the dimension of correct descriptive statement but in that of experience itself. Poetry and prose, literal photography and painting, operate in different media to distinct ends. Prose is set forth in propositions. The logic of poetry is super-propositional. The latter have intent; art is an immediate realization of intent. (Dewey 1934, p. 85)

Granted, not all artists intend to edify; but art that endures causes the observer to experience growth in ways that can eventually lead to edification. As Greene explains, "If questions beat inside us about whether or not something is to be called good art or bad art, what context has to do with an artwork, and what constitute good reasons, we are likely to wonder and to perceive even more" (1995, p. 139). These kinds of wondering and perceiving are the prerequisites to edification. One knows that edification has occurred when there is communion with a work of art, a form of communion that happens at the moment the observer sees the unity and the multiplicity together and senses a oneness that otherwise would be out of reach (see Zwicky 1992). Wendell Berry describes the communicative act between observer and art object as a conversation:

Works of art participate in our lives; we are not just distant observers of *their* lives. They are in conversation among themselves and with us. This is part of the description of human life; we do the way we do partly because of things that have been said to us by works of art, and because of things that we have said in reply. (Berry 1990, p. 64)

Berry's words show that aesthetic experience involves more than feelings or emotions. It involves the observer in complete wholeness. Thought and feeling merge as the conversation develops; they are inseparable not only because they occur simultaneously but because they are mutually dependent. I have called this whole-souled learning, "the education of the heart," an education that begins when one is captured by a question, searches for an answer, and experiences the indirect fruits of learning, such as edification (see Osguthorpe 1996). It occurs far too seldom in schools and homes, largely because most people understand neither what it means to learn in this way nor the role of the arts and humanities in such learning.

When I saw Gustav Klimt's painting, *The Park,* in the New York Museum of Art, I experienced the type of communication that Berry has referred to and that can lead to the education of the heart. Just prior to the visit, I had been drafting an outline for a chapter titled, "Surrounded in Life." While writing, I kept imagining a stroll along a pathway lined with locust trees spreading their branches overhead. The moment I saw Klimt's painting, I thought, "Here's my image, but in even more splendor than I had supposed." The painting is composed primarily of leaves of various shades, and the two trunks in the foreground almost take on human qualities. The first time I looked at the painting, I thought the trunk on the left was a person surrounded by trees. This is the feeling a park can give you — life on all sides, coming out of the ground, encircling you with branches — a botanical submersion in which you feel at one with the world, a fusion with all life.

Like poetry, Klimt's painting was "super-propositional" for me. It took me beyond the point of a literal photograph. In Maxine Greene's words, it helped to "release my imagination." I was not acquainted with Klimt's life; but the moment I saw his painting, I knew that I had understood at least part of his message and that he had experienced feelings akin to mine when walking through a park.

The artist. Just as a single artistic message can edify, so too can the life of the artist. Recognizing that another human being has created a work of lasting beauty — be it a painting, a poem, a novel, a dance, or a musical score — our own creative instincts can be nurtured. Not only do artists mentor each other directly; they also can lead indirectly by their works, as well as by their example, real or imagined (Gardner 1995).

During a visit to Kiev, Ukrainian educators made me acutely aware of Taras Sevcenko's influence on the national psyche. Not only did I see paintings and statues of the poet in museums and parks, but upon my departure I was given a book containing an extensive collection of his poetry. Grabowicz (1982) reminds us that poets like Sevcenko may become "mythmakers" for a culture not only through their poems, but through the iconic status the poet is afforded. In addition to Sevcenko in the Ukraine, such mythmakers abound, for example, Hugo in France, Michelangelo in Italy, Confucius in China, Chopin in Poland.

Following my encounter with Klimt's work in New York, I became better acquainted with his work and his life. I learned that at a critical point in Klimt's career, he gave up the security of receiving government payments for his work in order to pursue what he believed was his primary purpose as an artist: to explore the purpose of human existence (see Sarmany-Parsons 1987). His adherence to principle, to following his "question of the heart," as I refer to it, can edify an observer as much as Klimt's paintings can.

Long before Berry came under Wallace Stegner's formal tutelage, Berry describes how he learned from Stegner's example:

> And so Wallace Stegner became my teacher before I ever laid eyes on him, and he was already teaching me in a way that I have come to see as characteristic of him: by bestowing a kindness that implied an expectation, and by setting an example. (Berry 1990, p. 49)

But one does not need to be an author of Berry's or Stegner's renown, nor a sculptor of Michelangelo's fame, to benefit educationally from another artist's example. Anyone's creative power can be aided by the life of an artist, because one cannot regard the product of artistic endeavor without simultaneously being influenced by the one who produced it. As Greene has said:

> It is not necessary to be a sculptor to share the feeling of discovery by entering a new space, bringing together images of knives, chisels, and mallets so that the star itself can become a carver, a sculptor, as it shines through leaves. It is not only our thoughts of starlight that may be changed through such figurative work. So may our idea or image of

the sculptor, becoming an image of one who makes unpredictable forms. (1995, p. 141)

I am acquainted with an internationally acclaimed artist who, while talking to a group of young people about how he found his niche, said:

> When I was your age I kept drawing these pictures of strange little creatures and hiding them under my bed. I never showed them to anybody because to me the pictures were just doodling. Frankly, I didn't think anybody else would ever want to look at them. But I kept on drawing them because it felt like that was what I was supposed to be doing. And then one day I showed my little creatures to someone and I was shocked to find that he liked them. I started painting these little creatures and people actually started paying money for my pictures. The way I see it, I'm just getting paid now to do what I enjoyed doing when I was your age. (James Christensen, personal communication, 23 September 1993)

As my friend spoke to the teenage audience, he showed slides of his work and explained how he developed the ideas that led to each painting. He also talked about the messages that he was trying to convey with his work. Nearly everyone in the audience had seen at least one of his paintings prior to the lecture, but few had heard the artist himself describe the creative process that lay behind his work. Of particular importance for the young audience was the artist's description of how many preliminary attempts were required before completing the final painting. Although he did not use the word, my friend was producing *etudes* that would later be the centerpieces of his work as an artist. Like musicians who practice etudes before performing a concerto, my friend was sketching etudes prior to completing his larger paintings. In either case, the artist or the musician is finding the form or developing technique — working out the detail — so that the final work in its wholeness will be "right." Thus the artist may teach on at least three levels: 1) through the message of the art object, 2) by explaining the creative process that led to the object, and 3) by mentoring others in their own creative endeavors.

126

The pedagogy. There are specialized pedagogies associated with the teaching of art, music, drama, dance, and writing. Shulman (1990) has used the term *subject-specific pedagogy* to describe such teaching methodologies.

These are the approaches that Stegner might have used when teaching Wendell Berry to write or that Laufberger might have employed when mentoring Gustav Klimt. But I will not discuss such pedagogies in this paper. Rather, I wish to focus on what I am calling *edifying pedagogy* — approaches to teaching and learning that are integrative rather than discipline-specific, methodologies that emphasize the needs of the learner first and the requirements of the content to be taught second. Such approaches become less and less visible in formal educational settings the older the student becomes. But this type of teaching always has been apparent in the younger grades.

During a visit to a French maternal school, I watched as a teacher read poetry to a group of five-year-olds. She spoke in whispered tones as she prepared the children to listen to a poem titled, "The Secret." She kept whispering as she began reciting the poem from memory, motioning with her hands for each student to watch and to listen carefully. Spellbound by her recitation, the children leaned forward on their seats so they could hear every word and see every expression on the teacher's face. As soon as she had finished, one of the children said, "Now will you read the one in the red book — the one you read yesterday?" The teacher, somewhat surprised at the request, looked over at me and said, "I'm astonished that he would remember which book this poem was in; yesterday was the first time I've ever read from that book."

The boy delighted in every word of the poem; and when he asked to hear it again, the teacher said: "Instead of reading it again right now, I'll help you make a poster with the poem on it; you can paint a picture on it and take it home and hang it on the wall so you can see it every day. Someday you'll be able to read every word of the poem, but in the meantime your parents can help you with the words." The boy was satisfied.

The teacher continued to recite one poem after another, sometimes completely from memory, other times looking at the page periodically for a cue. She read a humorous poem about impossible events, each line ending with *"Ça n'existe pas, Ça n'existe pas"* (That just couldn't be, That just couldn't be). The children waited for these lines at the end of each stanza so they could chant them with the teacher and laugh at the absurdity of the images that came to their minds. They wanted to hear the poem again and again; but the teacher explained that while some poems were funny, others were sad. She then read a poem titled, "The King Is Sad," which told the story of a king who had lost a loved one, and how no amount of money or fame could soothe the pain of his loss.

As I watched and listened, I wondered how many teachers in America were reading poems to their students at the same moment. I could imagine many singing songs with young children, but I doubted that many were sharing poems with their students — poems that they had learned by heart. And by laying aside this part of learning, teachers cause students to miss out on the kind of edification that these young French children were receiving — a kind of edification that comes from words that are joined together in ways that remind us that life is sacred and that learning can be sacred, too. I wondered about how different education would be if we could eliminate the lewd and vulgar language of the media and the flat and uninspired language of school texts and replace them with the language of poetry.

The French maternal school teacher was reciting poetry, not necessarily to teach her students the skills of writing poems, but to expand their ability to make meaning of their world, to release their own creative potential in whatever form, and to bring them a little joy. As Greene has said:

> We are fully present to art when we understand what is there to be noticed in the work at hand, release our imaginations to create order in the field of what is perceived, and allow our feelings to inform and illuminate what is there to be realized. I would like to see one pedagogy feeding into the other: the pedagogy that empowers them to attend (and, perhaps, to appreciate) and vice versa. I would like to see

both pedagogies carried on with a sense of both learner and teacher as seeker and questioner . . . turning toward the clearing that might (or might not) lie ahead. The ends in view are multiple, but they surely include the stimulation of imagination and perception, a sensitivity to various modes of seeing and sense making, and a grounding in the situations of lived life. (1995, p. 138)

Although the French maternal school teacher was not attempting to teach the writing process directly, she was clearly "stimulating their imagination and perception" and increasing their "sensitivity to various modes of seeing" the world around them. When such stimulation occurs, the creative process will naturally follow, not by a forced, artificial assignment from a teacher, but from an irresistible "call" that may be recognized only by the listener. The call usually comes in the form of a question, as it did to Klimt — a tension between the way things are and the way things should be.

The creative act. The edification that can come by observing an artistic product, by contemplating the artist's life, and by experiencing effective pedagogy all eventually lead to the act of creation — painting, writing, designing, or composing something that has not existed before. Romain Rolland said that "there is no joy but in creation" (Rolland 1910, p. 364). It is everyone's purpose to create, to leave something to those who will follow. In the education of the heart all creative work is truth seeking work, the kind of work that edifies.

When a composer hears a new melody, an artist sees a new image, or a poet finds a new phrase, all may be discovering truth. Each one knows when truth has been found because the discovery, though it is new, seems familiar — like finding a favorite toy one lost as a child. For the musician the melody will endure if it is "singable," if it fits a pattern that is already inside the composer and the listener; the poet's phrase will find its way into everyday speech (think of Shakespeare); the artist's image will be recalled by viewers even when the painting or sculpture is not present.

Like Wendell Berry, my father was a farmer at heart. Although he always enjoyed growing vegetables, his most favored plants were straw flowers. He grew a wide variety of these flowers every summer, harvested them, hung them upside down in the garage to dry, and then spent the winter months preparing and arranging them. The onset of Parkinson's disease did not slow his propensity to plant and harvest. In fact, I always wondered if the flowers actually slowed the progress of the disease. A thing of beauty can help us see beyond our individual difficulties in a way that diminishes not only the pain but the cause of the pain as well.

My father's flower arrangements found their way into hundreds of homes, hospital rooms, and offices. Although the arrangements will probably not be regarded as great art, they continue to send a message of life and beauty even though my father is no longer living. No one assigned my father to engage in the creative act. If one had asked him to explain why he was growing and arranging the flowers, he would likely not have been able to give an adequate answer. He was simply responding to an internal call, doing what he felt he should be doing at the moment. And through his efforts he reaped the *indirect* benefits that always come when one is involved in acts of creation that edify. As King has said:

> One of the mistakes we make over and over again in life is to go directly for the things we think are important. But if we aim at self-fulfillment, we shall never be fulfilled. If we aim at education, we shall never become educated. If we aim at salvation, we shall never be saved. These things are indirect, supreme results of doing something else; and the something else is service, it is righteousness, it is trying to do the right thing, the thing that needs to be done at each moment. (1986, p. 255)

Edification and the Schools

My father did not learn to grow and arrange straw flowers in schools, but schools played a critical role, I believe, in helping him learn about living in a society in which people can pursue creative acts of their own choice. I like John Goodlad's explanation of the purpose of schooling, "to enculturate" the young into a democracy (Goodlad 1990, p. 48). What does it mean to "enculturate?" Can the process occur in the absence of learning in the arts and humanities? Can we help our youth become productive members of a democracy by having them study only the "new technologies?" Many have warned convincingly about the dangers of embracing a technological mindset in a postmodern world. Jacques Ellul (1965), Ivan Illich (1992), Neil Postman (1992), and others have cautioned against over-regimentation, over-reliance on gadgetry to solve our problems, and over-commitment to a sterile "outcome-based" morality that de-emphasizes simple acts of kindness because such acts are not seen to keep us at the "competitive edge." This kind of thinking leads to an impoverishment of the human condition even in a land of plenty. In the preface to Patrick Troude-Chastenet's book, *Sur Jacques Ellul*, Illich says:

> The subjugation of feelings seems to me an inevitable condition in a society of technical mirages. To counteract this subjugation, I must read sacred text, fight against the technological nightmare that separates me from reality; and [learn to look] in the only mirror in which I [can] rediscover myself, the pupil in the eye of the other, my friend. The preservation of feelings, this promptness to obey, this chaste look that the rule of Beno't opposes at the *cupiditae oculorum*, seems to be the fundamental condition for the repudiation of technique as long as it opposes an obstacle defined as friendship. (p. ii)

This means that our schools cannot be content to deliver information in an atmosphere of disregard for human needs, no matter how *efficient* such teaching might be. The pedagogical act has always been and will continue to be a moral act, and therefore cannot be conducted by those who are afraid to teach what is right and good. Like Mrs. Rockland, who taught her high school students that teenage pregnancy was a wrong thing to do, our schools must recapture the moral ground that has been slipping away during the positivist era. In 1899 Dewey said that "our social life has undergone a thorough and radical change. If our education is to have any meaning for life, it must pass through an equally complete transformation" (p. 19).

Dewey was referring to the need at the turn of the century for our society to adapt our schools to the requirements of an industrialized, modernist world. His words are equally applicable today; but instead of learning to adapt to a positivist technological approach, we must now confront a world that has in the view of many gone too far, to a point that our humanity has somehow been damaged. We must nurture a kind of imagination and a type of morality that place the needs of "the other" before our own (see Levinas 1993). This kind of education demands that we draw upon the arts and humanities to kindle the kind of creativity that will lead to improvements in the ways we live, not just in the ways we make a living. Thomas Green said:

> Persons who count themselves well educated because of their technical skill and their professional standing, but who lack vision, who do not dream, who assume that the world as it is is as the world must be — such persons are not morally educated, however much we may count them to be "good men and women." Lacking visions and lacking dreams, however rooted they may be, they cannot lead. Where would they lead us? (1984, p. 24)

Green's question should give all educators pause, because our young will be the ones leading in the future. It will be their imaginations, their morality that will combine to create the world of the next millennium. Are we adequately preparing them for the task? The move to democracy in Eastern Europe shows at once the appeal of freedom and the fragility of the system to endure in nations where democratic traditions are weak. The difficulties these new governments are facing raise awareness of those in our own country who cannot live inside the system because they have not been properly enculturated into it. Education seems the only answer, but not just any kind of education. As Goodlad has said:

The message is clear: "There will be no liberty, no equality, no social justice without democracy, and there will be no democracy without citizens and the schools that forge civic identity and democratic responsibility." . . . If education were merely some kind of training — such as to paddle a canoe, ride a bicycle, or even add numbers — we could afford to be somewhat relaxed about its context. Yet even under such circumstances, we cannot afford not to address the question of ultimate use. My incarcerated students in the industrial school for (delinquent) boys frequently offered to teach me the craft of lock picking. They offered no accompanying manual or lessons regarding the moral circumstances under which use of my new skill would be legitimate. (see Soder 1996, pp. 93-94)

So schooling in a postmodern world must pay ever-increasing attention to principles of morality if our society is to endure. But we must pay equal attention to helping students find their questions and their creative potential to seek answers; otherwise, as Thomas Green suggests, they will have no place to lead us. These two roles, the task of adhering to universal moral principles while simultaneously nurturing each individual's call to create, constitute the central paradox for postmodern schooling. In the premodernist period, art was the servant of either the state or the church — which were typically so closely linked that the artist had to please both. In the modernist period, art became increasingly privatized, an atmosphere which led to a "market-driven morality" where profits replaced prophets as the primary definers of how one should live. And as the artists began distancing themselves from both government and religious influences, they often moved further away from the foundational values that actually gave them the right to experiment in new ways.

Rather than eliminating disputes between artists and their governments or churches, modernism actually widened the gulf between prevailing beliefs about what constitutes acceptable morality and what made for good art. Ongoing battles among the National Endowment for the Humanities, its grant recipients, and Congress or among the Federal Communication Commission, parents, and television broadcasters regularly remind us of the clash between creativity and morality. Some would say that the clash is inescapable, that the creative person inevitably comes into conflict with prevailing moral thought because *creativity*, by definition, means to make something new, while *morality* implies that we must conform with the old. Believing that creativity and morality are opposed to each other is similar to believing that human intellect and feelings are distinct from one another — a belief that has resulted from modernist philosophies.

However, as educators in the postmodern world, we cannot continue to subscribe to such dichotomies. We must develop integrative, balanced approaches that help students to "see with both eyes," as Palmer (1993) has suggested. We need to reflect on the examples of those who, like Mrs. Rockland and the French maternal school teacher, rely on pedagogies that edify. Only then will we educate the whole person; only then can we begin to educate the heart. As we learn and teach in this way, we will be sifting the primitive that can pull us down from the eternal that can lift us up. And at such moments we will be helping students to develop their own "messages," based on a kind of creativity that is morally grounded and rooted — messages in the form of a painting, a dance, a song, or a poem; messages that have the power to edify.

References

Berry, Wendell. *What Are People For?* San Francisco: North Point Press, 1990.

Dewey, J. "The School and Society." Lectures delivered at Brigham Young University, Provo, Utah, 1899.

Dewey, J. *Art as Experience.* New York: Capricorn Books, 1934.

Ellul, J. *The Technological Society.* New York: Alfred A. Knopf, 1965.

Gardner, H. *Leading Minds: An Anatomy of Leadership.* New York: Basic Books, 1995.

Goodlad, J.I. *Teachers for Our Nation's Schools.* San Francisco: Jossey-Bass, 1990.

Grabowicz, G.G. *The Poet as Mythmaker: A Study of Symbolic Meaning in Taras Sevcenko.* Cambridge, Mass.: Harvard University Press, 1982.

Green, T.F. *The Formation of Conscience in an Age of Technology. The 1984 John Dewey Lecture.* Syracuse, N.Y.: Syracuse University, 1984.

Greene, Maxine. *Releasing the Imagination.* San Francisco: Jossey-Bass, 1995.

Illich, I. *Ivan Illich in Conversation.* Concord, Ontario: Amansi, 1992.

Jones, E.P. *Lost in the City.* New York: Harper Perennial, 1993.

King, A.H. *The Abundance of the Heart.* Salt Lake City: Bookcraft, 1986.

Levinas, E. *L'etique Comme Philosophie Premiere: Coloque de Cerixyla Salle Sous la Direction de Jean Greisch et Jacques Rolland.* Paris: Les Editions du Cerf, 1993.

Osguthorpe, R.T. *The Education of the Heart: Rediscovering the Spiritual Roots of Learning.* American Fork, Utah: Covenant Communications, 1996.

Palmer, P.J. *To Know as We Are Known: Education as a Spiritual Journey.* San Francisco: HarperCollins, 1993.

Postman, N. *Technopoly.* New York: Alfred A. Knopf, 1992.

Rolland, R. *Jean-Christophe: Dawn, Morning, Youth, Revolt.* New York: Henry Holt, 1910.

Sarmany-Parsons, I. *Gustav Klimt.* New York: Crown, 1987.

Shulman, L. *Aristotle Had It Right: On Knowledge and Pedagogy.* Occasional paper. East Lansing, Mich.: Holmes Group, 1990.

Simpson, J.A., and Weinere, E.S.C. *The Oxford English Dictionary: Second Edition.* Oxford: Clarendon Press, 1989.

Soder, R., ed. *Democracy, Education, and the Schools.* San Francisco: Jossey-Bass, 1996.

Troude-Chastenet, P. *Sur Jacques Ellul.* Pessac: L'Esprit du Temps, 1994.

Zwicky, J. *Lyric Philosophy.* Toronto: University of Toronto Press, 1992.

PART II

Raising the Roof Beams

Lights in the Trees

BY STEPHANIE B. PERRIN

Stephanie B. Perrin is head of the Walnut Hill School in Natick, Massachusetts.

"School teaches us to undermine our own aspirations, a lesson we labor all our lives to unlearn."
— Lynne Sharon Schwartz

The following thoughts are not the product of research on my part, though I have relied on the research of others. They are observations (sometimes sweeping) based on my experience as the head of a boarding high school for the arts. I also am covering a great deal of territory and simplifying complex concepts in the interest of raising broad questions. I am reminded of the yogi who, when asked if he had "scientific proof" of a concept, said, "No, but we have observed it to be true for thousands of years, so it must be true." I do not claim the same sagacity but feel that observation in the field does yield its own "truths."

This spring I found myself walking across campus late one evening. As I walked, I could see lights in all the buildings and students everywhere. I heard the sounds of violins and pianos in the practice rooms. I passed two young dancers working on a piece in a dark dance studio, boom box blaring. I heard the sound of a buzz saw in the theater and hoped it was someone working on a set. I saw a group of students winding lights over some old apple trees and was assured it was a sculpture project.

All this was going on at 9:30 at night, "free time" in terms of the school's schedule. Yet here they all were, working. What I saw and felt as I walked around on that campus was the heart of the school and the essence of education. These students were working on their own, making things that mattered to them and, in the process, making themselves. Defying every stereotype about "youth today" — lazy, unmotivated, net-heads permanently seated in front of a computer or TV — these students were working with passion, skill, and focus on what they were learning in school — in this case, the making of art.

A faculty member here once said that the motion — the *process* — of education should mirror the motion of life. That is, it should build on the natural desire of young people to learn, to grow, to achieve, to be respected, and to do meaningful work in the world. Everything we do in schools should move students toward greater differentiation *and* integration, should keep them moving forward with more and more of themselves available to themselves as they grow. And we should do that by engaging, whenever possible, with their natural movement toward greater intellectual, artistic, social, and emotional maturity. Their growth and transformation will go on whether schools engage with that process or not, but the most powerful educational models build on young people's desire to learn.

The education I received, on the other hand, often seemed counter to the motion of life. By high school it felt, in fact, lifeless and irrelevant, a holding action keeping us out of the workforce (or at least out of trouble) until we could be moved into college or jobs. Rather than capitalizing on the energy of youth, my schools seemed bent on restraining and dampening the big ideas and feelings of adolescence. The process of education did not mirror adolescent development. It often seemed to mirror the fears and limited vision of adults. And, until quite recently, the education I received in high school during the late 1950s had not substantially changed. I think we in America are in agreement that new times call for new models of education. The discourse now is not *if* we need reform, but what directions such reform should take.

140

I have come to see that *one* model of education that mirrors the motion of life, building on a student's natural forward momentum in all areas of life, is that of intensive training in the arts. At Walnut Hill we call this concept "education *through* the arts." By this we mean that the *intensive* study of the arts — defined as the training to mastery in music, dance, theater, creative writing, or visual arts — helps young people learn not only to be artists but also very effectively prepares them for life. They learn to be good citizens and workers in the postmodern world, no matter what their ultimate career. Such students have, from the start, ownership of their work (in this case, the arts) and a strong desire to learn (in this case, to be an artist). Therefore the motion of their education does mirror the motion of their lives, and a school can build on such motion, such desire, to educate in the broadest sense.

Education through the arts also requires the active engagement of the whole student — body, mind, and spirit — so that all aspects of the self are kept in motion. All schools must actively educate the whole child, paying attention to intellectual, artistic, and physical growth as well as the development of "character," that elusive yet crucial aspect of an educated young person that encompasses spirituality, a sense of personal and civic responsibility, and the tools to make ethical choices. Learning to play the violin or to act, while living in a school community that shares his or her deepest values, engages the whole child.

The assertion that intensive arts training might be the basis of good *general* education, as is routinely assumed of liberal arts study, at best usually is met with polite skepticism. Of course, the arts are "nice," a pleasant refinement enjoyed by the elite few who can understand or afford them and the very rare and talented people who are artists. But can an arts education serve as a model for general education in the 21st century? Not likely! Furthermore, since schools are cutting the arts dramatically these days, clearly educators do not feel that the arts are anything but a frill or, worse yet from the point of view of the artist, mere "enrichment."

No matter what we say about the arts in education (after all, who would be *against* art?), it is what educators *do* that matters.

And what we have done is virtually eliminate the arts from schools.

Obviously lost when the arts are cut are the young artists of the next generation whose talent and interest would have been noted and nurtured in public schools. They also would have become the arts audience. Not so obvious is the loss of access to a mode of learning, a way of developing the whole child, that is effective in ways we are just beginning to understand. For example, the study of music, begun in the lower grades, helps students develop many skills in addition to making music, such as dexterity, listening skills, focus, and persistence. It has been suggested in recent studies that early music training, or simply listening to music, increases a student's level of cognitive functioning and that students who study the arts score a significant 31 to 50 points higher on Scholastic Achievement Tests. Researchers in Germany have found that string players have larger areas of brain tissue devoted to touch and that the nerve fibers that carry signals between the two brain hemispheres is 12% thicker in students who began music study before the age of seven. Experienced teachers, those "researchers" in the field, will tell you that music students are good at math, and new research is just now emerging in that area. As a society and as educators, are we, at just the moment when new ideas are much needed, turning from a path that we should explore further? I would suggest that we are.

What I would like to comment on is the position of adolescents and schools in postmodern society and the role I believe that education through the arts could play in school reform. In the process I will raise more questions than answers; but, as Rilke wrote, I will "try to love the questions themselves . . . live the questions . . . and then perhaps someday . . . you will live your way into the answer."

Adolescence in America

A 15-year-old pianist at Walnut Hill School commented, "The freedom and love at . . . school . . . have opened my heart and mind in many ways that unfortunately . . . most . . . American teenagers are never exposed to. It allows for any and all growth spiritually, emotionally, intellectually, a teenager needs — person, musician, friend. It has bred the passion that now lives in me and allowed me to share it with the people around me."

In the past, the role of schools has been to bring young people into the common culture, a culture whose basic values were agreed on by its major institutions of family, church, and state. What is different in postmodern America is that the values of these institutions often are at odds with the violence-prone, quick-fix, MTV values of media culture. David Denby wrote: "Most high schools cannot even begin to compete against the torrent of imagery and sound . . . on TV . . . that makes every moment but the present seem quaint, bloodless or dead." In teaching a young dancer that it takes skill, patience, and hard work over a long period of time to achieve mastery, schools go against the pervasive media messages of our society. The American dream has changed from working hard to be successful to waiting to win the lottery. Schools usually do not think of themselves as counter-culture, but in postmodern America they often are. Among adolescents the results of this schizophrenic cultural split are confusion, at best, and disengagement and despair at worst. It is a hard time to be young in America.

The Carnegie Commission's 1995 report on adolescence in America presents an alarming picture of a society that neglects and discounts adolescents. The report describes American parents as often dismissive, preoccupied, and fearful of their own future, unable to cope with the troubles of their children. This attitude seems to hold as true for teens who enjoy every economic advantage, but who see their parents only while being driven from swimming lesson to dance class to tutoring, as it is for adolescents who live in poverty and whose parents often are absent because they must work long hours and hold multiple jobs to survive. Findings from this report and the Institute for Educational Leadership describe the level of crisis in American society as it relates to schools, families, and adolescents:

- America leads developed nations in two areas with regard to school children: hours of TV watched and number of school days missed.
- In 1992 the math and reading test scores of half of all 17-year-olds were too low to get them a job in an auto plant.
- In Los Angeles, an 18-year-old African-American male is three times more likely to be murdered than to matriculate at a University of California campus. Handgun deaths of young adolescent African-Americans have doubled since 1982.
- In 1965, 85% of American families fit the profile of a mother at home and a father working to support the family. Today only 7% of American families fit that profile. Eighty-two percent of all children under the age of 18 have working mothers, and 60% will live with a single parent before they reach age 18.
- In 1995, 33% of all children in America were born to unmarried parents, mostly adolescents and mostly white.
- By mid-adolescence, students will have watched about 15,000 hours of TV — more time than they spend with their teachers, their friends, and their parents.
- Suicide by adolescents increased 120% from 1980 to 1992.

Most of these changes have occurred since the early 1980s, yet schools and society are still operating as if it were 1960 and June Cleaver was still at home in the kitchen making a peanut butter sandwich for the Beaver. If we consider *only* the shift from the 85% "Cleaver" families of the 1960s to the 7% of such families in 1992 and note that there has been no significant response to this change from the culture, such as adequate day or health care for all young children, we can see that we still long for the past, do nothing in the present, and squander the future of our children. We are the richest nation in the world, with the most resources available to us, yet we tolerate a disparity between the wealthy and the poor that is incomprehensible to other developed nations. To them, it appears that we do not care for, or about, our children. Could that perception be the truth?

These statistics — and the reports themselves — describe a culture that is certainly not meeting the needs of its adolescent children. They describe a national crisis.

As to why our children act as they do: although we may wish to deny it, our children imitate us. If we kill, drop out, abuse drugs, mistake material things for happiness, and are filled with rage and despair, so are they. If we are apathetic, exhausted, and lonely for family, so are they. If we sing, dance, laugh, struggle to make meaning of our lives, are kind to one another, and look to the future with hope and confidence, even if the shape of that future is not clear, so can they. Our children mirror us; and if we do not like what we see, then we must look to ourselves.

The late Bart Giammati, former president of Yale and the baseball commissioner, said that "leadership is essentially a moral act," the assertion of a vision of what ought to be. The previous dismal litany indicates that America does not have a vision, moral or otherwise, for American youth. The Bible notes that "without vision the people perish." If we consider our children the future, we are in danger of perishing. When children die in the streets, they are buried in days. When they die in the schools because of low expectations and a failure to take their aspirations seriously, the results are not seen for many years. We are seeing those results now in the suicide and dropout rates, in reports that adolescents feel uncared for and so do not care for themselves or others. Postmodern culture is a period of great flux and transition, and we see the difficulty of these changing times reflected in the lives of our children.

Postmodern Culture and Education

A young violinist at our school commented, "When I first . . . joined the orchestra . . . I was 12 years old and was overwhelmed and inspired. There was an enthusiasm and joy in . . . playing . . . that I had never experienced; and I thought, 'Wow! I love this!' Being around so many inspirational people has given me a deep love not only of music but of life itself."

The definition of "postmodern culture" is an elusive one. It is characterized by a rapid rate of worldwide economic and social change, by an internationalist point of view, by both secularism and a tendency toward religious extremism, and by great difficulty in agreeing on norms, values, and the meaning of it all. It is characterized, in fact, by difficulty in characterization!

In the visual arts, for example, since the late 1960s the content and form of what is called "art" has expanded exponentially so that even the definition of art is debated constantly, whether by Jesse Helms and Jane Alexander or by artists themselves. The venue for art is now international, with no center of the art world as was New York in the postwar period or Paris before World War II. Rather, art is made all over the world; and its "language" of form and content is multicultural, rather than almost exclusively European. No "movement" dominates.

We are in transition as we move toward the millennium, a time of excitement and fear, rather like waiting for a comet that promises to be spectacular. This fluid situation could augur a new age of world peace or the apocalypse. It could bring further chaos and dissent or a more inclusive view of the world and its inhabitants. The symbolic weight of this "turn" of the century cannot be underestimated.

In America one of the biggest changes has been the relatively recent movement from an industrial and rural economy to an urban and suburban one, built on technology and service. It has long been clear that the American system of public education — developed in a mid-19th century industrial culture, well before the information explosion, and focused largely on intellectual development through the rote learning of an agreed-on canon of Eurocentric ideas — is not applicable to a postmodern culture. In the postmodern culture most workers at all levels will have an average of seven significant jobs over the course of their working lives and will come from many different racial and ethnic backgrounds.

In 1992 the U.S. Department of Labor published a document called, *What Work Requires at School for Workers in the Year 2000*. The authors of the report identified three categories of abil-

146

ities and attitudes. The first category, "Basic Skills," incorporates such skills as reading, writing, mathematics, and speaking. The second, "Thinking Skills," includes creative thinking, the ability to solve problems and make decisions, the capacity to reason and "see things in the mind's eye" (which I take to mean imagination), and knowing how to learn. Finally, under "Personal Qualities," the authors see a need for workers who are responsible, sociable, and able to work with others, who have integrity and a sense of self-esteem, and who are honest and skilled at self-management.

The report's authors suggest that a technological, service-based, and international postmodern culture requires workers who are flexible, creative, problem solvers able to take action on behalf of themselves and others; they are people who are imaginative and critical thinkers. Postmodern workers need to be able to function in changing and ambiguous situations, to envision new realities and solutions to problems, and to act with confidence on their ideas.

The bottom line is that workers in postmodern society will be required to learn all their lives. From Wall Street to the garage down the street, those habits of mind and heart that support lifelong learning are needed and are what schools must help students to develop. In the "old days" one learned math and, as a byproduct, may have learned to think critically. What schools now must do is not only to teach content (math) but also to teach the process of learning so that students emerge knowing *what* they have learned and, crucial to lifelong learning, *how* they learned it.

We in America have known for some time that the old models of schooling are inadequate and that school reform is necessary to meet the demands of this new age. The only skills developed in the schools over the last hundred years, according to the Department of Labor list, have been those in the first category of "Basic Skills," with the exception of "speaking." If schools are truly to develop other capabilities, skills, and attitudes toward self and others, then school reform on all levels is necessary.

However, when one thinks of education reform, high schools for the arts do not leap immediately to mind. On the contrary, the arts are disappearing from public schools at a rapid rate. I want to suggest that such schools for the arts *do* offer a model that works for many students, educating them both as artists and as citizens, and that, in some form, this model may work for more students than one might think — and not only the "talented."

Consider, for example, that in cities such as Dallas and Washington, the arts magnet high schools (even those that do not require an audition for entrance) have consistently higher retention rates, lower absenteeism, and a greater number of graduates going on to further training when compared to other high schools in the district. The reason is that these schools are able to engage students by capitalizing on the students' own passion: the motion of education mirroring the motion of life. Students in these schools want to go to school and to stay in school. They want to learn what adults have to teach. Without that motivation, that "wanting," engaging students in their own education is difficult. In these schools, the arts provide the motivation, and the schools build on that desire to learn and do.

Intensive arts training, far from being impractical and elitist, can prepare students for life and work by developing in them the general skills and attitudes, the habits of heart and mind that they will need to prevail in postmodern society, no matter what career they choose. Intensive arts training in high school increases, not decreases, options. If you want a motivated, organized, hard-working, flexible, smart, creative worker, who is able to work well alone or in groups, then hire a young violinist.

Furthermore, the philosophy and process of arts training, a far older system of education than that of American high schools, also mirrors the motion of many current education reform movements and concerns, such as the need for standards, the concepts of student as worker and teacher as coach, the development of character, the necessity of addressing diverse learning styles, meaningful assessment, and the importance of responding to multiculturalism in schools.

Education Through the Arts

A 16-year-old harpist at Walnut Hill School commented, "The study of music . . . pushes us to see ourselves more deeply. Sometimes it is painful to know more about yourself. You can't stand the way you are. But it is also great to discover the deepest place in your heart."

Let me go back for a moment to those students that I noticed hanging lights in the trees at night: How are they being educated through the arts? How will their arts training help develop the skills and attitudes they will need to flourish in the next millennium? Following are some observations from the field.

Ownership of the work is a driving force in arts training. Students have chosen their paths and know that they will stand or fall based on personal vision and effort. They challenge themselves to succeed at tasks they have set. They take their work seriously and know that true motivation comes from within. They understand that they must sustain themselves when the going gets rough. They understand that hard work and discipline are required to succeed. If it takes six hours of practice a day, that is what they do. They are the keepers of their own vision.

Study of the arts helps young people develop *a full knowledge of the self*, a self that is understood, reflected on, and able to be shared. A mature self-awareness is the foundation on which personal artistic vision is built, and it is that vision that distinguishes the artist from the technician. In traditional schools, the self often is not engaged in the classroom; it comes into play, as it were, after school, where the real passion in life is located for most adolescents.

Young artists *learn by doing*, truly active learning. It is impossible for students to learn to play the piano by watching the teacher. They learn to play by playing and the "doing" involves body, mind, and spirit. Further, students have to put themselves out in the world and perform in order to grow, and that takes courage and a willingness to risk. You cannot cheat in the arts. You cannot send someone else to play your recital.

149

Arts students are able *to use failure to learn*. Pianists must make mistakes if they are to improve. Error is an indication of where the work is. Going too fast in a passage means "slow down," not "you are a failure." Schools have not looked at failure as a teaching tool, yet it is the most powerful corrective in life, if it is used as a part of learning and not as a punishment. These students also have to be critical thinkers and judges of their performance. Ongoing assessment, by students as well as teachers, is a part of learning in the arts.

A student once asked me if there was any such thing as a positive learning experience. I had to say I thought not, because once you get it "right," there is no learning to be had. "Failure" that does not overwhelm us pulls us forward and keeps us in motion.

Arts students *understand adversity* and struggle far better than many their age. Am I good enough? What happens if I don't make it? Will I be too tall, too heavy, too short? What if I can't get over this injury? I can't spend time with my family for the second summer in a row because I have to go to music camp. I didn't get cast again! The choice to pursue the arts leads to hard choices and realities early on and actually helps these students be more mature, more accurate about what the world is all about than are most of their peers.

Students of the arts are asked to do *real work* that is judged against a high professional standard. A young violinist is not preparing to be a musician; he or she *is* a musician. Students know the importance of real work as opposed to always preparing for a future that seems far off. Adolescents want to do real work in their lives, but too often there is none for them.

Arts training develops in students an understanding that *learning is an ongoing process* and therefore is never "done." The goal is not to find the right answer. Rather, it is to ask the next, best, question. Students often speak of having "had" history after a course. For a young musician, the study of music does not end with graduation.

Arts students have *high ideals* and strive for excellence, admiring and wishing to emulate their teachers. They have the gift of heroes

150

and *role models*, such as Yo-Yo Ma and Meryl Streep. Such positive and respectful engagement with adults is something all adolescents long for and need. This faith in accomplished adults helps young people to be eager to mature and to join the adult world.

Passion is a concept that is very real to young artists. They are focused and intense about what they do and what they believe. They are sometimes skeptical, but seldom cynical. They believe that their lives and work matter and that caring deeply about one's work is essential.

The capacity to *persist over time* in order to reach a goal is developed in intensive arts training. Training in ballet, for example, begins as early as age five. A young dancer knows he or she must work for years to develop enough skill and technique to support the artistry of dance. Success is not a matter of a lucky break or a quick fix, as the media would have young people believe. It is the result of constant hard work. As Woody Allen once pointed out, "Ninety percent of success is just showing up." Respect for hard work and a self-motivated capacity to stick to the task are qualities needed in the working world.

Young artists have the gift of a *positive sense of identity* based on what they do, not who their family is or who they hang out with. The young dancer is a *dancer*, and he or she belongs to the world of dancers, one that also includes Suzanne Farrell and Alvin Ailey. The young dancers and their work are taken seriously by themselves and their teachers, something that seldom happens to adolescents these days. Self-esteem and self-confidence come from the students' personal accomplishments.

Young artists are *big and detailed thinkers* and can work on many levels. They are asked to see the whole of an ensemble or a play, as well as all the components that make it up. They understand all the notes in a piece and how to play them in order; and they can see the integrity of the whole, the "line" that moves throughout the piece and makes it "music," a work of art, not just notes strung together.

Arts students learn to *work well with others*. You cannot play in an orchestra alone any more than you can be the football team all by yourself. The high level of responsiveness, sensitivity to others, and coordinated interaction is very clear in a theater piece or a string quartet. All members of an ensemble know that the success of the whole depends on the productivity of each member. Age, sex, country of origin, or ethnic group does not matter; the quality of the work does. This aspect of arts training is mirrored in the recent interest in schools in cooperative learning in the classroom as an effective technique for using the richness of heterogeneous groups to learn. Interestingly, cooperative learning, contrary to the thinking of many parents, increases the achievement level of all participants, including the "brightest" students. The same is true in a quartet, where the experience is often synergistic, the whole being greater than the sum of its parts.

In this context it is interesting to note that educators who have studied schooling in Japan have suggested that the most important skill Japanese children learn in school is how to work together for the success of the group. This ability has allowed Japan to emerge as an economic power in the world and is certainly a crucial attribute for a postmodern, internationalist culture, where the capacity to work together for common goals is a necessity. America has a lot of learning to do in this area, because we tend to love the *Lone* Ranger, not Ranger Troop 100.

Peer pressure is a powerful force in schools, having, some say, more influence on how a student behaves than does any other factor. Often peer pressure is spoken of negatively, but it can be positive. In schools for the arts, *peer pressure is focused on high achievement and seriousness of purpose.* The worst crime in a school for the arts is a lack of seriousness about the work. Students who want merely to "be artists," rather than actually producing work, are quickly frozen out.

Students of the arts must develop their *imagination* to a high degree. One of the primary tasks of the artist is to envision new realities, new forms, new interpretations, and to make something where there was nothing. No one has ever hung lights in trees in *this* way before. Paradoxically, the unknown is familiar and exciting territory for young artists, an advantageous attitude for the 21st century.

The study of the arts teaches students to be good *communicators* of their thoughts, feelings, and ideas. If the audience does not "get" the character of Macbeth, then the actor is not doing his job. If the song does not move the audience, then the singer is failing. Art students do not just sit around and think about things, mumbling to themselves — at least not for long. They communicate, they perform, they exhibit, they put themselves and their ideas out in the world. They act. We may not usually think of artists as activists, but serious artists are both dreamers and doers. They need a vision and the courage to act on it.

Actress Ruth Gordon told about the importance of acting on faith in one's vision. When she was a young girl, Gordon was short and, charitably, plain. She was told to "face the facts" that, given these shortcomings, she should not pursue her desire to be an actress. She did not follow that advice and had a long and successful career on stage and screen. Later in life she attributed her success to three guiding principles: 1) Work harder than anybody else, 2) never give up, and 3) never face the facts.

It has been said that studying to be an artist is a failure to "face the facts" of stiff competition for the few, low-paying jobs available. However, to fail to encourage a young person to pursue his or her own highest aspirations is both counter-intuitive and, finally, counter-productive.

Students' ambitions and visions need to be pursued. If in the end they do not choose a career in the arts, they still will have had the experience of an education that, among other things, taught all the skills they need in order to follow any career path. And that education did so by taking the students' dreams — and the students themselves — seriously.

Not facing the facts, in the sense that Gordon uses the phrase, is necessary if we are to move ourselves beyond any present "reality." If we really "faced the facts," we would, given the grim statistics we see, never marry and certainly not have children. But we take such leaps of faith because it is the nature of humanity for us to follow our hopes. Not facing the facts can allow us to imagine the world in new ways and to create new "truths." At present, American educators are struggling to get beyond the "facts" that often seem to overwhelm efforts at reform, "facts" such as "These kids don't want to learn!" "We can't make up for the ills of society!" "We can't handle so many different cultures." We educators need to go beyond these "facts" in order to re-envision American schools so that they can become places that nurture and educate all children.

To go beyond "the facts" is the heart of the matter in the arts and for all people who seek change. Not facing the facts can be an act of courage. To imagine things to be different is the first step toward change, and artists are taught to develop their imagination and act on it. Society needs such dreamers and doers.

Writer Donald Murray, in the *Boston Globe* for 13 September 1996, suggested that, of all citizens, artists are the most capable of engaging with the 21st century. He wrote that we need to educate people who can "discover meaning in confusion, pattern in chaos, instruction in failure, and vision in doubt . . . [who continue to] believe while questioning and have faith that beauty and order exist in confusion and ugliness." He suggests, therefore, that schools teach arts as the main curriculum, with "math appreciation" in the afternoon.

Education Through the Arts and School Reform

There is a general movement in education today that focuses not only on what students know but also what we want them to be able to do as a result of their education. The Coalition of Essential Schools is one such model, and many of the concepts that inform the thinking in the coalition are reflected in the process by which students have been trained in the arts for centuries. For example, the notion of students as workers and teachers as coaches is seen in the relationship of the young violinist to his or her teacher. The student learns by doing, by playing the violin, not by reading about it. The teacher teaches by coaching and demonstration. Also, the notion that the process of learning, as well as content, must be of comparable weight in a young artist's training is one that the arts always have assumed.

154

The issue of content and process, or content versus process, is a lively topic in education thinking. One extreme is the demand that all students must learn the same information and that there should be national standards and tests of such knowledge. The other is a focus on teaching students only process skills, such as how to frame a question, how to think creatively, or how to write a paper, without reference to any particular content. Clearly, there needs to be a balance between the two. Students need to "know" the history of their culture and civilization. They also need to know how they learn so that they can continue to learn. Young violinists need to develop their personal technique and their way of working (process), and they need constantly to build a personal repertoire (content). The arts, while they focus on creative process, also are about content and context.

Assessment. Given a focus on what students should be able to do, the question of how we assess their progress is critical. Concepts such as outcome-based education, assessment by demonstration, and portfolios long have been a part of arts training. Young violinists are judged on what they can do at a given time, and they demonstrate achievement by performing for a master teacher or teachers. In music, such demonstrations are called juries and are the basis on which progress is assessed. Further, in a jury the question is not did the performer do it wrong or right (as in a paper-and-pencil quiz), but did the student perform well, or less well, and learn from the jury where he or she is in the process of learning and what he or she needs to do to improve. Such a process of assessment encourages lifelong learning and is far more indicative of real-life skills than paper-and-pencil tests. Outcome-based assessment, such as the jury, is being much more widely used in high school classrooms these days. Although such assessment takes longer, it is much more individualized than paper-and-pencil tests; and it has the crucial element of not only telling students how they are doing in their work, but also teaching them the process of assessment so that the process can be used in other life situations.

Standards. Some time ago, I heard Diane Ravitch speak eloquently in favor of national standards for all schools. As I listened,

I realized that much of what she was suggesting always has been done in the arts. One of the concepts underlying the standards movement is that if we want students to achieve at a high level, we must set high and clear standards for them. High standards in schools are seen as important not only in measuring achievement but also in motivating students. Studies consistently have indicated that high and clear expectations, coupled with expert teaching, lead to high achievement, something that is assumed about serious training in the arts.

In recent years there has been much discussion about the nature of "motivation" in students. The complexity of this issue has led some, sadly, to conclude that certain children or classes of children cannot respond to high standards. This conclusion leads to lower expectations and, predictably, low achievement. The recent self-esteem movement in schools appears to suggest that children should be told they are doing well even if their work is of poor quality, because they will perform better when they feel good about themselves. The result of this seems to be happy students who cannot spell and who are not good judges of the true quality of their work.

Arts training, on the other hand, has never lost sight of the importance of high standards or of what it takes to achieve them. There is no quick and easy way to learn to play the violin, no "new violin." Arts training has followed the same principles for achievement for centuries: Respect your teacher, work hard, and always aim to be the best you can be. High achievement is the result of some talent, good coaching, and a great deal of hard work. Furthermore, these standards must be internalized by the student if he or she wishes to progress. Standards become an aspect of character, not something externally imposed.

Talent. An understandably common perception is that intensive arts training is only for the gifted and talented few, rather than an opportunity for learning that should be offered to all children from the earliest grades onward. We do not assume that only "talented" children can be taught to read, write, and figure, yet we call ability in the arts "talent," not intelligence, and assume that only a few children possess that mysterious commodity.

I often am asked why there are so many Asian musicians in American conservatories and orchestras. The explanation for the emergence of so much Asian talent is that in countries such as Korea, China, Taiwan, and Japan all children are taught from the earliest grades to play an instrument, to draw, and to sing. The issue of "talent" is set aside until later in their schooling, because that issue places too much emphasis on individual differences. It is assumed that all children can and should be taught to play, sing, dance, and draw to a high degree of proficiency, just as Americans assume that all children can be taught to read, write, and cipher. Furthermore, proficiency in the arts in Asian culture is considered an important characteristic of an educated person. Knowledge and ability in the arts is necessary to fully participate in one's culture.

If you ask American children at the age of five if they can dance, sing, and draw, they will reply enthusiastically, "Yes!" When asked the same question in middle school, they say, "No." These skills appear to be unlearned in American schools.

It is well documented that the number of students who report participation in the arts drops from about 50% in the first grade to below 5% in middle school when, apparently, it is time to buckle down and study such "real" subjects as math and science. Talent in America is not rare; it simply is unidentified and unnurtured. How many songs remain unsung by American children because their society and their schools, unlike those of many Asian countries, separate the arts from other areas of human experience considered essential to a civilized culture? This is particularly ironic when one considers that it is often only through the artistic achievements of past cultures that we know what mattered to those who preceded us.

Varieties of Learning Experience

These observations about talent and the arts are related to an area in education research where we have gained much greater understanding in recent years, that is, how children learn and therefore how we should teach. We now understand that every child learns differently. Some are visual learners, others aural; some cannot focus on one thing for more than a minute or two or must be in motion to pay attention; some appear to think in the linear fashion, while others seem to start in the middle of a concept and work their way out.

Until quite recently, schools, particularly secondary schools, were structured to accommodate only "linear" learners. Students who could sit still, write from the blackboard, keep their books in order, and listen without fidgeting to someone talking for a long time did well in these schools. (What they learned is another question.) Students who did not learn in this way often were labeled as stupid, rebellious, or mentally ill.

Happily, we now know that children learn in a variety of ways and that the task of teachers is to understand how each child learns and to teach to each child's strengths while helping all children overcome their weaknesses. This is not easy; it was much easier to assume that all children learned in the same way. However, this more complex view not only is truer to the reality of human experience, it also is essential if we are to fully educate all children.

Related to our increasing understanding of the true complexity of learning styles are the theories of Howard Gardner about the nature of intelligence. Gardner suggested some time ago that there are at least seven "intelligences" — not just the two (logical-mathematical and linguistic) emphasized in most traditional schooling. He suggests that schools should strive to identify and develop all intelligences in children, including those that he calls bodily-kinesthetic, musical, spatial, interpersonal, and intra-personal. Different children have different arrays of "intelligences," and schools need to teach to the child's strengths, using a variety of methods and providing a variety of means of expression and evaluation through such "intelligences."

Gardner also raises the interesting point that, while we call logical-mathematical and linguistic abilities "intelligence" in the generic sense, we label the rest of the intelligences, such as musical intelligence, "talent." This distinction suggests that we view non-mathematical/non-linguistic intelligences as rare — particular to the few, not the many — and therefore not "real" ways of learning.

Schools for the arts, or schools where the arts are a significant aspect of the curriculum, are able to offer students many more opportunities to develop more intelligences than are schools that do not include work with the body, with music, or with developing the understanding of self and others — intelligences that are required of the good actor or the ensemble musician. Gardner's work makes it clear once again that in removing the arts from the schools, many children lose access to modes of learning that are as valid in terms of developing essential general skills as is the study of any of the traditional academic disciplines. Moreover, these neglected intelligences may be a more effective match with some learning styles. The opportunity to teach the whole child is diminished.

The Multicultural School

A 14-year-old violinist said, "Music is a lifelong language, one that does not discriminate against cultural heritage, race, or country. The only other non-discriminatory entity is death, and my music is something I will have until then."

Multiculturalism in schools, especially in urban areas, has become a concern in recent years. According to the *Carnegie Commission Report on Adolescence*, one-third of American adolescents today are of non-European descent, coming from a wide variety of religious, ethnic, and national backgrounds. By the year 2050, nearly 50% of the American population will be non-Caucasian. Currently, in 26 California cities there is no single racial or ethnic majority. Learning to live peacefully while respecting diversity will be a major task for adults in the 21st century, adults who are the current children and adolescents in our schools.

Under these circumstances, creating a school community that recognizes differences yet supports commonly accepted goals

159

and values is a challenge. High schools, where peer groups are the most influential factor in many youngsters' lives, are particularly vulnerable to cliques, mistrust, and hostility. The fact that students come from families that also often have widely differing values and experiences in the society adds to the difficulty of creating community within schools. This is not just a problem of inner-city black-white-Latino conflict. Anyone who has heard white students in wealthy suburban schools talk with envy and derision about the superior performance of Asian students understands that such wounding and divisive stereotypes are found everywhere.

In a school for the arts, the identity of students is based on their arts discipline; and their merit is judged on how serious they are in the pursuit of their work. Students are dancers, musicians, artists, actors, and writers, not rich kids, poor kids, nerds, jocks, blacks, Asians, or Latinos.

Of course, there are stereotypes among arts students. Dancers are smart but quiet in class, only responding if they are sure they have the right answer. Musicians hum to themselves and operate half in and half out of the real environment. Visual artists don't talk much and tend to be holistic and non-linear thinkers. A young actor will offer a long and convincing explanation of a book he hasn't read. However, contrary to popular belief, serious arts students are very supportive of each other, even when competing for roles on stage or seats in an orchestra. This may be because their common identity as artists and their need for peer support and affirmation is greater than their need to compete, at least in a school community.

It is a cliché to say that art is a universal language, but it is my observation that students from many cultures are able to appreciate not only the content of the arts cross-culturally but also the processes and aspirations of other young artists, no matter what their background. A school where one can communicate by playing an instrument, singing, dancing, and painting is a school where there are many opportunities for all students to be seen in the fullest sense by their peers. For example, placement in a string quartet is based on skill level, not age, class, or nationality. Consequently, it is not uncommon to find players from 12 to 18 years old and from several different countries in a single group, all relating and learning under the best possible circumstance, because they *must* if they want to play well. Their common goals, techniques, and training help them overcome, in a natural way, the barriers that would normally separate them. They come to see and understand each other through their work, not through the eat-the-food, national-costume "international days" so common in many school settings.

The relevance of students coming to such an understanding through direct experience is obvious for postmodern society. True mutual understanding comes through working together in an endeavor that has meaning for all, using a "language" — in this case, music — common to all. It is experience, understanding, and changed feelings, growing from that experience, that bind people together and break the stereotypes that keep them apart. It is not rhetoric, rules, or the pleas of school administrators to "just get along." New experience changes perception and leads to new understanding. Intensive arts training offers a natural venue for such experience and therefore for such understanding.

Moral Education

A 14-year-old pianist commented, "From playing, one learns not only the music, but the meaning of living."

One of the most difficult issues with which our society and schools must struggle is the role of schools in the moral and ethical development of adolescents. In this secular and multicultural society, there are no easy answers. We do not, as a nation, agree on what moral education is, let alone offer a cohesive moral education curriculum. How, then, do we support the development of good character in students? A bright, well-educated, talented young person who has no moral center, who does not have the tools and understanding to lead an ethical life committed to the good of others as well as to himself, ultimately is useless, often dangerous. Adolph Hitler, for example, was bright, charismatic, reasonably well-educated, and talented, but also greatly flawed. Character is destiny, and character is significantly shaped by experience.

Most young people, no matter what their behavior, want to be "good," want to behave in an ethical way, and want to be respected and to respect others. It is up to adults in schools and society to develop and nurture that impulse toward health and goodness that is, admittedly, buried very deep in some. We must all help young people to develop tools for making ethical choices in a world that will continue to present them with fluctuating and often competing values.

How *do* schools take on the task of "teaching" young people how to be ethical and responsible citizens? Not, I think, in ethics classes. Morality is embedded in life, not in an academic discipline. Students learn what it means to be ethical human beings by working with adults who strive to live ethical lives and to accept responsibility for fostering that desire in others. Students learn about morality by observing how adults act, how they treat each other in the hall or cafeteria, as well as in the classroom and studio. Teachers always are under the scrutiny of the sharp and unforgiving adolescent eye; and though they deny it, adolescents imitate what they see, not what they hear. Arts students have an advantage in that they are quite ready to honor and follow their teachers (even when they don't like them, which, for long stretches of time, they often don't). Their teachers consider it part of their teaching responsibilities to foster the development of a reflective self, because good art is the product of such a self.

All schools need to assert that the kind of person you are is as important as what you know and can do. Education does not equal goodness, and the importance of goodness needs to be made explicit wherever and whenever one can. Nor does goodness, like any true accomplishment, come from a timid failure to take risks, thereby avoiding censure, mistakes, and incidentally, any growth. Goodness, like playing the violin well, does not come by default.

All schools need to teach young people that what we call our conscience, our awareness of right and wrong, resides within us and not in rules and laws, important as these are to a civilized society. Young artists are asked all the time to listen to themselves, know themselves, and take responsibility for themselves. No one else can learn an actor's lines or appear for him in *Macbeth*. No one else can practice, alone, night after night. It is up to that actor at that time.

The development of character, of a moral center, means encouraging students to be true to their own beliefs, acknowledging how hard that can be, especially when there is great pressure to betray oneself for others. The study of the arts is about clarifying and being true to oneself, to one's own vision, even when there is little apparent support for that vision. In the long run, moral education and character development are accomplished by young people living with adults who struggle to live moral lives and who take it upon themselves to articulate these beliefs and standards, in word and deed, as a central aspect of the education process.

Related to the issue of moral development is the more complex one of spirituality. "Spiritual" experience in postmodern America ranges from born-again Christians to the late Timothy Leary's cult of LSD. The only area about which there seems to be any agreement is that spiritual life for many people, especially adolescents, is not a meaningful part of daily life. No easy answer is apparent. What is clear at this time in our history, however, is the longing people have for meaning in their lives and the sense of an often frantic search for such meaning.

William James said that all persons have a "will to faith," a desire to believe in something greater than themselves. Certainly one of the most positive characteristics of adolescents is their idealism, as expressed in their desire to seek greater meaning in life. Arts schools have an advantage in this realm because the study of the arts naturally leads students to questions and experiences that I would define as spiritual. The arts strive to make visible the invisible, to allow us to see and to experience what we "know" but cannot see.

The study of the arts demands that students engage actively with developing an understanding of such concepts as "meaning" and "beauty." Performance can allow both participant and viewer an experience of transcendence rarely felt in schools or society at large.

Think of the effect of the opening notes of Handel's *Messiah* or Lawrence Olivier's first speech as Macbeth. These experiences go straight to the soul and express and engender feelings that can not be captured in any other way. An accomplished singer once remarked that what he was searching for in his work was the feeling he had as a small child when, as a member of a gospel choir, he opened his mouth and, together with all the others, sang the first note. He called this experience "a state of grace; being in the presence of God." That ecstasy of being fully part of something larger and deeper than oneself, that glimpse into the transcendent, can come through the arts.

Spiritual life is concerned with the meaning of things, of events, and of ideas. It is important to spiritual development to seek meaning and to be able to articulate that meaning to oneself and to others. Young artists are asked all the time to search for and articulate the deeper meaning of the work and to find the impulse that inspires creation.

In this sprawling and hard-to-define area of school life variously called moral development, ethics, and spiritual life, another advantage of a school for the arts is that it is not only all right, it is *necessary* to talk about love and passion. It is not "cool" for a young artist to appear indifferent, a stance toward life that many adolescents cultivate, rather than allow their fears, vulnerability, and aspirations to be seen in an adolescent culture that often seems cynical and pragmatic.

We do not talk enough about love in our schools. We talk about sex and drugs, about relationships and responsibilities, as indeed we should, because these are important aspects of living. But it is also the task of schools to teach about passion, about love, about the growth of the spirit, because it is that part of young people that moves them toward greater dreams and wider worlds. Love is the spark that ignites the spirit and fosters transformation; and students in the arts love their work, even while they sometimes seem to hate it.

I am aware that I have chosen not to discuss the obvious fact that the study of the arts, like the arts themselves, is intrinsically good and does not need to be justified in terms other than its own. Study of the arts is useful in enriching the disciplines and, as has been the focus of this discussion, such study is a powerful vehicle for general education, for developing in young people the skills, habits, and attitudes that will help them lead better lives no matter what their career. But the study of the arts also should be available to all children because the arts in themselves offer experiences that cannot be found elsewhere. Through singing, dancing, playing, writing, painting, drawing, and all manner of making something where there was nothing and of expressing that which cannot be expressed in any other way, we become more fully ourselves, more able to partake of the human community, more fully *human*. We see the bison on the cave wall and feel the human connection across the millennia. It is a beautiful image, a message to the gods or, perhaps, to other hunters. Certainly it is a message to us.

Conclusion

In *Doctor Faustus*, Thomas Mann wrote, "To be young means to be original, to have remained nearer to the sources of life; it means being able to stand up and shake off the fetters of an outlived civilization, to dare — where others lack the courage — to plunge again into the elemental."

Postmodern society, service-oriented, technologically sophisticated, and full of unknown opportunities, needs people who are artists and people who think and live like artists, people who are creative and critical thinkers, risk-takers, hard workers, imaginative and inventive, and open to new experiences. The new century requires people who have faith in themselves and the future and who want to be involved. It is not about specific training for

165

specialized lifetime jobs. It is about flexible skills and attitudes, yet with a firm grounding in the self and confidence built on a sense of agency in the world and in one's ability to ask the right questions and find an answer. Artists are not afraid of what they don't know. In fact, it is what is unknown that is most inviting to the artist.

What I have suggested in this essay is that the process of intensive training in the arts develops in young people many of these skills and attitudes. It is one of the most effective methods of educating a young person I have observed and one that finds itself in concert with many current ideas about school reform. My purpose has not been to suggest that such study is the only path; rather, it is to point out that it is a path.

Many schools are realizing that the process of teaching as the master musician has taught since the Greeks — learning by doing, teacher as coach, building on the desires of the student, working in groups, evaluation as part of learning, and assuming that learning never stops — is an effective educational process in many ways. Education through the arts is not the only model that uses these concepts, but it is a powerful model and one that might be used much more widely.

How?

First, arts schools should remain an option for some, and all schools should continue to develop arts infusion curricula to enlarge and enrich the study of other disciplines and also to give students an opportunity to learn and be assessed in other modes. On a national level, we not only should restore but should increase and deepen arts instruction in all schools for all students at every grade. At the high school, for example, intensive training in the arts is, as I have indicated, a powerful method of educating no matter what career a student intends to pursue.

I also would suggest that some "regular" high schools include in their curriculum intensive training in the arts — as part of the education program, not as an after-school activity, not somewhere else, but right along with the liberal arts and sports. Not all students would be involved, just as not all play a varsity sport; but such an expansion of the curriculum would not only train young artists in the context of school, rather than apart from it, but it also would give the whole school the particular tone that one finds in a school where many students are involved the arts, an atmosphere of intensity, color, and positive energy. Such a school might become a community resource, a cultural center for performance and arts lessons for community members. Schools and conservatories have developed separately in most cultures. What would it look like if these two systems joined? It seems a radical idea; but so, at one time, was the notion of compulsory free education for all children.

These are a few ideas about how we might use education through the arts in schools. "Arts education" in its many forms is a fertile field these days, and from it may grow some unexpected crops. However, there is no doubt that school reform is a matter of urgency. We need to find ways to educate young people so that they become active and ethical citizens in postmodern America, citizens who once again have faith in themselves and therefore in their society. We are in danger of losing this generation and, in so doing, of losing the future. The sense of urgency we feel is real.

One of the functions of art is to show us where we are as a society, to reflect us to ourselves. In America we do not generally think of artists as political or social activists. However, it is no mistake that one of the first things totalitarian regimes do when they come to power is regulate the arts, because the arts do speak a "truth" that is often other than that of those in power. The arts are a powerful voice, a clear reflection of where we are if we can bring ourselves to look.

The reason postmodern art often seems so alienating, discordant, and deconstructionist is because those are deep elements in the culture that we do not wish to see, a poverty of soul and spirit that is more wounding than any physical limitation. It is the lack of a common civic and spiritual vision that leads to hunger, poverty, and the dead-end world of drugs, not a lack of resources or technology. We live in the richest nation in the world, yet in the name of individualism, we tolerate disparities of resources and human care between our poorest and richest citizens that stagger the imagination, especially when compared to other developed countries. Statistics indicate that it is not race or ethnic grouping that create low test scores and poor achievement in schools and in life; it is poverty. As John Frohnmayer remarked, "We are not in an economic depression; we are in a depression of courage."

America needs a greater vision for itself and faith in its own capacity for right action. We need to use what we have learned from our past and revise our vision of the future in a way that leads us forward, rather than remaining, as we sometimes seem to be, mired in hopelessness and a dysfunctional nostalgia for the past, a past that was not all that good for most citizens. America in 1960 was great for Beaver Cleaver but not for Eldridge Cleaver. Artists — and those who live and think like artists — can provide that vision and can demonstrate the value of acting on one's beliefs, on the power of faith. Artists *expect* their work and lives to have meaning and importance; they expect to struggle to reach their goals. America needs to do the same if we are to go forward.

When I walk across the campus at night, these thoughts are held by the sights and sounds of students working, on their own, to realize their deepest personal and collective aspirations. Education must mirror and support this natural motion of life, the desire of all young people to grow. These young artists need to be kept in motion by respect, love, high expectations, safe boundaries, and faith in the future. They must not be frozen by low expectations, dangerous streets, cynicism, and neglect. The motion of life that I see here is powerful and, nurtured and supported by a culture that cares for and about its youth, will help us move to the new millennium with the same high expectations, hope, and passion they display — the passion that keeps them up at night hanging lights in the trees and dancing in the dark.

Adult Literacy and the American Political Culture

BY GEORGE DEMETRION

George Demetrion is director of materials development at Literacy Volunteers of America in Syracuse, New York. Previously, he managed the Bob Steele Reading Center in Hartford, Connecticut.

> No educational practice takes place in a vacuum, only in a real context — historical, economic, political, and not necessarily identical to any other context. — Paulo Freire

In the 1980s, the problem of illiteracy gained national prominence through the advocacy of Barbara Bush and the perceived "crisis" in education, which linked the failure of schooling to the declining ability of the United States to compete effectively in a global economy. In response, the U.S. Congress passed the National Literacy Act of 1991. This legislation provides evidence of the value, whether rhetorical or more fundamental, that the U.S. government places on achieving the stated national goal "to eliminate illiteracy by the year 2000 . . ." (S1310, 1990).

Nonreaders nationwide have enrolled in adult literacy basic education and community-based organizations, with thousands of volunteers and part-time instructors contributing hours of valued time. In addition to such national agencies as the Literacy Volunteers of America (LVA) and Laubauch Literacy Association (LLA), regional literacy resource and research centers have sprung up to help coordinate efforts and to provide intellectual coherence and practical support for practitioners.

On the face of it, there appears to be a national consensus on the problem of illiteracy that transcends issues of class and ideology. But that is far from the case. In fact, wide gaps exists between the actions of the policy elites and the viewpoints of progressive and radical literacy scholars and practitioners. The national discourse is further complicated by the various perspectives of adult literacy learners who, as a new body of research is beginning to document (Beder and Valentine 1990; Eberle and Robinson 1980; Fingeret and Danin 1991; Ziegahn 1992), seek inclusion into the mainstream through approaches to literacy that integrate practical, personal, aesthetic, and cultural knowledge in ways that correspond to the concrete particularity of each learner.

In this essay I examine the prevailing discourse through an exploration of two key "voices" that structure the current debate. First is the work of policy advocate Forrest P. Chisman, whose structural-functionalist ideology played a pivotal role in shaping the U.S. government's literacy policy in the early 1990s. Next is the radical critique of functional literacy through Paulo Freire's "foundational" opus, *Pedagogy of the Oppressed* (1970).

Freire's early work presented a compelling counter-voice to a pervasive post-World War II "modernization" theory, wherein the "developed" world would provide aid to the "underdeveloped" world, in part by linking literacy to national economic development (Graff 1987; Street 1984). Freire's text still is drawn on widely by radical and progressive educators intent on resisting the hegemonization of a structural-functional ideology, currently expressed through a "post-industrial" vision reflecting the contemporary "realities" of an information-age society (McLaren and Leonard 1993).

As a progressive educator in the Deweyan tradition, I share a certain affinity with some of Freire's views, including the inextricable connection that he identifies between pedagogical theory and political ideology. My progressivism, however, is more firmly linked with the Progressive Movement of the early 20th century and is clearly reformist rather than radical in scope. I value both individual consciousness and collaborative efforts to enact change within capitalism as, to use Freire's term, the "limit-situation" in which mainstream literacy programs within the United States operate. While I share Freire's quest for "humanization" through the transformation of limit-situations, I remain critical of his overall "revolutionary" political project as it may pertain to adult literacy education in the United States. I also dispute the emancipatory/oppressive polarity that shapes the core of his utopian praxeology.

For a portion of this essay I will focus on the values that students at the Bob Steele Reading Center in Hartford, Connecticut, ascribe to literacy. Although it is not my intent to privilege the "naive" interpretations of learners, I take their views seriously. Through this, I question Freire's concept of "false consciousness," that the "oppressed" lack sufficient knowledge to act in their best interests and, instead, are compelled to internalize the "voices" of their oppressors. Rather, I adopt the position that adult literacy learners in "mainstream" programs are embedded in ambiguous historical milieus that simultaneously contain emancipatory and oppressive dimensions. I argue that their essentially "individualistic" aspirations reflect less an apolitical ideology than an acute "reading of the world" based on "horizons of possibility" within their reach (Lestz, Demetrion, and Smith 1994; Demetrion and Gruner 1995).

Rejecting the utilitarian reductionism of Chisman's structural-functional vision and Freire's radical "pedagogy of the oppressed," the students throughout Literacy Volunteers of Greater Hartford (LVGH) articulate a middle-ground quest for inclusion into the American mainstream. This consists not only of the desire for enhanced functional competency in ways that have application in the real world of adult literacy learners. The middle ground also includes a focus on personal and aesthetic development and a broad understanding of culture and society in ways that make sense to new readers. My thesis, therefore, is grounded in the progressive education theory of John Dewey, particularly his notion of "growth."

171

A Structural-Functional Vision:
Forrest P. Chisman and the Federal Politics of Literacy

Forrest P. Chisman does not present the most sophisticated view of functional literacy. Yet his interpretation is important because his policy advocacy exerted a significant influence in shaping the National Literacy Act of 1991. His "voice," therefore, is amplified through the federal government and indirectly plays a prominent role in shaping public perceptions. According to Chisman:

> There is no way that the United States can remain competitive in a global economy, maintain its standard of living, and shoulder the burden of the retirement of the baby boom generation unless we mount a forceful national effort to help adults upgrade their basic skills in the very near future. (1989, p. iii)

At the core of Chisman's view is a post-industrial, "human resource" vision, in which the nation's economy will be enhanced by creating more productive workers for the "informational processing" economy of the present and the foreseeable future. Stated negatively, unless the nation resolves the problem of worker readiness in the near future, the United States will no longer compete effectively in the global economy. In Chisman's cataclysmic dystopia, the nation has until about 2010 — when the baby boom generation will retire — to get its economic act in order (Chisman 1989, p. 3). Otherwise, the gap between the demands of an increasing technological workplace and the numbers of those ill-equipped to master the skills necessary to function effectively will result in a national crisis. In order to establish a competitive workforce to equip the nation to compete effectively in a global economy, Chisman believes that the government needs to play a direct, proactive role:

> Federal leadership is required because of the enormous social and economic stakes involved. The problem of adult literacy poses a severe threat to the well-being of the nation as a whole, and only government at the national level can

172

lead a nationwide attack in a problem of this scale. (Chisman et al. 1990, p. 221)

In order to address this economic crisis, Chisman argues that
the federal government must shift more resources from the unemployed to "the most seriously neglected national priority in
this field: basic skills of the workforce" (1989, pp. iv-v). While
Chisman seeks not to "abandon" other literacy efforts, he argues
for a major reallocation of resources from the unemployed to the
employed as the most efficient means of revitalizing the flagging
American economy. It is with such a national goal in mind that
Chisman articulates a "definitional tour de force" (1990, p. 3).
Chisman is concerned not about literacy in its literal sense, but,
as he says:

> *functional literacy*: mastering basic skills well enough to
> meet individual goals and societal demands. . . . [T]he terms
> *literacy* and *basic skills* will refer to functional literacy,
> understood in this sense. (1990, p. 3, emphasis in original)

Chisman continues:

> Unless we take steps to upgrade *their* skills in the very
> near future, all of us will be very worse off. Our rate of eco-
> nomic growth will stagnate, welfare costs will escalate, for-
> eign competition will make more rapid inroads, and our
> national standard of living will fall (or at least it will not
> keep pace with increased standards of living elsewhere in
> the world). (1990, pp. 8-9, emphasis added)

In response Chisman laid out a plan of action for the federal
government, much of which Congress drew on for the National
Literacy Act of 1991. At the center of Chisman's proposal is a
"leadership role" for the federal government. Specifically, he called
for a "federal coordinating body" (1990, p. 239) to decide how
"to improve the effectiveness of the nation's literacy system as a
whole," to "set measurable nationwide goals for upgrading basic
skills," to "monitor progress toward those goals," and to "refine
the guidelines of federal programs" (p. 239). Chisman recognized
the inherent political tensions between a uniform policy and "a

robust, pluralistic system," but felt such a coordinating body would at least "provide a high-level forum in which tensions in the field can be aired and, hopefully, channeled in constructive directions" (p. 240).

Because of such pluralism and limited fiscal resources, Chisman proposed that the federal government also should mandate state governments to deal with illiteracy at the local level in accordance to the purposes established in Washington, linked to national economic revitalization. Chisman's recommendations and policy formulations had a major effect on the National Literacy Act (NLA) of 1991, in which the utilitarian values of functional literacy were pervasive. Title II of the NLA focuses on workforce literacy and is intended to encourage small and medium-size businesses to offer basic skill literacy programs to employees "to advance the productivity of the labor force" (National Literacy Act 1991, sec. 202). Each state is expected to develop a literacy plan, "especially with respect to the needs of the labor market [and] economic development goals" (National Literacy Act 1991, sec. 332). The NLA also established the National Institute for Literacy to conduct research, to identify and disseminate information on promising practices, to facilitate staff training, and, in general, to help coordinate the field (Quigley 1991, p. 114). The NLA also provided a definition of literacy that, in certain key respects, emulated the "self-evident" utilitarian ethos of the functionalist paradigm. At the prompting of literacy educators in the field, Congress developed an expanded definition. Specifically:

> Literacy means an individual's ability to read, write, and speak in English, and compute and solve problems at levels of proficiency necessary to function on the job and in society, to achieve one's goals, and develop one's knowledge and potential. (Amendment in the Nature of a Substitute 1991, p. 2; quoted in Quigley 1991, p. 112)

A far cry from Paulo Freire's "emancipatory" vision of literacy, the expanded definition at least legitimizes personal development and moves beyond the narrow utilitarian functionalism espoused by Chisman. While recognizing that the NLA of 1991 provided certain windows of opportunity for progressive literacy educators, Quigley wonders whether such "centralized, more systematized models of federal and state support . . . will really bring us closer to what we so desperately need in the field" (1991, p. 116). Perhaps a certain skepticism is warranted that any sophisticated understanding of literacy, which seriously takes into account the experiences and worldviews of adult literacy learners, can come out of Washington, D.C.

Chisman played a significant policy role in defining literacy as a major national problem. His "demand" for high professional standards in the field and the need for major gains in basic skill development among learners point to certain challenges that require some type of resolution; however, Chisman's thinking on literacy remains problematic on a number of key respects.

Most poignant, perhaps, is the enduring gap that Chisman fails to realize between the vast preponderance of adult new readers and the skills required to enter into even the lowest strata of the "informational processing" sectors of the post-industrial economy. According to the federal government's own statistics, literacy programs reach only about 19% of the potential adult student body that might benefit from such services (National Literacy Act 1991, sec. 2). Of those, a sizable proportion "drop out" (or "resist," depending on your ideology) before making significant progress toward sustainable literacy, which based on current standards is approximately one-and-a-half grade levels of reading improvement per year of instruction (Chisman 1990, p. 15). For those who do stay, it may take three to five years for a lower-level student to achieve anything resembling fluent, independent, functional literacy. Without continuous involvement by the student in learning, a significant degree of atrophy occurs. Of those who do "succeed," very few enter informational sectors of the economy, such as banking, insurance, and financial institutions. Chisman's proposal for a major reallocation of resources is meant to mitigate these problems, but the extent to which even a major infusion of resources can significantly alter these current realities remains questionable.

In Chisman's approach, more resources would be extended to individuals most likely to enter into the post-industrial economy: employed learners, perhaps at the G.E.D. level of reading and writing proficiency. Chisman might better have placed more emphasis on lower-level skills and the implications for policy formulation that would affect people who may never enter into the "informational" sectors of the post-industrial economy.

An equally troubling implication is Chisman's assertion that the major burden for developing a competitive economy rests on the skills of the workforce. That might be the case for a potentially booming economy based on extensive internal and external markets for American products and services. But the economic crisis that the nation has experienced since the 1970s is not attributable so much to the lack of sufficiently trained employees as it is a result of the failure of a market reconstruction based on emerging "post-industrial" realities that cannot match the vitality of the post-World War II boom period that carried the nation through the 1960s.

With the precipitous decline of manufacturing, the rising "service" economy (whether low- or high-tech) has lacked sufficient vitality to keep the nation at the competitive edge that it enjoyed in the 1950s and 1960s. Tremendous downsizing of major corporations over the past several years and the enduring problem of unemployment and underemployment lead one to conclude that the current workforce is both sufficient and sufficiently well-trained to meet the employment needs of the sluggish economy of the present and the foreseeable future.

The more perplexing problem is a lack of sufficient jobs. On this reality, upgrading the skills of the marginally literate is much less a concern than is the need for a more diversified economy to meet the many challenges of a complex society. Instead of focusing on the single track of the post-industrial utopia offered by popular forecasters, such as Alvin Toffler (1971) and John Naisbett (1984), policy makers need to concentrate systematically on constructing a more diverse economy based on manufacturing, building trades, service, and information. Such an economy not only would better match the various skills and aptitudes of our increasingly diverse population, it also could provide the infrastructure for the stabilization of a more vibrant internal market, which is essential for economic revitalization, even in a trade-oriented economy that requires an expanded complex of products for an increasingly diverse world marketplace. Given this more realistic framework, human resource development could take on other patterns than those suggested by Chisman and his "post-industrial" cohorts.

A final problem with Chisman's view is the narrowness of his utilitarian focus. In *Leadership for Literacy* (1990) he acknowledges the "humanitarian" and "civic stake" that the nation has in promoting a literate society. He alludes to "the pathos of people unable to read stories to their children or covering up their lack of basic skills on the job, the isolation of people with limited literacy skills . . ." (Chisman et al. 1990, p. 5) — stereotypes that Hanna Fingeret, for example, has worked so diligently over the years to deconstruct. Chisman also bewails the civic cost in his difficulty "to imagine how people with limited literacy can be well-informed voters or how they can even learn enough about the issues of the day to be motivated to vote at all" (1990, p. 5). On this point he dismisses the importance of oral communication and the ability of people to think critically, even without possessing extensive reading and writing skills.

For Chisman, though, the primary stake is utilitarian. While "humanitarian and civic concerns . . . lead us to *care* about literacy," (emphasis added) clearly that is not "enough to make the United States mount a substantial response to the problem" (1990, p. 6). Rather, there is a concern of more fundamental proportions:

> Why should we do something about adult literacy? The most persuasive answer appears to be that literacy is a life-and-death economic issue for the United States, both now and in the coming years, because it is closely linked to economic productivity. (1990, p. 6)

I would argue against any direct relationship between adult literacy and the economic imperatives that Chisman foresees. I place the humanitarian and civic consequences of literacy, which Chisman tends to patronize, at a higher level of national importance in order to establish a more enlightened society and to extend a more participatory democracy into the body politic. Furthermore, I question Chisman's bureaucratic imperative that the personal needs, interests, and aspirations of individual literacy learners should be subordinated to a "national interest" defined by policy elites. Essentially, I agree with David Harman:

> Literacy itself cannot be forced upon a people. A demand for its acquisition — on the part of the people to be taught — is a necessary precondition. Such demand is not born in a vacuum. It reflects people's social, cultural, and individual needs; it is intricately interwoven with the learners' past and their vision of the future; it occurs only when the learner feels an inner need for it; it is self-reinforcing; it is accepted only because the learner wants it, not because some other person says it is important; and it relates to time and space. Unless these conditions are met, literacy will not be acquired. . . . A strategy based on the needs of the people — as they themselves perceive them — can transform the vision of universal literacy into reality. (Harman 1987, p. 73)

I will examine some of these issues further after exploring counter-currents in the work of Paulo Freire.

The Radical, Critical Pedagogy of Paulo Freire

Paulo Freire wrote that "the task of the humanists is to see that the oppressed become aware of the fact that as dual beings, 'housing' the oppressors within themselves, they cannot be truly human" (Freire 1970, p. 84).

Pedagogy of the Oppressed (Freire 1970) is clearly a foundational text among contemporary progressive literacy educators. Freire's engaging persona greatly aided the dissemination of his ideas. He traveled the world to promote them. Translated into many languages, *Pedagogy of the Oppressed* has served as a potent stimulus among all educators seeking to promote "bottom-up" literacy programs, that is, programs whose premise is the inherent intelligence of even "illiterate" adults, an intelligence often blocked by years of domination by social and political elites. More than anyone else, Brazilian educator Paulo Freire drew out the connections between political ideology and pedagogical theory. Whether or not we agree with his views, all of us concerned about these issues owe Freire a debt of gratitude for his pioneering work.

In the United States, Freire achieved a "founding" role in the school of "radical, critical pedagogy" and stimulated the scholarship, among others, of Henry Giroux, Peter McLaren, Ira Shor, and Donaldo Macedo (McLaren and Leonard 1993). These theorists have drawn on the political critique of Freire and the role of the educator as a "transformative intellectual" to develop a so-called radical pedagogy that challenges the fundamental assumptions of the "normative" political culture of the United States. Adult literacy educators also have drawn on Freire's work as a basis for developing participatory approaches to instruction and program management (Fingeret and Jurmo 1989). The political assumptions from which they operate are more reformist than radical in that they "privilege" the "lived experiences" of learners as the foundational basis for program development.

It will be useful to explore Freire's core assumptions and to develop a critique grounded in a contradiction between Freire's concept of false consciousness and his quest for a participatory model of education. Specifically, I question the oppressive/emancipatory polarity on which Freire's politics of literacy is based and argue that, at least within mainstream programs in the United States, the consciousness of adult literacy learners, as well as the "objective" historical situation in which both learners and teachers are engaged, is more ambiguous than Freire was willing to allow. On these grounds, the "duality" of consciousness that Freire sought to transform among the "oppressed" represents an acute "reading of the world," one that deserves considerable respect.

In the four passionate chapters of *Pedagogy of the Oppressed*, Freire laid out the framework for a politics of literacy that, with some important modifications, has remained consistent in its direction over 25 years. In his opening salvo, Freire declared "humanization" as the true vocation of all people and laid the foundation for this highly charged polemic, drawing deeply on the European intellectual traditions of existentialism, humanism, and neo-Marxism to create a Latin American text analogous to Frantz Fanon's anti-colonialist work, *Wretched of the Earth*.

For Freire, humanization refered less to a completed state of being than a process of continual "becoming" through "praxis" wherein people, both individually and collectively, critically reflect on their ongoing experiences for the purpose of constructing a more liberated society and culture that frees the "oppressed" and the "oppressor" from an "unauthentic" existence. While only "humanization" is "man's [true] vocation" (p. 28), dehumanization remains a distinct possibility, which reflects much of the actual socioeconomic conditions in Latin America among both the rural peasants and the urban proletariat.

At the core of such dehumanization is the oppressive force of "objective reality," particularly crushing poverty that keeps intact the dominating power of social, political, and economic elites. Such power includes a vastly unequal distribution of material goods between the elite and impoverished, which Freire never minimized. More perniciously, the oppressed have incorporated the image of the elite within their own consciousness and they lack the power within themselves to expel the invader from within. "Freedom would require them to eject this image and replace it with autonomy and responsibility" (p. 31).

Viewing freedom more as a process than an accomplished fact, Freire placed a larger degree of responsibility on authentic revolutionary leadership to play a liberating role. For this reason, the place of a critical, dialogical pedagogy also plays a central role in Freire's conception of a cultural revolution. Although radical educators have a more accurate sociological understanding of the sources of oppression than the "people," enduring political, social, and cultural transformation can take place only through a constructive dialogue that attains their full participation. In Freire's vision, leaders and the people are embraced in an epiphany of mutual love and interdependency. In their present condition, the people need the leaders to begin the arduous process of ejecting the invader from within. Without the full participation of the people, in turn, the leaders are subject to "vanguardism." In Freire's utopian view:

> the teacher-of-the students and the students-of-the teacher cease to exist and a new term emerges: teacher-student with students-teachers. The teacher is not merely the one who teaches, but one who is himself taught in dialogue with the students, who in turn while being taught also teaches. They become jointly responsible for a process in which all grow. . . . Here, no one teaches another, nor is anyone self-taught. Men teach each other, mediated by the world, by the cognizable objects which in banking education are 'owned' by the teacher. (p. 67)

Freire posited a sharp dichotomy between "banking" and "dialogical" education that conforms precisely to his polarized political ideology. On Freire's reading, banking education enacts "communiqués" wherein those with knowledge bestow it upon those who lack it:

> Projecting an absolute ignorance onto others, a characteristic of the ideology of oppression, [the banking educator] negates education and knowledge as processes of inquiry. [Instead, t]he teacher presents himself to his students as their necessary opposite. (p. 58)

In the banking model, the curriculum reflects the values of the educators and, more broadly, the dominant elite for whom education serves a normative function to "fit" students into their "appropriate" subordinate roles. As part of this "oppressive" ideology, the banking model mirrors the social hierarchy. Thus teachers talk while students passively listen; teachers select content materials that students unquestionable accept; and, most pernicious, in a parallel structure to the broader macro world "the teacher is the subject of the learning process, while the pupils are mere objects" (p. 59).

The opposite of the banking model is not the "celebratory" voices of students, though they serve as a critical starting ground for a dynamic "pedagogy of the oppressed." The problem is that the people are so oppressed that they have incorporated the ideology of the elite inside their own heads. The opposite of banking education, therefore, requires the expulsion of those "inauthentic" voices by the embrace of a new praxeology, wherein people progressively enact their authentic vocation, "humanization," through identification with the cultural revolution. To accomplish this, the people and the leadership of the cultural revolution need to work in a close, synergistic relationship through a "problematized" and thoroughly dialogical critical pedagogy to expel the invader from within and to initiate concrete action to overcome the oppressiveness of any given "objective" reality that masks the contingent nature of all historical experience.

As a postmodern Deweyan progressive, I find much in Freire's work that I seek to emulate. Like Freire, I believe that the connection between politics and education is ineradicable. Moreover, I share his passion for praxis, that education has the capacity to change reality, as he puts it, "however small" (Freire and Macedo 1987, p. 126). I share his belief in dialogue and the importance of student voice in the development of an instructional program so that education is *with* rather than *for* students, and I agree that "humanization" is a fundamental human vocation that education should facilitate. Similarly, I am in accord with Freire's understanding that literacy is fundamentally a "meaning-making" process whereby we "read the word" in order to more fully "read the world." Finally, I agree with him that the educator plays a fundamental role as a change agent by encouraging students to exercise a critical intelligence in their exploration of the world.

My fundamental disagreement resides in the oppressive/emancipatory polarity that still characterizes Freire's project, notwithstanding certain modifications of his earlier views, such as his diminishment of revolutionary rhetoric and his acceptance, where necessary, of pragmatic, reformist tactics. It is not his utopian perspective *per se* that is at issue. Rather, it is its radical/revolutionary framework that pits "critical intelligence" and "lived experience" in basic opposition to each other. This opposition often is the case in adult literacy programs in the United States, when they reflect a prevailing ethos of "late"-capitalistic formation in the consciousness of the vast majority of students and instructors. While Freire and, more generally, the Girouxian school of radical critical pedagogy have retreated somewhat from such simplistic antipathies, the overwhelming impetus of their work is still characterized by a hegemonic/counterhegemonious polarity with "resistance" playing more of a role than "revolutionary" praxis as a mode of operating in a profoundly nonrevolutionary society.

Such polarities remain coherent within traditional Marxian and neo-Marxian perspectives, with theory playing predominantly a critical rather than praxeological role. Given Freire's respect for the lived experiences of the oppressed and the unlikelihood of any sustainable, significant social movement toward radicalism in the United States in the foreseeable future, it seems unlikely that the radical stance can result in a meaningful "transformative" praxis, particularly in mainstream adult literacy programs, however progressive in tone they seem.

Middle Ground: Literacy as Growth and Art

Dewey wrote:

> [Growth] is essentially the ability to learn from experience; the power to retain from one experience something which is of avail in coping with the difficulties of a later situation. This means power to modify actions on the basis of the results of prior experiences, the power to develop dispositions. Without it, the acquisition of habits is impossible. (1916, p. 44)

I set this essay in a "hermeneutics of hope," rather than on any foundational position, on the assumption that such space provides the best chance of realizing an "emancipatory" pedagogy in a profoundly ambivalent, at best reformist, political culture. This culture contains both untold opportunities and incredible constraints, unevenly distributed across the social landscape. My intention is not to replace radical, critical pedagogy with my own reformist project, as it remains uncertain whether even this more temperate political ideology contains sufficient potency to reconstruct the field of adult literacy education within a more realistic, yet reconstructive paradigm. Given the limitations of both the post-industrial vision of functional literacy and the radical camp of Freire, I argue that this reformist temper for a middle way represents "the last best hope" for adult literacy in the United States for the foreseeable future.

In the effort to chart such a course I embrace certain of Freire's key ideas, such as humanization, dialogue, critical reflection, ontological openness, and the ineradicable connection between political ideology and pedagogical theory. On my reading of the world, I interpret these core characteristics through a reformist vision as the horizon of possibility, as the force field of potentiality that allows us to move "forward" into being and becoming. Therefore, from such a reading, in the next few paragraphs I shall attempt to reconstruct Freire's emancipatory pedagogy through the progressive gaze of John Dewey's philosophy of education. It is Dewey's core concept of growth, enunciated at the height of Progressive Era optimism at the beginning of this century, that I seek to appropriate for the more pessimistic climate of this century's end. Dewey characterized growth in the following way:

> If education is growth, it must progressively realize present possibilities, and thus make individuals better fitted to cope with later requirements. Growing is not something that is completed in odd moments; it is a continuous leading into the future. If the environment, in school and out, supplies conditions which utilize adequately the present capacities of [for our purposes, adult literacy learners] . . . the future which grows out of the present is surely taken care of. The mistake is not in attaching importance to preparation for

184

future need, but in making it the mainspring of present effort. Because the need of preparation for a continually developing life is great, it is imperative that every energy should be bent to making the present experience as rich and significant as possible. Then as the present merges into the future, the future is taken care of. (1916, p. 56)

Dewey's philosophy of education was undergirded by a broad consensus that the American political and social landscape had the capacity to create a progressively better society. It is much more difficult to be sanguine about that now, and the collective work of Freire, Giroux, McLaren, and Shor have made an important contribution in deconstructing the benign influence of liberalism on education theory and practice. In pointing to the broad structural inequalities of life in the United States, the school of radical, critical pedagogy remains compelling, though far from wholly convincing.

I cannot provide a path through the wilderness that leads to or even progressively moves toward the promised land of justice and emancipation, the hallmarks of Freire's utopia. There is no evolutionary teleology implicit in my appropriation of Dewey's progressive, pragmatic philosophy for our times. I draw on it almost symbolically, simply as the most compelling intellectual and praxeological space available, from my reading, for making progress at all in any sustainable cultural and institutional sense; and my reading admits considerable pessimism.

I draw therefore on Dewey's notion of "growth" as the primary hermeneutical space available for mainstream adult literacy programs in the United States. This assumption, in turn, is based on the belief that the gap between the "literacy myth" (Graff 1979) and what literacy actually delivers for people who persist in the effort long enough is not so wide as to prevent the kind of growth to which Dewey refers. One of the key dimensions to this is "making the present experience as rich and significant as possible," with the goal of transforming lived experience into an art form that leads to a feeling of transcendence. Whether this is an innate human capacity or an especially pronounced phenomenon of the American cultural landscape, we nurtured such an aspiration at the Bob Steele Reading Center, particularly through a variety of student narratives in which learners become authors and establish part of the curriculum for other learners, who then are challenged to engage in similar art forms. Thus the synergistic relationship between experience and art represents an essential component of growth and can be incorporated into a reformist adult literacy curriculum, particularly on Dewey's notion of art as the "consummation" of lived experience. Cultural critic Giles Gunn provides keen insight on Dewey's philosophy of art:

> The point he [Dewey] was emphatically interested in defending is that aesthetic experience is no different in kind but only in degree from all other experience. It is an attempt to refine, intensify, and subsidize the satisfactions potential to, but not possible for, nature itself. These satisfactions are at least potential to nature because all natural processes contain within themselves, as essential to their continuation and development, the capacity to convert obstacles or impediments into instruments for further growth. Yet these satisfactions are still not possible for many natural processes because they do not include within this capacity the ability to create new experiences out of meanings derived from earlier experiences. What enables the transformation of the one into the other, according to Dewey, is the agency of the imagination which he understood to be an element in all conscious experience. (Gunn 1992, pp. 88-89)

Such stimulation of the imagination through the enhancement of new experience represents an important, often overlooked component of adult literacy education. When such enhancement crosses a certain threshold, experience, according to Dewey, is transformed into art. Admittedly, this transformation is subjective, because art is a matter of taste and is understood more through intuition than cognition. Still, consider the depth of expression articulated by one of Hartford's former "illiterates":

> Sun set and the night roll around, I can feel my emotion come down, but now as I pull back the cover of my bed say-

ing to myself tonight I'll forget tears falling like the rain, tears — another hardly knows my pain — tears — all the tears your heart wouldn't hide — tears — now the tears become a good nice rain. If I could go back and change the hand on the clock, my heart would be saying you heard it, tick dock. For the one I love has gone far away. It gets harder and harder to face another day — tears falling like the rain, tears — another hardly knows my pain — tears — all the tears you wouldn't hide — tears — now the tears become a nicc good rain, every night when I lay my head down to sleep. (Smith 1991, p. 15)

Although this piece is particularly poignant, it is far from unique in the depth of emotion it depicts in the emerging genre of student-generated material created by adult literacy learners and their tutors. This growing body of literature portrays a vehicle that can enable new adult writers and readers to achieve provocatively innovative art forms through powerful acts of reading and writing that is as aesthetic, if not more so, than the experiences offered by the so-called classics of any traditional canon.

In addition to transforming experience into art, what Dewey refers to as a "consummatory" experience, the other purpose, according to Dewey, of making "present experience as rich and significant as possible" is that such a focus serves as the best possible ground for preparing people to meet the varied exigencies of the future. It is difficult to accept Dewey's notion that given such an approach, "the future is taken care of," considering the present unstable economy and the persistence of poverty, particularly in the nation's urban areas. Without profound structural change, the future likely will remain precarious for many adult literacy learners. Yet in starting with the present, rather than with a utopian ideal, this approach offers a way to help people prepare for the future by establishing opportunities for them to enhance their aesthetic sensibilities through literacy. This, in turn, may enable them to develop the wide array of skills, aptitudes, and perceptions needed to meet the challenges of coping with a complex and ambiguous social world.

Consider David, a Guyanese student who entered the Reading Center program at age 19, soon after migrating to Hartford. When he entered the program, he possessed virtually no reading and writing skills; but he had obtained a job stocking shelves at a supermarket. He was offered a new position there loading trucks but turned it down because of his inability to read meat labels, which would have prevented him from performing the job adequately. Later, as David increased his literacy (as well as his work experience), he was able to take a better job at a meat-packing company (Smith, Ball, Demetrion, and Michelson 1993, pp. 14-24; Demetrion 1994, pp. 25-31).

Although David's new job may not require much reading, becoming literate played an important role in enabling him to seek and obtain the new position. That is, literacy had an *indirect* effect that advocates of competency-based programs need to ponder. There is not always (perhaps not even typically) a direct correspondence between measurable increases in reading and writing aptitude and the ability to function more effectively in society. The critical and somewhat mysterious intervening variable is the concrete particularity by which individuals mediate affective, social, and cognitive development through the emerging social construct of the self. Some of the factors that enabled David to seek and obtain the new position included the ability to read maps and road signs, which expanded his knowledge of local geography; the ability to fill out job applications, thereby increasing confidence in communicating effectively; and an overall expanding self-perception, which was the result of a combination of increasing literacy, the empathy of his supportive family, and general maturation. David's future goals include obtaining his GED, becoming a nurse's aide, and to "communicate good with my wife and my son" (Demetrion and Gruner 1995, p. 42). It is clear that David is future-oriented and wants to accomplish a variety of important objectives through literacy. But the primary way that he has developed his aptitude has been through concentration on more immediate interests.

Among the things that David enjoyed during his program were oral history texts, an abridged volume of *Moby Dick*, and news stories, such as the Clarence Thomas Supreme Court hearings and the O.J. Simpson trial, all of which provided abundant opportunities for him to develop critical reflectiveness as well as basic skills (Demetrion and Gruner 1995, pp. 36-42). Interestingly, none of these topics have any direct relationship to increasing functionality within society, which is the primary objective of competency-based adult basic education. Yet they all potentially may play a pivotal role in the enhancement of his "growth," if their educational value is exploited to help David develop a variety of skills, aptitudes, and perceptions that then may be transferred to "real world" settings.

Of particular interest was David's affinity for science. The sheer wonder of it stimulated his curiosity. Although his understanding of science still is vague — he defines it as "how something is situated" — he senses that it represents a world of knowledge that could expand his own horizon; and he has learned enough to realize that there are "different ways to put science on my level." Even though "I don't have a clear picture of what I want to say," it is evident that he is intrigued by a body of knowledge that apparently has little or no direct application to any functional goal that motivates him. Yet he insists, "I want to experiment with science. That kind of science I like" (Demetrion and Gruner 1995, p. 36).

By tapping into his curiosity and wonder, the horizon of David's learning may be expanded, enabling him to develop broader capacities to "function" more effectively in other areas. This is what Dewey meant by *growth*; "to utilize adequately the *present* capacities" (Dewey 1916, p. 56; my emphasis) in order to expand on experience and to stimulate further learning as the most effective way of preparing for the future. The key for David's ongoing literacy development is the stimulation of his current interest. As he puts it, "If the story is interesting, I read better. If not I put it back" (Demetrion and Gruner 1995, p. 36). These simple sentences capture the essence of David's learning history, which is remarkably congruent with the sophisticated pedagogical philosophy of John Dewey.

We have abundant documentation of the value that learners at the Bob Steele Reading Center attribute to literacy in areas that are midway between the epistemology and social reductionism of Forrest Chisman's concept of functional literacy and the radical cultural revolution that undergirds Paulo Freire's utopian praxeology.

I define this middle ground through the ontological openness of John Dewey's vision of growth. In such a space the quest for community plays an important supportive role, but only in a context wherein each person's individual goals are enhanced through literacy. On this I am turning Dewey's social theory on its head on the ground that in the late 20th century, "post-industrial" era, the quest for the "Great Community" has considerably eroded. What is left, I argue, is an individualism that nonetheless seeks "completion" through what I would like to call "the better" community. It remains individualism, by and large, and with notable exceptions, which drives the quest for community in much of contemporary life in the United States and certainly within mainstream adult literacy programs. If that becomes obstructed, a fundamental source of motivation for participating in the program — some form of self-development, albeit often for profoundly social purposes — is eroded. As part of a broad ideology of "growth," adult literacy learners also are predominantly motivated by a quest for inclusion into the mainstream, rather than by any radical restructuring of the social institutions and cultural assumptions of "late" capitalism.

On this last point, I take the position that the quest for inclusion represents a powerful "reading of the world," rather than a manifestation of "false consciousness" in an utterly non-revolutionary, neo-conservative society with limited options for fundamental structural change, yet with windows of opportunity (however small at times) for enhancement and growth. In arguing thus, I take a praxeological rather than "critical" stance from the vantage point of practitioners and participants in "mainstream" programs, trying to improve the situation from within.

I do not deny the value of Freire's "reading of the world" as critique and as possessing a certain praxeological value in given places and certain periods of time. However, I contend that *development* over radical structural transformation represents the current "limit-situation" and "force field of potentiality" that characterizes

190

the primary opportunity structures of mainstream adult literacy programs in the United States at this time. And even this limited reformist space is, at best, precarious.

References

Beder, H.W., and Valentine, J. "Motivational Profiles of Adult Basic Education Students." *Adult Education Quarterly* 40 (Winter 1990): 78-94.

Chisman, F.P. *Jump Start: The Federal Role in Adult Literacy.* Southport, Conn.: Southport Institute, 1989.

Chisman, F.P., and Associates. *Leadership for Literacy: The Agenda for the 1990s.* San Francisco: Jossey-Bass, 1990.

Demetrion, G. *Motivation and the Adult Reader: Becoming Literate at the Bob Steele Reading Center.* Hartford, Conn.: Literacy Volunteers of Greater Hartford, 1994. ERIC No. ED 372 224.

Demetrion, G., and Gruner, A. *Dialogues in Literacy Interviews with New Readers.* Hartford, Conn.: Literacy Volunteers of Greater Hartford, 1995.

Dewey, J. *Democracy and Education.* New York: Free Press, 1916.

Eberle, A., and Robinson, S. *The Adult Illiterate Speaks Out: Personal Perspectives on Learning to Read and Write.* Washington, D.C.: National Institute of Education, 1980.

Fingeret, H.A., and Danin, S.T. *They Really Put a Hurtin' on My Brain: Learning in Literacy Volunteers of New York City.* Raleigh, N.C.: Literacy South, 1991.

Fingeret, A., and Jurmo, P., eds. *Participatory Literacy Education.* San Francisco: Jossey-Bass, 1989.

Freire, P. *Pedagogy of the Oppressed.* New York: Seabury, 1970.

Freire, P., and Macedo, D. *Literacy: Reading the Word and the World.* Amherst, Mass.: Bergin & Garvey, 1987.

Graff, H.J. *The Literacy Myth: Literacy and Social Structure in the Nineteenth Century City.* New York: Academic Press, 1979.

Graff, H.J. *The Labyrinths of Literacy.* New York: Falmer, 1987.

Gunn, G. *Thinking Across the American Grain: Ideology, Intellect, and the New Pragmatism.* Chicago: University of Chicago Press, 1992.

Harman, D. *Illiteracy: A National Dilemma.* New York: Cambridge Books, 1987.

Lestz, M.; Demetrion, G.; and Smith, S.W. *"Reading the World:" Life Narratives by Adult New Readers*. 2 vols. Hartford, Conn.: Literacy Volunteers of Greater Hartford, 1994.

McLaren, P., and Leonard, P., eds. *Paulo Freire: A Critical Encounter*. New York: Routledge, 1993.

Naisbett, J. *Megatrends: Ten New Directions Transforming Our Lives*. New York: Warner, 1984.

Quigley, B.A. "The Sleep of Reason: Adult Literacy and the S-2 Omnibus Education Bill." *Adult Basic Education* 1 (Summer 1991): 109-17.

Smith, S.W. *Welcome to Our World: A Book of Writings by and for Students and Their Tutors*. Hartford, Conn.: Literacy Volunteers of Greater Hartford, 1991.

Smith, S.W.; Ball, E.; Demetrion, G.; and Michelson, G. *Life Stories by and for New Readers*. Hartford, Conn.: Literacy Volunteers of Greater Hartford, 1993.

Street, B.V. *Literacy into Theory and Practice*. Cambridge: Cambridge University Press, 1984.

Toffler, A. *Future Shock*. New York: Bantam, 1971.

Ziegahn, L. "Learning Literacy and Participation: Sorting Out Priorities." *Adult Education Quarterly* 43 (Fall 1992): 30-50.

A Postmodern Feminist Perspective on Visual Arts in Elementary Teacher Education

BY CHRISTINE B. MORRIS
AND IRIS M. STRIEDIECK

Christine B. Morris is an assistant professor of art education at Ohio State University. Iris M. Striedieck is an assistant professor of education at Lock Haven University.

Today, many schools of education call for prospective teachers to demonstrate such understandings as the historical, social, and political contexts by which local and global learning communities define and value knowledge and action. The arts and humanities offer a powerful vehicle for creating such understandings.

In this essay, we present one possibility for creating a holistic perspective of knowing in the context of an elementary arts methods course. We begin by presenting the conceptual framework that guided the decisions and actions of this class. Included are highlights of critical events in the class and their meanings, as viewed from Christine's perspective. She is the teacher educator around whom this case study was focused. Offering another window into the events is a portrait crafted by Iris from interviews with Christine. Together, these stories share how one teacher educator responded to using the arts and humanities as critical tools of inquiry.

Cultural pedagogy is a combination of cultural issues, critical analysis, arts, and humanities (Trend 1992). From a community-based perspective, central issues of world concern and solutions to those issues are what need to be addressed. The use of central issues focuses the notion of multiplicity, a concept fostered by John Dewey. Cultures and art can be examined from a multitude of perspectives, including contemporary, historical, regional, and worldwide. The issues addressed through the study of culture, the arts, and multiple perspectives can be integrated into all subjects, thereby serving to connect subjects, to bridge book learning and practical application, and to foster students' understanding of the world's people and how people are connected to them through similarities and possibilities. The educator's job is to connect children not only to their own culture, but to the world — to create world-makers.

Christine: Experiences Create Intentions

As a cultural pedagogue, my teaching philosophy has been heavily influenced by the "vision of what teaching and schooling ought to be, and the reality of working in a large bureaucratic institution" (Weiler 1988, p. 101). My overall educational objective is to create an environment in which all students' cultures and multiple intelligences are equally valued, reflected in the curriculum, and developed as an integral and integrated part of society.

As a public school teacher I encouraged independence, gender and cultural justice, and growth and evolution by eliminating hierarchical systems that promote fear, dependency, and ignorance. Central to my teaching was, and is, critical thinking, a reflective process based on experience, rather than an analytical exercise. From my elementary classroom experience, I soon felt a need to reach a larger audience, to inspire students that want to be elementary teachers to be responsible, productive, and culturally and visually literate. I want to create thinking teachers who value cultural diversity, multiple intelligences, critical analysis, and connecting all subjects for optimum learning.

In the sections that follow, I explain how the elementary education majors with whom I worked embarked on their exploration and rethinking of traditional concepts of curriculum and knowledge production, arts, humanities, aesthetics, and critical analysis through cultural pedagogy.

Making Connections

Education's functional roots have been promoted as *the* tool to obtain the "American Dream." Thus teachers who question the legitimacy of the "Dream" propaganda find themselves outside the basic curriculum. These "outsider" teachers — of theater arts and media arts, as well as artists and musicians — often are perceived as irrelevant (Trend 1992). Arts and humanities critics, such as Newt Gingrich, Allan Bloom, E.D. Hirsch, Jr., Diane Ravitch, and William Bennett, sometimes go so far as to blame education problems on the arts and artists (Trend 1992; Giroux 1994; Apple and Weis 1983). But arts and humanities educators rightly ask, Since when have the arts and humanities had control of the education system?

Trend points out:

> Conventional schooling begins the process of depersonalization and control by fragmenting knowledge into categories and units of measurement. Not only are the relationships among different ways of thinking removed, but learning is conceived as something that occurs in school and at a specific point in one's life. In these and other ways, schooling positions teachers and students within what might be called "official." Young people are expected to respect this major instrument of socialization, even though it often denies the legitimacy of their own desire, experience, and cultural heritage. (1992, p. 123)

Conventional schooling has produced generations of passive learners who see schools as oppressive and irrelevant to their lives and graduate with limited skills in all areas (Giroux 1994). Consequently, many students in college and young teachers in the classrooms have been exposed to this type of learning, values, and socialization and are themselves passive learners.

On the first day of class, I explained to my education majors that the course was theirs to mold and that I was to be seen as a facilitator. I explained how their diverse interests, knowledge, and past education experience would be incorporated into the class.

The next step was to determine their knowledge of the arts and humanities and cultures. It was not surprising to find the majority of students' experience with arts and humanities had stopped after the eighth grade, and for some as early as the end of sixth grade. The majority of students believed that the arts were for the talented and had little or no educational significance other than that the arts could provide "relief from the real subjects." Most students had limited exposure to cultural diversity and defined culture by racial, far away, and "other" components. When I asked students to identify their culture, they either responded that they did not have a culture or referred to countries where their ancestors were born. In short, these future teachers had limited experiences with the arts, limited exposure to diversity, and limited exploration of critical analysis, ethics, and aesthetics.

Howard Gardner states that for understanding to occur, "students must encounter individual benchmarks on the trail from novice to expert, as well as road maps of how to get from one milestone to the next" (1994, p. 17). For education majors to value the arts and to understand the importance of the humanities and multiple cultural perspectives, they must experience that kind of education. And so, that was the experience I provided. The prospective teachers in my class also developed an instructional web to follow, as a kind of road map for teaching and learning.

I organized the semester around five portfolios. Each portfolio was designed to build on the others in terms of issues, philosophy, pedagogy, art, humanities, whole language, aesthetics, critical analysis, and curriculum development. At the same time, each portfolio had a particular, individual emphasis that was designed to create conflicting experiential knowledge and encourage change through "the discourse of possibility" (Giroux 1994).

I divided the class into groups based on their interest in teaching certain grades. Group emphasis was on teamwork and peer teaching so that each student was exposed to multiple perspectives and an environment in which it would be safe to share ideas, feelings, and frustrations.

The first portfolio was the *Quilt Portfolio*, which explored artistic and aesthetic development, multiple cultural presentations in the classroom, and the language of art. The students read articles about these topics and discussed them in small and large groups. We explored the quilt as an art form from sociological, cultural, gender, artistic, and personal perspectives, as well as the variety of expressions that quilts have inspired, including poetry, dance, festivals, music, and movies. Students experienced making a quilt square, participating in a quilting bee, and creating works about their quilting experience through poetry, music, dance, or story.

The students also were given the task of creating a unit web that would use quilts as the theme or issue to create one lesson. Up to this point, students had enjoyed the creating aspects of the unit, but they could not yet transfer their excitement to developing a unit or lesson. They were so concerned with the notion of pleasing me or trying to regurgitate a right format that this assignment established the beginning of conflict. As students asked questions, I would pose my answer as a question back to them, asking students what they thought. Of course, this was frustrating to them. Empowerment is hard to accept: "For their own empowerment and in order to organize against the increasing bureaucratization of schools . . . teachers must seek out ways of working collectively and collaboratively" (Weiler 1988, p. 152). Students' shared frustration helped the students to bond within the groups. By the second portfolio, they had gained the power to challenge me. The learning began in earnest.

The next two portfolios explored cultural issues, including aesthetic pluralism, cultural importance to education, teaching cultural arts, valuing voices, cultural biases, and determining stu-

197

dents' cultures. The objectives were to expand students' notion that cultures had to be exotic; to dispel students' misconceptions that they had no cultural identity; to conceive of multicultural education as more than a token day, week, or month; to question the absence of multiple voices; to discern personal cultural biases; and to determine how all of these factors can affect their teaching and children's learning. We critically examined art textbooks, concluding that the lessons presented in many were simplistic, predictable, and stereotyped the art and the people.

Through a variety of lessons that were built on my own cultures, Cherokee and Appalachian, students experienced a sense of cultural inclusion that enabled them to relate these topics to their own lives in a variety of ways. We related getting ready for a date and the rituals it entails — such as showering, using perfume or cologne, applying make-up, picking out clothing, and playing music, singing, and dancing to lift the spirits — to the rituals and traditions of adornment of a variety of cultures. Encouraging such a broadened and connected perspective-taking proved to be very frustrating. Few students were able to develop this portfolio well during the semester. I had presented a new way of seeing the world that challenged what they had always thought to be the Truth. But if, as Trend (1992) suggests, knowledge is created through critical analysis and by examining ideas, then I would have to be satisfied with planting the seeds. And, in fact, the students' frustration with developing units and lessons did decrease as their empowerment increased.

The last two portfolios were designed to encourage prospective teachers to develop their own teaching philosophy and pedagogy, as well as to develop as artists. An example, illustrated by the figure, is one group's unit web, which also included learning objectives and a description of learning activities.

The theme of this sixth-grade unit is violence; the word *violence* sits at the center of the web. The group's reason for exploring violence was based on their need to understand the mechanics of violence and the complacency with which students and adults often view violence. Trend (1992) states that students

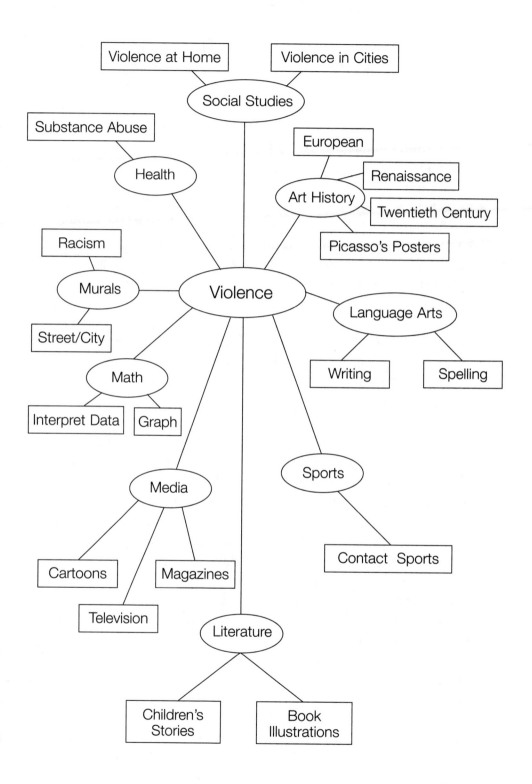

need to critically examine themselves and to use that analysis to make responsible, reasonable changes that will improve their social and cultural environment.

The group believed that the unit was age-appropriate, based on Piaget's theory that fifth- and sixth-graders are shifting from a single-dimensional emphasis on perception to a greater reliance on logical thinking about concrete events. While many children in this age group will have reached the stage of reasoning about hypothetical situations and be able to discuss events, others will not have reached this stage. Because these children also are becoming aware of sexual differences, are confronted with adult situations, and are beginning to view the world through an adult perspective, the group felt that violence was an important and appropriate topic of exploration.

The ovals that spoke off the central word, *violence*, represent the subjects of violence that the group targeted to explore. The rectangles represent resources and specific topics to be developed in lessons and activities.

This web is an example of one subject in the media unit web. Part of the web represents the media exploration, while another part shows how the other subjects in the web are integrated with each other and support each other, making connections not only across disciplines but with current events. The group provided a wide variety of media examples that illustrate or glorify violence: news, television shows, advertising, and movies, such as John Hughes' *Home Alone*, Steven Spielberg's *Jurassic Park*, Walt Disney's *The Lion King* and *The Little Mermaid*, and Gary Propper and Steve Barron's *Teenage Mutant Ninja Turtles*. They connected these examples to historical events, such classic stories as "Snow White," and social issues that contribute to violence and drug and alcohol abuse.

The students also were required throughout this unit to analyze themselves as individuals and to examine themselves in the larger context of a society.

The lessons were sequenced by subjects, with the first lesson exploring violence on television and in the movies. This lesson

200

required the future teachers to obtain excerpts from various sporting events and television shows. One student stated:

> I picked these clips to show the different forms of violence that children are exposed to every day. The movies range in ratings from PG-13 to G so that they are all available to the children that this lesson is directed towards. The clips from the television shows were all taken before 9:00 p.m. [in other words, during the designated "family hours"].

For the elementary students, this lesson begins with a discussion of their thoughts about the extent of violence in the media The students then view the movie and television show clips and discuss if and how their views have changed regarding violence in media. Next the students are asked to write a paragraph describing their views on violence and its effects and to explain their reasoning. The teacher then reads the paragraphs aloud and emphasizes that the purpose of the activity is to accentuate that violence is a serious subject for study. This then directs the discussion toward society's complacency toward violence.

The second lesson is an extension of the media lesson and looks at advertising. The future teachers chose commercials, such as the movie promotion for *Bad Boys* and commercials for *Laser Tag* and various toys. The objective of this lesson is to learn to read advertisements for the "hidden" messages that are conveyed through the use of color, images, and sounds that try to persuade viewers. For the elementary students, then, the lesson begins with viewing a compilation of videotaped commercials, stopping the tape after each commercial and analyzing the hidden messages. Next, in small groups, the children are asked to do the same activity with magazine ads. Finally, the children are asked to redesign, display, and explain the ads in ways that promote peaceful conflict resolution instead of violence.

The third lesson connects present-day views of violence in the popular culture to views of violence in past cultures. For example, the future teachers recognized that violence has been a part of art since the beginning of history. They chose to illustrate this with works such *The Battle of San Romano* by Paolo Uccello, *Perseus with Medusa's Head* by Benvenuto Cellini, and *Guernica* by Pablo Picasso. For the elementary students, this lesson requires them to learn about the historical, social, and cultural contexts that influence each of these paintings. They explore such questions as, "Are there similarities between the past and the present?" "What are the differences?" and "What are the solutions?" These historical, cultural, social concepts lead naturally to aesthetic exploration. The extension of this lesson is to have groups of children find a piece of art depicting violence and then create a response to the violence, such as a peaceful solution to the portrayed conflict.

The fourth lesson deals with violence in children's literature. The elementary students are invited to compare two versions of "Snow White" — one by Paul Heins and the other by Walt Disney. Questions are posed, such as, "Is this children's literature?" and "Are there offensive passages or illustrations contained in these stories?" Using a chart system, the children are asked to record the story's mood swings (for example, from calmness to violence) and then to interpret their data.

Later, the elementary students will go to the library and choose a picture book to read to a class of kindergartners, and in their choice they will be more aware of the book's contents in terms of violence. They will read the book with a peer partner first and chart the book page by page for the moods of violence. If the book is deemed unacceptable by the partners, they write a short paper about why they found it inappropriate and how it could be changed to make it a better book to be read to younger students.

I had a difficult time knowing for certain how successful these lessons might be, because the lesson would be influenced by several factors not present in the academic setting of the university, such as community attitudes and the attitudes of future co-workers. Instead, I evaluated the future teachers on their intentions, initial exploration of critical pedagogy, and multiple cultural perspectives. Certainly, the prospective teachers' intention of exploring violence is excellent. Giroux (1992) states that students must be given the opportunity to explore resources that affirm and interrogate their own culture and history. Knowing that this was the first time these prospective teachers had dealt with cultural pedagogy and that they have not yet taught in the public schools, I took into account that there were naive expectations. However, my overall reaction was that their use of cultural pedagogy was good. The lessons are embedded with self-, cultural, and social analysis.

Although the underlying theme is empowerment, the weakness was that this concept was not explored. Also, the topic of political responsibility regarding violence in a democratic society is not addressed. I asked myself whether my students could obtain only a superficial view of cultural pedagogy at this point, or did I present the political nature of this pedagogy in a way that could not or did not relate to their lives at this time? In the end, I was not certain of the answer.

A final issue that was addressed regarding their unit was the use of multiple cultural perspectives. Considerable class time was spent on the theme of inclusion through images, text, and discussion. The images and text that they chose were primarily Caucasian (reflecting self). This was a disappointment. After four portfolios of demonstrating how multiple perspectives could be achieved, I still saw no internalization of the concept of comparing contemporary and past cultures. I continue to wonder why this concept was, in a sense, rejected by these students?

A Room with Multiple Views

Calls for the inclusion of multiple cultures and perspectives in teacher education are varied. Taking a view that underscores the significance of considering social and political influences, Gollnick (1992) asserts:

> The task for teacher education is to help teacher candidates begin the process of critical examination of the practices of educators and schools . . . understand the influence of culture on their teaching styles and on the learning styles of students. . . and develop and model good cross-cultural communication skills. (pp. 65, 69, 71)

Clarken and Hirst observe that "we know much about diverse cultures, but our schools of education teach little to help teachers understand these cultures" (1992, p. 8).

In part, it is in response to such calls that this case study was designed — to describe and interpret how one teacher educator defines and makes meaning of the concept of multiple cultures and perspectives in the context of her elementary art education methods course. Following is a portrait of Christine that was crafted by Iris through three in-depth interviews. We attempt in this manner to capture the essence of Christine's journey to become an effective teacher educator and to offer a window into Christine's classroom.

This portrait is read from a postmodern feminist perspective, from which the themes of conflict, voice, position, and power emerge. In crafting this portrait, the following questions served as a basis for inquiry:

- What is the context of participants' past experience that shapes their meaning of education that imbues multiple cultures and perspectives?
- How does one teacher educator describe the concrete details of her present teaching experiences in light of her goal to address issues of multiple cultures and perspectives?
- How do the factors of participants' lives interact to help them understand education that imbues multiple cultures and perspectives?

The tools of inquiry used in this interpretive, semester-long case study included in-depth phenomenological interviewing of the teacher educator and selected prospective elementary teachers, participant observation of the methods course, and document analysis of the course syllabus for assumptions of Western cultural beliefs. (For a complete report of this case study finding, readers may refer to Striedieck 1995.)

We present in this essay an excerpt from the larger study, a portrait of Christine's theory of education, reflecting her postmodern feminist viewpoint. Portraiture, as defined in this study, is a tool of data representation that offers a collection of detailed stories told in an attempt to illuminate a more general phenomenon, capturing the insider's views (Lightfoot 1983). As a logical display of case study, the use of portraiture to represent data has the potential to capture the multiplicity of asking, telling, writing, and reading stories. Hence, as a locally situated creation, this portrait portrays the cultural values that structure and integrate individual experiences and their representation in the teacher education class. The study included a critical reading of this portrait from a postmodern feminist perspective, resulting in four themes: conflict, voice, position, and power. These four concepts are briefly addressed as a strand of themes, following this portrait.

Iris: A Portrait of Christine

"I'm telling a story and everyone has stories and people really like to tell their story. In my culture that's what you have. Your wisdom comes from your stories and your experience. When you tell stories, everyone has one then that they can relate to. That's really the essence. We all want to tell our story. And in that, we relate, we appreciate, and we understand. It makes us feel as one when you allow that." — Christine

Christine is a 40-year-old woman with ethnic connections to Cherokee and Appalachian cultures. Considered a member of the middle class nowadays, Christine's family history reflects the working class. She is a wife and mother with two teenage sons. Her teaching experience spans 15 years and ranges from working with elementary-age children to teaching adults, all of various abilities. Christine has worked as an educator in public schools, higher education, and museums. She also teaches informally, as a cultural role model in her daily life.

At the time of this study, Christine was teaching an art education methods course designed for prospective elementary teachers at Pennsylvania State University. She provides the following narrative.

Christine's Narrative

[I taught] in art museums first. [Later I taught] in an urban school [where] I didn't have any experience in that situation. I didn't have experience in teaching behavior disorder students, none. Not a class, no theory, no nothing, [I] just recogniz[ed], "the kid's troubled here, we [have to] take care of this."

When I was teaching in [another school district] I was called a cultural arts teacher. I had no idea what a cultural arts teacher was . . . and to this day I don't know why the cultural aspect was applied to the course. "But . . . ," I responded. I don't know if I responded to the label or responded to my own experiences. I'm sure it was my own experiences, that I taught from a cultural base. And. . . I never put anything really together [about] what I was doing [or] my approaches until much later. Now I can look back and read it and see theory in it. I certainly didn't have that at all in my mind when I was doing it. I was doing it **by** gut.

When I look back to my undergraduate years . . . I think I've done it backwards, in a sense, because I had the experience and then I came to school to put a label to it. I don't think I was given any theoretical information. I didn't even know the word, *theory*. I was taught subjects.

What a shock it was for me the first time going into a classroom! There was all these things that you had to deal with [and] I thought I was supposed to know this stuff. So a lot of it came from . . . experiences and I would just go home and start analyzing what happened in my classroom today, [asking myself] "What do I need to do tomorrow?" and learning how to deal with those situations and coming up with solutions that *worked for me* in becoming a teacher that I wanted to be. So it was a lot of reflection . . . [a] re-evaluation process, to get to where I wanted to be.

[It is this process of reflection that I still engage in when planning my lessons now. What happens in my upcoming class] . . . depends upon what went on in my last class. I think about students' responses [and] about the dynamics of the class. Then I think about what I need to do to get it to where I want it to go. I try to stay one step ahead, but still on that same track, trying to take them from one place to the next.

[Essentially, as a teacher I try] to help people to reach their potential, to be happy with who they are, to know who they are and to [help them] see their strengths, utilize those strengths and be aware of weaknesses. When you are aware of those weaknesses or your biases, you're opening yourself up to change, to check yourself, to evaluate yourself, to question your choices. And I think that's very important for teachers to always do. It gives you the opportunity to always make sure that you're doing right by your students.

[I also try to provide students with] unconditional support and unconditional love. There are students that I see do things that I don't believe in. But if that's what they believe in . . . and they can defend it, and they're comfortable with it, then that's the teacher they have to be. And it's not up to me to judge them. And that's the unconditional support.

In education, getting people to think is not very easy. It's very simple to give people the answer. But people don't take the answers. Any time you challenge people to think you're going to get those [who] drag their feet or [suggest that] maybe you don't know the answer. So then it's [a] challenge and a little hard to take, because you do know the answer, but that's not your job to give it. It's going to take them a while to work all this out, [but] they don't want to hear that.

I was in a graduate class [recently] — aesthetics, philosophy. And someone [there] used the word — and they were meaning this, is what got me. I mean these are people that have lived the world and these are graduate students, they're my peers — and they used the words *primitive* and *highly advanced*. And that primitive people don't have aesthetics. And I'm sitting there, trying to take this in, thinking, "Okay, I'm not really taking this course, I'm just sitting in here, learning how to teach aesthetics. I'm trying not to become a part of this. But after listening to them, going back and forth about highly advanced and primitive people, I came up out of there and I said, "I think that you are all presumptuous, elitist. How dare you even think that you have the right to even talk about these issues that you know nothing about. If you're going talk about highly advanced, as you put it, limit your conversation to that, because obviously that's where you think you are. And don't talk about things you don't know anything about. I don't want to hear whether you think it's okay that Cherokee is a jeep, because that's not up to you to make this judgment. Or whether or not you think these people are making a big deal out of it. I see no jeep called Pale Face, I see no jeep called Honky . . . they're not an issue that you deal with, therefore, why do you think you should deal with the issue. And I really came up out of there — it was a good class for me to get it out, because then I'm able to sit there and listen to the undergraduates, and I don't pounce on them.

For me to jump down on students is very negative and turns them off. For them to experience my culture in a positive way, in an open way [allows them to be] more responsive to change . . . and it doesn't become a personal attack. [T]hey have to evaluate themselves. It's not up to me to judge them, they have to judge themselves. [But I can] encourage them to see other ways.

And I do that by bringing David, my husband, in. The two of us perform for them and have them listen to the songs telling about my cultures in both places, and then I talk about my experience. I told them about how I felt as a child finding out the word, *hillbilly*, or finding out how people thought [I was] primitive or making fun of the way I talked. [I also talked about] how it affected me and why I do what I do in the schools today. And why it was important for them to do and why it was important for them to be proud of the cultures that they were from. And that every child should walk around being proud of who they are.

I do [all of this] to illustrate how hard that is to connect dots and why it's so important that they connect the dots for their students. And I model for them. But I don't bring it out directly. I just keep demonstrating and at the very end [I] tell them [what this process is], 'cause they go through frustration levels. [My] purpose is to give them a space to explore . . . difference and for them to see the value of . . . difference and to be glad for who they are and not to try to erase it.

[So I don't want to jump on people or be controlling]. I don't like control. I don't particularly like power in that sense. [One way I try to minimize my power in the classroom is for students] to come up with their grading criteria. And for me, this is their responsibility.

[Sometimes my students have difficulty accepting this role and this responsibility, like] the student who was upset over the fact that he had to set the grading criteria, because "teachers only do that." That student never connected [and] . . . denied ownership. That student didn't want ownership, he wanted dictatorship. Because to him that's how school has always been. He was rejecting that part of responsibility and ownership to the class.

I [recently] showed [my students] a documentary [about the human species' need to be creative and play]. Desmond Morris, [who is a zoologist,] shows all these cultures all mixed up. Exactly what I'm talking about. We were all over the world. And guess what? We were the same. Different packages, but we were all the same. And I said [to my students], "Isn't it amazing, we watched this for thirty minutes and he showed us thirty cultures and there was really no choices." Not one was better than the other. And we learned that all these cultures had things in common. And how he looked at that was through an issue. He asked a question and then answered it in all these different ways.

And that's a multicultural approach. And not one of us had to learn to be an African [or] Hawaiians. But that this is another way of looking at multicultural education. And this can work in your classroom from pre-school through high school through college. We don't have to make decisions about which cultures to concentrate on. And that's what he showed. It's just by the multiple visuals that you use. Be aware of those particular choices that you make. And . . . that goes back to your biases, . . . maybe [you] need to add [something] and be a little open and grow . . . with your students.

Students love to know that teachers don't know everything . . . they love to know that they've just taught you something. [And by doing so] you give that child . . . empowerment.

And they have ownership now [which] . . . really opens those doors to having that in and out communication, you know the feminist pedagogy of being able to learn together and being responsive.

Sometimes . . . people . . . are very adamant about what they've experienced was wonderful and that that's what they want to do. They don't understand that it may have been wonderful for them, but what about the one child that it wasn't [wonderful for]. I was the one child, so I'm always concerned with the one child, I'm not as concerned with majority. The majority will survive, they don't need reaffirmed. And I don't mean they don't need it, but they have a great deal of affirmation because our culture provides that for them.

At this time, with the students that I have to work with, [I try to get them] to understand that there is a term called Other. And that their job is to get rid of that term. And by allowing them, in the comfort of the classroom, to be honest about themselves, to know who they are, to respect or attempt to respect and appreciate diversity, even within that classroom — as homogeneous as it may seem — it's not. And that looks are very deceiving . . . be careful of assumptions. What you may think is a homogeneous group of people, may not be. And if you look further, we're not at all.

[I recently attended an international art educators conference and] one of the things that they were talking was the fact that cultures from all around are going through a stage of cultural protectiveness because of the massive amount of misappropriation . . . and exploitation that has occurred.

Jaune Quick-to-See Smith, a Native American contemporary artist, was one of our speakers [at this conference and] she was talking about the fact that she traveled all over the United States and . . . that she's sick and tired of seeing what people were doing with Kachina dolls. "Why were they teaching Kachina dolls?" [she asked. It's] okay to show Kachina dolls [and] to talk about the tradition of Kachina dolls, which is what I advocate. You teach the history of it, . . . the spiritualness of it, . . . the cultural aspect of it, but why . . . would you [have] kids make one? What . . . [has] that got to do with their life? And she said, "Why aren't they making Christian dolls?"

Change is going to come whether people want it to or not. And those . . . grandiose lessons that perpetuate "dominant culture knows all" are going to be eliminated

. . . whether they're going to admit it or not and whether they want it or not, it's going to happen. [T]hose world-wide sounds are different than what's being echoed here, whether it's the Latino culture, the Native American culture, [or] the Appalachian culture. We're going to have to really listen to that as teachers. So that reaffirmed for me . . . that I was okay [as a teacher].

Multicultural to me, and the essence of it is beliefs and values. That's what separates us when we misunderstand each other. It's not looks. It's fear. And that goes either way — you think they're all like you and then you find out they're not like you, as far as [sharing the] same values and beliefs. Or because they look at you and automatically determine you're different. And then if you look further they might be just like you [and] . . . have the same values and beliefs as you do. So it's trying to get [students] to understand that those first assumptions are not always the right [ones]. That goes back to the biases again. [W]e all have common things and what separates us is our reactions. And that's all culture is. Culture is a reaction to our time and place.

It is all about our heart and soul. There's a lot of people walking around . . . without that. And that's where a lot of the problems stem from, they don't have their roots [and] they don't see their future. They have nothing to grasp onto. [People] don't know what their values are. I know there's a lot of controversy about whether morals should be taught in schools. I'm not sure about that myself. But I am sure that children should have an opportunity to be proud of who they are and they should be able to go into any public place and feel free — if we are a democracy — and be able to be that person.

I'm looking at a wide definition of multicultural, which is more postmodern than the modernist view. And I think we're still dealing with that modernist view of multicultural, which is . . . very patronizing, stereo-typical and sterile.

[T]he schools here, when they have what they call . . . multicultural education, they always talk about Other. One of the effects of that mindset is that these kids don't know they have a culture. Any time the word culture has been mentioned, it's been about somewhere far away. Therefore they think to have a culture you have to be from Africa, [or] . . . you have to so different.

What I'm feeling, and hearing [from] teachers and . . . students in classrooms, and finding in research — I'm talking elementary and junior high — [is that students] are culturally void because of this. And [yet there are] . . . people that want to instill a national culture; they want to eliminate diversity. [P]opular culture [then becomes] the only thing kids have at this point to hang onto, and it's not answering their needs or their place. If we really look at what is culture, it is a reaction to place. So if they are without their place, if the culture is not being transmitted to them, or it is being told it's wrong, or it doesn't exist, then you go someplace else to try to find one. But when you go and take someone else's, it doesn't answer to your place. And they become cultur-ally void.

I think it's awful that my students can sit there for two or three weeks trying to figure out what their cul-ture is. They don't know. . . . That's why it's important for us to really widen our view and quit giving that message to students that culture is something someone else has.

And I want people to understand that when I say cul-tural pedagogy I mean to begin with what is in that classroom and recognize the multiplicity within that classroom and then go out and look. Once students can value themselves and others that they know in their community, then that gives them the skills to see all

Others in that same perspective. So you don't have to teach something that they don't know or they may never know.

I think it's great to educate children about things in the world. I have nothing against bringing in a group from Africa or Japan. [B]ut if they don't have a perspective of how to view it then it was nothing more than a 45-minute entertainment. I think you need to give them the context in which to view it.

[In] education, the whole thing that we're supposedly giving is lifelong skills. And that's not what [is happening]. What [we] need to do is educate the educators [about how to teach through multiple cultures] . . . instead of taking it all away, because it could be very meaningful if the teachers knew how to use it. And they don't know that because we don't teach them that, [it's] a lack of training. [I]t takes a long time to find out about.

Collectively, the themes of conflict, voice, position, and power are critical components of the essence of who Christine is as a teacher educator. As her portrait conveys, the evolution of Christine as a contemporary teacher educator was and continues to be influenced by her cultural identity and historical past. Christine's approach to teaching is one that recognizes that "every class has its own process of getting to where they're going" and attempts "to always connect things back to [students'] own experience."

In exploring notions of difference and similarity in her predominantly white, middle-class classroom, Christine finds it important to "get the class to admit . . . that their experiences are very limited," and so she invites students into dialogue to better "understand that there is a term *Other*." Her goal for prospective teachers is to develop a grounded and global perspective of multiplicity and culture and to recognize that "Change is going to come whether people want it or not."

Taken together, the themes that emerge from this portrait suggest that Christine's personal life is a foundation for both her teaching and her concepts of how students learn. The process of building this foundation represents the essence of what Papert (1990) describes as his passion for learning:

> Understanding learning is my life-long passion. . . . But interestingly I find that what helps most is not the proliferation of abstract principles. I gain more by extending my collection of "learnings" — concrete learning situations that I can use as "objects to think with." (p. ix)

Christine's collection of learnings have served to help her understand the importance of contextualizing her prospective teachers' education in their own life processes and positions. She develops her praxis by engaging in processes of self-reflectivity and critique, two skills that Bowers (1984) asserts are necessary for helping students demystify notions of culture. Furthermore, her selection of issues, art content, and pedagogy reflect assumptions of multiple problem-posing and problem-solving, thus allowing for the multiplicity of experience that her prospective teachers bring to the classroom as learning tools.

What Teaching and Schooling Can and Ought to Be

The role of the arts and humanities in fostering acceptance of multiple cultures and perspectives offers teacher educators a myriad ways of viewing and knowing the world. As Ernest Boyer poignantly stated in his keynote speech to the Association for Supervision and Curriculum Development conference in 1993, a coherent view of knowledge requires, in part, an ability to respond to the aesthetic as a core commonality or shared experience. By viewing artifacts and the languages of art, dance, and music, for example, both as unique and shared forms of expression and as they are embedded in various social issues, the process of teaching and learning necessarily invites a perspective that transcends the piecemeal and controlling approach evident in so many contemporary classrooms. As such, the postmodern feminist perspective espoused in this writing is a fundamental movement for emancipation from hierarchical structures of knowledge and power. This perspective is

215

a commitment to morality, social justice, and equality for all individuals. Such a perspective stresses the need for a greater degree of participatory interaction between learners and providers of education, drawing attention to the fact that diverse groups and individuals may participate differently in educational programs.

References

Apple, M., and Weis, L. "Ideology and Practice in Schooling: A Political and Conceptual Introduction." In *Ideology and Practice in Schooling*, edited by M. Apple and L. Weis. Philadelphia: Temple University Press, 1983.

Bowers, C.A. *The Promise of Theory: Education and the Politics of Cultural Change*. New York: Longman, 1984.

Clarken, R.H., and Hirst, L.A. "Enhancing Multicultural Education in Teacher Preparation Programs." Paper presented at the Annual Meeting of the American Association of Colleges for Teacher Education, San Antonio, 1992.

Gardner, H. "Teaching for Understanding: Within and Across the Disciplines." *Educational Leadership* 51, no. 5 (1994): 14-18.

Giroux, H.A. *Border Crossings*. New York: Routledge, 1992.

Giroux, H.A. "Living Dangerously: Identity Politics and the New Cultural Racism." In *Between Borders: Pedagogy and the Politics of Cultural Studies*, edited by H.A. Giroux and P. McLaren. New York: Routledge, 1994.

Gollnick, D.M. "Understanding the Dynamics of Race, Class, and Gender." In *Diversity in Teacher Education: New Expectations*, edited by Mary E. Dilworth. San Francisco, Calif.: Jossey-Bass, 1992.

Lightfoot, S.L. *The Good High School: Portraits of Character and Culture*. New York: Basic Books, 1983.

Papert, S. *This Too Is Music*. Portsmouth, N.H.: Heinemann, 1990.

Striedieck, Iris M. "A Narrative Portrayal of How Multiple Cultures and Perspectives Are Represented in One Elementary Teacher Education Class: A Postmodern Feminist Perspective." Doctoral dissertation, Pennsylvania State University, 1995.

Trend, D. *Cultural Pedagogy: Art/Education/Politics*. New York: Bergin & Garvey, 1992.

Weiler, K. *Women Teaching for Change: Gender, Class, and Power*. New York: Bergin & Garvey, 1988.

The Family Myth in the Postmodern Humanities Curriculum

BY DONOVAN R. WALLING

Donovan R. Walling is editor of special publications for Phi Delta Kappa International and previously taught art and English and was an education administrator over the course of two decades in public schools in the United States and abroad.

Lamentations over the demise of the "traditional family" are the leitmotif of the 1990s. Variations on the theme are played in the halls of Congress, on the talk-radio airwaves, in television and newspaper commentaries, from church pulpits, and in board rooms so often that they seem surely not to merit further media exploitation. Yet the headlines and sound bites cry on. Politicians and pundits blame the deterioration of the traditional family for low school achievement, continuing — indeed increasing — child poverty, escalating crime, and a host of other social ills. What few of these decriers realize and even fewer admit is that the archetypal, so-called traditional family as a predominant family type no longer exists and cannot be revived.

In fact, it never really did exist. The predominance of the traditional family is a comfortable fiction elevated to the level of myth by past generations of politicians and other soothsayers too willing to find scapegoats instead of solutions for basic societal problems.

In this essay I will argue that it is necessary to dismantle the traditional family myth of modernist lore and to recognize the postmodern family — what David Elkind refers to as the "permeable family" (1995, p. 12) — as a major part of the diverse reality basis for the school curriculum. In particular, this understanding is needed in order to develop a humanities curriculum that will meet the needs and match the interests and experiences of a diverse student population.

Key Principles of Postmodernism

Charles Jencks became one of the first definers of postmodernism with the publication in 1977 of his book, *The Language of Post-Modern Architecture*. That book helped to set in place a linguistic framework on which general definitions of postmodernism have been built in other disciplines. The two seminal concepts in Jencks' language are "complexity" and "pluralism."

Modernism, which characterizes much of Western history during this century, was an outgrowth of converging 19th century "isms" — humanism, rationalism, and individualism, among others. Elkind (1995) contrasts the three basic beliefs of modernity — progress, universals, and regularity — with the beliefs of postmodernity, which he posits are the articulation of sociocultural differences rather than linear social progress, cultural particulars rather than universals, and the irregular as being "legitimate and as worthy of exploration as the regular" (pp. 9-10).

When Elkind announces that "the [postmodernism] movement represents a fundamental paradigmatic shift in our abiding world view" (p. 8), he echoes Jencks' characterization of urban architectural settings:

> [D]uring the industrial age Modernism became the most important *episteme*; while in the post-industrial period none of these competing cultures — High, Low, Traditional, Mass, Pop, Ethnic or Other — speaks for the majority of urban dwellers. Most of the time in the huge megalopolis we are all minorities — yes, even those who have cornered what

used to be called 'the ruling taste,' the Establishment. This can be alienating, and many people deplore the competition of language games and values, and the retreat into a previous orthodoxy, whether Modern or Traditional. But those with a Post-Modern sensibility enjoy the diversity, and know why it is necessary and positive. (1991, p. 10)

"What is at stake in this situation, what constitutes the new world view?" Jencks asks rhetorically. He responds: "Fundamentally it is the growing understanding that pluralism creates meaning . . ." (p. 10).

Jencks' megalopolis can serve as a metaphor for today's schools, particularly urban schools, which are microcosms of the larger urban society. Today, in many urban schools — and increasingly in all types of schools regardless of setting — the student majority is composed of former minorities. Collectively, students from nonwhite racial minorities outnumber white students in many schools. Likewise, the number of students from language-minority homes and culturally different families, without regard to race, are increasing in proportion as the number of students from "traditional," native English-speaking families are decreasing. More students arrive at school each new school term from single-parent and blended families. If "the school is the mirror of society and of the family," Elkind suggests, then "as society and the family change, so too must the school" (p. 8).

Unfortunately, permeating much of the public dialogue about the nature of American society and, especially, in radical conservative rhetoric, there is a profound failure to reconceptualize the family based on today's reality. Thus critics of postmodernist definitions of family, school, and society perpetuate a traditional family myth. In so doing, they substitute breast-beating for solution-seeking to deal with societal problems. In order to move toward the reality base of the postmodern family, which can better inform educators about their students' lives and needs, it will be necessary to dismantle the modernist family myth and, in the words of Elkind, "modify and correct modern ideas that have been perverted and modern beliefs that have proved to be too broad or too narrow" (1995, p. 10).

Toward a Redefinition of Family

Janice Hamilton Outtz's work, *The Demographics of American Families* (1993), provides a statistical basis for debunking the traditional family myth. In it she concludes:

> The American family is diverse, there is no "typical" family structure. Instead, there are many work-family patterns and each pattern, or family type, has different needs. (pp. 18-19)

In the traditional family myth, the ideal American family is portrayed as a breadwinner father, a housewife mother, and two or three children, much like several popular 1950s sitcoms — "Ozzie and Harriet," "Leave It to Beaver," and others. Outtz points out that many of today's American families do not resemble this model. "In fact," writes Outtz, "fewer than one in ten families in the United States resemble the 'Ozzie and Harriet' prototype" (p. 1).

Indeed, the mythic notion that the traditional family — a married couple with children under age 18 — once was the predominant American family type is patently false. As Outtz demonstrates, in 1950 this "traditional" family constituted only 48% of all family households. Ironically, as the so-called Sexual Revolution of the 1960s peaked, the traditional family actually surged to 50% in 1970. But by 1990 the traditional family made up only 37% of family households (p. 6).

Clearly, a variety of family types always has existed. What has changed is that in recent years, the proportions of the various types in that diverse universe of families have changed. Also, these changes have been rendered more visible by the fact that the number of total families has increased dramatically over the past 40 years. Outtz notes: "Between 1950 and 1990, the total number of families increased 70 percent, from nearly 39 million to 66 million" (p. 5).

The changes in proportions of family types cannot be dismissed as insignificant. The recognition of such changes strengthens the case for discarding the traditional family myth and redefining our concept of family in order to better address the educational needs of all types of families. Following are some important proportionate changes (Outtz 1993, pp. 8-12).

- In 1990, 24% of families were headed by a single parent; in 1950 the comparable figure was 7.4%.
- In 1970 some 341,000 men headed single-parent households; by 1990 the comparable figure was 1.2 million, a 238% increase.
- In 1991, 71.7% of all children under age 18 lived with two parents (a number, between one-fourth and one-third, in "blended" families), 22.4% lived with a mother only, 3.1% with a father only, and 2.9% with some other relative or no parent.

Although they often are not recognized in official data counts as "families," gay and lesbian families today also are variously estimated to be rearing perhaps 8 million to 14 million children (p. 12).

Outtz concludes: "All of us must recognize the diversity of American families as well as the complexities surrounding the needs of this diverse group. Just because the family is *different*, does not mean that it is 'bad,' or that it is 'dysfunctional'."

Stephanie Coontz, in her *Kappan* Special Report, "The American Family and the Nostalgia Trap," echoes this sentiment when she writes:

> We cannot return to "traditional" family forms and expectations that were at least partly mythical in the first place. To help our children move successfully into the 21st century we need to stop organizing our institutions and values around the notion that every family can — or should — have one adult totally available at work and another totally available at home. We have to adjust our economic programs, schools, work policies, expectations of family life, and moral reasoning to the realities of family diversity and the challenges of global transformation. (1995, p. K18)

Changing How We View the Humanities

Both Outtz and Coontz also devote considerable space to addressing issues of increased family poverty as part of the larger picture of how families are changing. However, it is not my purpose here to examine that aspect of the education dynamic. Rather, my limited purpose is to discuss how a new framework for the teaching of the humanities might be built, in part, on a foundation of family-type diversity, which increasingly is characterized by nontraditional, "permeable" families. Thus I return to Jencks' "complexity" and "pluralism."

In a recent essay Joel Kupperman makes the case for a multicultural curriculum as fundamental to the social contract of Western democracy. He concludes that:

> every member of society must be considered in the design of society. The germ of an idea of equal, or approximately equal, rights for everyone is in this notion. The individual has these rights, furthermore, not because of a family or connections, but because she or he is a member of society. (1996, p. 58)

Kupperman argues for developing a "permeable" curriculum (not his words) as Elkind argues for recognizing the permeable family — that is, using *permeable* in Elkind's sense to mean a curriculum that is characterized by "themes of difference, particularity, and irregularity" (Elkind 1995, p. 10).

Kupperman and others, such as Samuel Fleischaker and Molefi Kete Asante in separate articles in the May-June 1996 issue of *Academe*, make the case that multiculturalism is basic to the Western education tradition. So also must the case be made for taking seriously the notion of family diversity as a norm of, rather than a departure from, the American (and to a large extent, Western) concept of family.

Conservative politicians and social critics may argue for a "return to the traditional family" and for nebulously but narrowly proposed "family values," but a fact of American family life always has been, and is, diversity. That diversity is one basis for the popular culture and, consequently, must be a basis for the arts and humanities in postmodern schooling. John R. Gillis, author of *A World of Their Own Making: Myth, Ritual, and the Quest for Family Values*, writes of family research:

> Researchers' focus on the nuclear family blinds them to the degree to which people turn friends into members of their "family," creating new kin that supplement their ties of blood and marriage. No wonder that when people wish to find visions of family life that bear some resemblance to their own experience, they turn to the messy, often disturbing accounts provided by contemporary novels and films, rather than to the abstractions offered by demographers and sociologists. (Gillis 1996, p. A40)

There, in a nutshell, is the matter at hand: The fictional neatness of nuclear modernity must be discarded for the reality of messy postmodernism. Critics of postmodernism tend to suffer, as Salman Rushdie recently wrote of some literary critics, "from culturally endemic golden-ageism: that recurring, bilious nostalgia for a literary past that at the time didn't seem much better than the present does now" (1996, p. 50).

The fiction of Ozzie and Harriet's "traditional family" of the 1950s was no more edifying then than the fiction of Murphy Brown's successful unwed mother/career woman of the 1990s is now. Both stretch viewer credulity. But, after all, that is what television sitcoms always have done. However, anti-postmodernists (recall former Vice President Dan Quayle's denunciation of Murphy Brown) view the former as worthy and the latter as unworthy out of a rooted notion that family diversity did not exist in the "good ol' days" and should not be held up in any positive light today.

That is a notion that must be rejected in the development of a "permeable" curriculum for the humanities. As film critic David Denby puts it:

> Well-educated American conservatives who vilify popular culture for political ends appear to want entertainment that is didactic, improving, hygienic.

In a true liberal-arts education, however, children are exposed to many stories, from many sources. They hear about all sorts of behavior — wickedness and goodness and the many fascinating varieties in between — and are taught what a narrative is and what its moral relation to life might be. (1996, p. 53)

Fleischaker says that "we who live in the West must study Western culture not because it is the 'best' of all cultures, but because it is ours" (1996, p. 16). In much the same spirit, educators must construct a postmodern humanities curriculum in full recognition of broad family-type diversity because such diversity — such complexity and pluralism — is our reality. Conservative critics of postmodernism may yearn, as Elkind says of some parents, "to go back to an earlier, less complicated time. But we will not get the postmodern genie back in the bottle" (Scherer 1996, p. 9).

Contexts, Processes, and the Curriculum

Discarding the traditional family myth is a first step toward constructing a "permeable" humanities curriculum. But then the problems begin. How should a humanities curriculum embrace complexity and pluralism without trivializing — one might compare this to "balkanizing" — the curriculum?

Arthur Applebee, in his recent book, *Curriculum as Conversation*, rightly observes:

Discussions of curriculum in American schools and colleges have usually focused on what is most worth knowing: Should we stress the Great Books, the richness of multiculturalism, the basic literacy needed in the worlds of work and leisure? But these arguments have been based on false premises. . . . They strip knowledge of the contexts that give it meaning and vitality. . . . In such a system, students are taught about traditions of the past, and not how to enter into and participate in those of the present and future. (1996, p. 3)

Framed in terms of contexts and processes, a postmodern curriculum for the humanities might take on a very different appearance. It might be characterized, for example, by a focus not on a canon of Great Literature, Great Art, or Great Music but, rather, on the processes by which writers, artists, and composers create authentic and valid works within a variety of contexts. Not least among these contexts will be the home and the family.

This is not to diminish the content of the works. On the contrary, the study of content is enriched by the study of how that content came to be and to what life themes it responds. These contextual "conversations" ("knowledge-in-action," to use Appleby's term) spring from a philosophically postmodern base of constructivism — in other words, that knowledge is constructed, conjectural, and fallible and grows through exposure (Zahorik 1995, pp. 11-12).

The constructivist approach harkens to Denby's "many stories, from many sources." Among those sources will be "subcultures" composed of nontraditional societies, including families that contradict the modernist myth of the traditional family. One might even go so far as to suggest a family-as-subculture stance in the face of conservative pressure to maintain and enlarge the traditional family myth to the detriment of nontraditional families. British educator Alan Sinfield, writing about gay and lesbian subculture, comments that a "subculture is where we may address, on terms that make sense to us, the problems that confront us" (Sinfield 1996, p. 100). This is the essence of family as well. Sinfield continues:

> Subculture is not just where oppression is registered and resisted, it is where self-understandings — fraught, as they inevitably are, with the self-oppression that stigma produces — may be explored and re-made. (p. 100)

Students from "broken" homes, single-parent families, blended families, gay or lesbian families, non-English-speaking families, or other "nontraditional" families are representatives of American subcultures, according to the conservative modernist viewpoint. Therefore, Sinfield's comments about the value of subcultures are pertinent. They also strengthen Appleby's notion that:

225

All of us benefit from the breadth of vision and sensitivity that we gain through learning to enter into alternative systems of knowledge-in-action, including those represented by other literary and cultural traditions than our own. (1996, p. 122)

One cannot help but call to mind literature that has been suppressed, either formally or, more often, by educators' self-censorship over fear of conflict or criticism. This certainly has been true in the area of children's literature that reflects gay and lesbian families, for example. Michael Willhoite's book, *Daddy's Roommate* (1990), often has been challenged by would-be censors. In John Warren Stewig's words, the book "is a pleasantly innocuous account of a young boy's life. . . . [H]e describes the things that his daddy and the roommate do, all of which seem commonplace" (Stewig 1996, p. 74). But the context of the child narrator's experience — that of living in a gay family — is outside the traditional family myth. Thus it also falls outside the modernist canon. However, that is precisely its value. Such stories, comments Stewig, "show child readers, no matter what their own family structure is, that families are as richly diverse as the people who make them up" (p. 77).

Vicky Greenbaum, a high school English teacher, comments similarly on dealing with gay-themed literature with older students:

> Love, sex, and family dynamics tend to be literary subject matter, worthy of taking a thesis on, writing a story about, or discussing in class. Why not banish fear and broaden the spectrum? Students — gay and straight — will benefit from inclusiveness of all kinds. (1996, p. 91)

Both Stewig and Greenbaum are pointing precisely in the direction that Applebee would have curriculum go when he says, "Through literature, we may develop a basis for understanding acts and points of view that otherwise would simply be seen as deviant" (p. 122).

This point is valid across the spectrum of the humanities. For example, Violet H. Harada urges the exploration of "alternative visions of what is offered as historical truth" (1996, p. 636) when she suggests that 10th-grade history students need to study the World War II internment by the U.S. government of 120,000 Japanese Americans whose only crime was "being Japanese." Harada points out that the internment story — as much a story of Japanese-American families as of individuals — is "a critical chapter in the American struggle to achieve freedom and equality in an ethnically diverse society" (p. 631).

Enlarging the Window of the Humanities

Postmodernism's themes of complexity and pluralism are forms for realizing an expanded worldview — as Elkind comments, "a paradigmatic shift" — from the more narrow modernist worldview circumscribed within a Western canon of art, literature, history, and so on. The "permeable" curriculum is just that, capable of being pervaded by that which heretofore was outside the myth and thus outside the curriculum.

In summing up, I turn again to Applebee, who says:

> Literature offers both contact zones and safe houses. When we read within familiar traditions, we experience the comfort of the predictable. When we read in alternative traditions, we are asked to step into another perspective, to view the world from an unfamiliar tradition of knowing and doing. In so doing, we broaden the "great conversations" about literature and life that encompass our knowledge of humankind and the wisdom of the cultures that comprise it. (p. 126)

The same can be said not merely of literature but of the arts and humanities in their entirety. Dismantling the traditional family myth is an essential undertaking for postmodernist educators. By tackling this formidable challenge, by taking on anti-postmodernists or reactionary modernists who promote and indeed would codify the myth, such workers enlarge the window on the world that education can offer children, youth, and adults.

The humanities can and should offer students of all ages a view into the real world, which is richly complex. Thus such studies

227

should offer many views — through literature, visual arts, theater, music, history, sociology. The "permeable" curriculum of the humanities should provide a panoply of *virtual* experience (to use cyberlingua). But in that panoply as well, students will find images and stories that resonate with (not necessarily resemble) their own experiences. Many of the most personal, most intimate of those experiences will be of families that are quite different from the mythic traditional family.

References

Applebee, Arthur N. *Curriculum as Conversation.* Chicago: University of Chicago Press, 1996.

Asante, Molefi Kete. "Multiculturalism and the Academy." *Academe* 82 (May-June 1996): 20-23.

Coontz, Stephanie. "The American Family and the Nostalgia Trap," *Phi Delta Kappan* 76 (March 1995): K1-K20.

Denby, David. "Buried Alive." *New Yorker*, 15 July 1996, pp. 48-58.

Elkind, David. "School and Family in the Postmodern World." *Phi Delta Kappan* 77 (September 1995): 8-14.

Fleischaker, Samuel. "Multiculturalism as a Western Tradition." *Academe* 82 (May-June 1996): 16-19, 65.

Gillis, John R. "The Study of Families Needs More-Relevant Questions." *Chronicle of Higher Education*, 2 August 1996, p. A40.

Greenbaum, Vicky. "Bringing Gay and Lesbian Literature Out of the Closet." In *Open Lives, Safe Schools*, edited by Donovan R. Walling. Bloomington, Ind.: Phi Delta Kappa Educational Foundation, 1996.

Harada, Violet H. "Breaking the Silence: Sharing the Japanese American Internment Experience with Adolescent Readers." *Journal of Adolescent & Adult Literacy* 39 (May 1996): 630-37.

Jencks, Charles. *The Language of Post-Modern Architecture.* 6th ed. New York: Rizzoli, 1991.

Kupperman, Joel. "Pluralism and the Tradition of Democracy." In *Can Democracy Be Taught?* edited by Andrew Oldenquist. Bloomington, Ind.: Phi Delta Kappa Educational Foundation, 1996.

Outtz, Janice Hamilton. *The Demographics of American Families.* Washington, D.C.: Institute for Educational Leadership, Center for Demographic Policy, 1993.

Rushdie, Salman. "In Defense of the Novel, Yet Again." *New Yorker*, 24 June and 1 July 1996, pp. 49-55.

Scherer, Marge. "On Our Changing Family Values: A Conversation with David Elkind." *Educational Leadership* 53 (April 1996): 4-9.

Sinfield, Alan. "The Sussex Program and Its Contexts." In *Open Lives, Safe Schools*, edited by Donovan R. Walling. Bloomington, Ind.: Phi Delta Kappa Educational Foundation, 1996.

Stewig, John Warren. "Self-Censorship of Picture Books About Gay and Lesbian Families." In *Open Lives, Safe Schools*, edited by Donovan R. Walling. Bloomington, Ind.: Phi Delta Kappa Educational Foundation, 1996.

Zahorik, John A. *Constructivist Teaching*. Fastback 390. Bloomington, Ind.: Phi Delta Kappa Educational Foundation, 1995.

Resolving the Paradox of Postmodern Education

BY RAYMOND PETTIT

Raymond Pettit has worked at all levels of schooling, having been a teacher, supervisor, and director of instruction during the past two decades. He recently earned a doctorate at the University of Illinois at Urbana-Champaign.

An essay that is fashioned to describe the role of the arts and humanities for the postmodern era in American schools and society runs several risks. The first is that the arts and humanities may be held up as a solution to all of the problems of education. Barzun (1974) has argued that this notion is unreasonable. And, indeed, such an expectation (or hope) is merely wishful thinking. The arts and humanities do not possess, as some have advanced, incredible healing, curative, or redemptive powers. The notion that the arts hold mysterious qualities that are missing from more scientific or pedantic educational pursuits is simply misleading. Smith suggests that the arts and humanities should be taught for "the characteristic effects [such study] is capable of inducing and not as a means for solving or ameliorating a host of social problems" (1992, p. 757). This is not to say that the arts and humanities are peripheral — indeed, the opposite is true, I will argue. But they are no panacea.

231

The second risk is that the role of the arts and humanities will be politically construed, that is, to advance social, business, or cultural values that are unrelated to the essence of education in a democratic society. Smith (1992) suggests that this essentially is what occurred in the past decade with the publication of a number of reports that attempted to define the importance of the study of the arts in American schools based on weak premises and an "ad hoc" philosophy.

The third risk is that promising ideas may be subjected to endless rounds of reviews, conferences, meetings, expert panels, and finally relegated to conference reports and commission recommendations. In short, bureaucracy may turn fertile soil into useless sand. The process of change often falters during either incubation or implementation. It behooves educators, policymakers, and other concerned individuals and groups to be aware of all three types of risk.

Education in a Postmodern Society

In recent books, a number of education critics have attempted to detail the necessity for reform of American public schools. Some have approached the problem from the perspective of social responsibility by depicting the imbalance between the schooling of the wealthy and the schooling of the poor (see Kozol 1991). Others have suggested that schools should be turned over to business and run as profit-making enterprises to encourage competition and stimulate the "best" possible performance (see Bacharach 1990). Still others have explored elaborate restructuring or revised governance initiatives in the hope of extracting better performance out of existing, but reformed, schools (see Sarason 1990). All of these plans have merits, but they all leave out the important issue of what children will need to know and be able to do in the future in order to achieve *personal fulfillment* — as well as to contribute to the good of American society, the economic health of the nation, and the betterment of the world in general.

Notable exceptions among these critics — such as Robert Reich and Arthur Wirth — illuminate the potential of the arts and humanities for altering the ethos and outcomes of schools. But I will touch on their work in a moment. First, it is important to acknowledge a predecessor to the current crop of education critics, Harry S. Broudy, who is well-known to students of aesthetic education. His ideas still hold potency for any deliberation on the importance of studying the arts and humanities in public schooling.

Broudy (1972), in his book *Enlightened Cherishing: An Essay on Aesthetic Education*, provided a foundation for thinking about how the arts and humanities contribute to a well-rounded education — just the sort of education necessary for a postmodern future. The humanities, according to Broudy, are a source of wisdom. They guide actions by teaching values. The aesthetic dimension inherent in experiencing the arts builds one's imagination. Thus the important activities in this type of process become valuing, prizing, desiring, and judging. The use of the imagination enables students to study the aesthetic image or symbol, its sensory properties, formal properties, and expressiveness. The possible course outcomes of an experience in aesthetics include disciplined perceiving, imagining, and thinking. However, the most important quality, according to Broudy, is that "the quality of life is measured by the repertory of feeling which pervades it" (p. 58). The ability of the arts and humanities to touch and to teach the affective side of human life thus becomes the most significant aspect of its study.

Robert Reich's book, *The Work of Nations* (1991), written while Reich was a professor at Harvard University, is not a book strictly about education. However, it offers an economic perspective on education and the abilities that citizens most likely will need in the near future. Reich speaks of the rise of the "symbolic manipulator," one who is skilled in identifying and solving problems in a symbolic domain. The "symbolic manipulator" that Reich describes has 1) skills that involve identifying and researching problems ("problems" in the broad sense to include economic, social, or political issues), 2) skills that involve

233

solving problems and meeting needs that already have been identified, and 3) skills that involve the "brokering" of problems,
solutions, and opportunities — "brokering" meaning that a match
is found between problem and solution that may involve diverse
individuals and groups. It may be assumed that "brokering"
requires a high level of managerial, executive, and communicative
skills; therefore, great stress is placed on the necessity for "symbolic manipulators" to be able to communicate and cooperate.

According to Reich, much of the work in the future will be at
the symbolic level and will involve mainly short- or moderate-
term projects designed to address a particular issue or need. This
contrasts with much of today's large-scale corporate approach.
Therefore cooperation among workers will be essential. Such
cooperation will require skills in working together in a variety of
situations, forms, and styles. This "symbolic" level of work in the
future, according to Reich, may be handled adequately by 10% to
20% of the worker population.

What about the other 80% of the labor force? Reich maintains
that the largest proportion of workers will be involved in the service
sector. This area of employment will not demand the same high
level of "symbolic" training and understanding that will be required
by the "symbolic manipulators," but such work still will require a
command of many symbolic manipulative skills, in addition to a
well-developed "service" orientation. Thus communication skills
and the motivation and desire to provide a quality service will
become paramount. Reich completes his scenario by describing a
small (10%) cohort of workers needed to do physical labor in the
future. However, even in the education of this last group, he stresses
the need for a minimal level of symbolic skill training.

One might ask, How does Reich's description of the nature of
human activity in the future correspond to the function of the arts
and humanities in the schools of the postmodern society? The
arts and humanities are built on the manipulations of symbols —
sounds, images, emotions, words, or physical movement. In addition, the arts and humanities, by definition, require a high-level of
communication and cooperation to be fully realized. An obvious

example is the symphony orchestra, where perhaps a hundred musicians must perform together with precision and high quality to reach the larger goal of an expressive, musical performance. This cooperation factor becomes even more evident (and crucial) when the arts are combined. A visit backstage to the Metropolitan Opera House is a lesson in cooperation, where skilled technicians, designers, singers, musicians, conductors, producers, and directors all are involved in delivering a successful production.

The arts and humanities represent the application of symbolic and communicative skills in a variety of situations, experiences, and forms. They correspond closely to the types of skills needed in the future, as Reich describes them. Thus an education that takes the building blocks of learning (verbal, mathematical, musical, spatial, and so on) and projects them into an applied arena of learning appears to hold significant promise for the future education of our children. Although some attempts have been made to expand the scope of education (see Gardner 1983), Reich's model of the "symbolic manipulator" suggests goals that can be realized only by the whole-hearted support and development of programs in and through the arts and humanities.

In *Education and Work for the Year 2000* (1992), Arthur Wirth extended Reich's concepts and, indirectly, provided support for teaching and learning in the arts and humanities. Wirth's description of the skills needed to do symbolic analysis includes:

- Abstraction — the capacity to order and make meaning of the massive flow of information
- System thinking — the capacity to see parts in relation to the whole to discover why problems arise and how components are linked together
- Experimental inquiry — the capacity to set up procedures to test and evaluate alternative ideas
- Collaboration — the need for active communication to get a variety of perspectives, as well as the capacity to create

All are part of education and experiences in the arts. What better way to learn than to undergo rich and meaningful experiences in the many facets of the arts and humanities curriculum? It appears that a well-crafted arts program at the secondary level might provide the synergy needed to actively support and reach goals and objectives of worth for the future citizen, worker, and contributor to the community. Even more promising, the question, "How can we sustain involvement of the whole range of human capacities of everyone in the system" (Wirth, p. 192), is answered. Through education in the arts and humanities, young people can be involved in a multitude of roles, responsibilities, learning situations, and educational paths as never before. The payoff comes in a variety of ways, not the least of which is the possible transformation of high schools into institutions that prepare students for the Information Age, rather than for the Industrial Age that is quickly disappearing.

According to Wirth, American society and specifically American high schools have an unprecedented opportunity to expand and enrich the education of *all* children, not just the schooling of a predefined or preselected technological elite. All the children in our schools must have the chance to develop and enhance their symbolic-analytic skills. In addition to the four values that were cited by Wirth, schools also should be asked to instill a capacity for disciplined effort and to cultivate an appreciation of the aesthetic in all children. Numerous education writers, such as Eisner (1990) and Moody (1990), would tend to agree. They add that the act of diversifying the outcomes of schooling leads to greater equity-in schooling. The arts and humanities provide multiple forms of representation that enable diversity of learning and experience to occur. Eisner adds that thinking in this way influences the aims of education, curricular decisions, teaching practices, and evaluation of instruction. In short, all major aspects of the education experience are affected.

Ripples in the Postmodern Current

So far, I have assumed that postmodern society, as it continues to develop, will hold diverse opportunities for employment for most of the working-age populace. This optimism is reinforced by such writers as Reich and Wirth. Other critics are not as optimistic. Jeremy Rifkin boldly writes of an evolving society in which technological and information-age jobs will be held by a small minority of worldwide workers, and the rest of the working-age population will be unemployed, underemployed, or involved in a new "Civil Society" (Slavin 1996). Rifkin writes eloquently about the need to educate children in schools "where the values of reciprocity, stewardship, participation in community, and caring for others holds sway" (p. 609). Social capital, as defined by Rifkin, becomes just as important as market capital, with the rewards of the former imminently more satisfying than the single-minded pursuit of material goods and services. According to Rifkin (Slavin 1996):

> Preparing the next generation for work in both the marketplace and the civil society may be the single most important task facing our school system as we make the transition into a new century and a new economic epoch. (p. 609)

While it is difficult to fully envision Rifkin's societal future, education in the arts and humanities brings a means for crafting a response to his "important task." Indeed, a well-conceived approach to learning and doing in the arts and humanities can provide the necessary structure for education in the types of societal, communal, and service values proposed by Rifkin, as well as in the more utilitarian skills demanded by life in the Information Age and required by the symbolic analyst.

If it becomes the case, as Rifkin suggests, that people "work" less and spend more time in community, family, or cultural activities, then the value of the arts and humanities in embracing, enriching, and broadening creative living is evident. Many people already are passionately committed to art clubs, orchestras, community theaters, service organizations, and the like. In a time of increased leisure, these activities and experiences will become a major part of life. Education and experience in the arts and humanities will be a necessity, not a frill.

Many who advocate a "market-based" approach to schooling seem bent on preserving only a cultural elite. To these critics, the future belongs to the 20% who will be fortunate enough to equip themselves with the skills needed to fill "high-value" professions and services. The fate of the rest of the population is not clear — and probably not very desirable. The arts and humanities offer a way to examine experience in a holistic and integrated fashion. Although this appears contrary to the notion of the separate disciplines of literature, theater, music, art, dance, and their specific performance domains, educationally they can be placed in a unified framework. That is, the basic principles underlying the *processes* of experience and learning in the arts and humanities can be extracted as a rationale on which to base an approach to education that may be imperative for our personal and societal future.

The Paradox of Unity and Fragmentation

Educators for a postmodern future would do well to recall that the arts and humanities originally formed a unity, which became fragmented in the West (Moffett 1994) through specialization and compartmentalization, both of which characterize the modernist approach to education. Such fragmentation served a purpose to focus attention on the various specific arts and humanities. However, the basic method of the arts — taken together — is to create and recreate, to help individuals and collectivities to explore the potential of life beyond the utilitarian. By tapping the creative and imaginative human impulses, the arts extend personal capacity. Education — in whatever discipline — occurs or is extended *through* experiences in the arts and humanities. Thus, too, the greater democratic value lies in a redesigned arts and humanities curriculum, because even the most basic question of the "public good" can be answered by a program based on the values and practices inherent in the arts and humanities.

Whether our society evolves as Reich and Wirth have envisioned or more in the manner of Rifkin's vision, the arts and humanities must be a vital part of every child's schooling. Only through an enhanced effort to develop meaningful, integrated arts programs can the possibility of meeting the complex, multifaceted demands of the postmodern society be met.

Finally, it will be only through efforts by local, state, and national leaders that the arts and humanities will assume their most effective place in postmodern society. Already some of the pieces are in place. For example, the Getty Foundation has established planned education research and dissemination in the domain of visual arts education. Their materials and information are readily available to arts educators, administrators, and other concerned citizens (Smith 1992). The music education profession, through the efforts of the Music Educators National Conference (MENC), also has made an effort to muster policy makers, music industry business leaders, performing artists, politicians, and music educators to build a national platform of standards in music education. Implementation and evaluation of new curricula in the arts and humanities are taking place at the state and local levels through a variety of coalitions and committees. Likewise, universities and colleges are supporting the study of the arts and humanities through their admission requirements and policies (Shuler 1996). With few exceptions, the nation's "movers and shakers" are beginning to understand the value inherent in the study of and experiences in the fine arts and humanities. The structure of a valid and responsive postmodern arts and humanities curriculum slowly is beginning to take shape.

Education's skeleton effort to resolve the paradox of postmodern schooling — to find the aesthetic through the utilitarian and the practical through the artistic — now needs to be reinforced, fleshed out. Three areas of support need to be firmly in place in order for meaningful, long-lasting change to occur. First is the philosophical, which concerns a massive effort to identify and come to terms with the rationale and purpose of an arts and humanities-oriented education for all children. Leaders in government (on all levels), business, education, and cultural and artistic organizations must forge a common bond of understand-

239

ing and an appreciation of the arts and humanities. Connections must be made from the bottom up *and* the top down.

Next is the political. Legislators and policy makers must be led to a nonpartisan understanding and acceptance of the idea of the "public good" and how the arts and humanities may fulfill that responsibility for the future. Knowing that a postmodern society requires skills, experience, and motivation that are different from modern society, those who possess political power must unite around a simple fact: The future of American society rests on the education of *all* our young people — not only the "best and brightest." All citizens must be contributors in the postmodern society, and so all must be educated in the arts and humanities if that role is to be fulfilled.

Finally, there is the financial. Through national involvement and leadership, through philosophical and rational debate, and through the voice of common concerns, a call must be raised for adequate financial support for changes in arts and humanities teaching that will be required if the needs of postmodern society are to be addressed. Only through solid financial support — putting our money where our mouth is — can the changes necessary for the bright future of society be realized. What vision can we achieve? What achievements can we support? More important, what achievements do we have to support to remain a viable culture in the future? These questions deserve our deepest examination.

In conclusion, I want to share a personal vision. Imagine a high school that offers a significant (perhaps 50%) arts and humanities component to all of its students. Besides individual or sequenced courses in art, music, drama, or dance, a vital experience would be to combine these skills in various types and levels of "productions." Students could "major" in an area (or areas) matched to their needs and interests. Students could write (stories, poems, plays, screenplays), compose music, perform (act, dance, sing, read, play instruments), use arts technology (record, film, produce, arrange lighting, build sets), and execute arts programs (direct, conduct, coach, rehearse). The forms of expression and experience might range from individual and small-group projects (a radio talk show) to large-group endeavors (musicals, plays, or festivals). My point is that, contrary to today's largely compartmentalized approach to school subjects, the arts and humanities open up the possibility to draw relationships and create interactions among significant "symbolic," expressive, interpretive, and communicative projects that will relate to students' future activities. In the past — and still in many schools — such activities were regarded as "extracurricular." In the postmodern schools, they should be part of the "basics," studied both for themselves and as a foundation for future learning.

The need for aesthetic learning combined with the utilitarian demand for "symbolic" skills in the future is less paradoxical than it may seem on the surface. Indeed, both should be viewed as complementary facets of all children's development. Inculcating the values of a new society — a postmodern society — demands that education be open-ended, life-enhancing, and growth-oriented. While in the past the goals of schooling may have been to "pass on" traditional values and ideas, the goals in the postmodern era require the type of imagination and freedom inherently generated in learning in the arts and humanities. Thus through the arts and humanities, technical, social, cultural, and political needs may be fulfilled in postmodern society.

References

Bacharach, S.B., ed. *Education Reform: Making Sense of It All*. Boston: Allyn and Bacon, 1990.

Barzun, J. *The Use and Abuse of Art*. Princeton, N.J.: Princeton University Press, 1974.

Broudy, H.S. *Enlightened Cherishing: An Essay on Aesthetic Education*. Urbana: University of Illinois Press, 1972.

Eisner, E.W. "Implications of Artistic Intelligences for Education." In *Artistic Intelligences: Implications for Education*, edited by W.J. Moody. New York: Teachers College Press, 1990.

Gardner, H.A. *Frames of Mind*. New York: Basic Books, 1983.

Kozol, J. *Savage Inequalities*. New York: Crown, 1991.

Moody, W.J., ed. *Artistic Intelligences: Implications for Education.* New York: Teachers College Press, 1990.

Moffett, J. *The Universal Schoolhouse.* San Francisco: Jossey-Bass, 1994.

Reich, R. *The Work of Nations.* New York: Alfred A. Knopf, 1991.

Sarason, S. *The Predictable Failure of Educational Reform.* San Francisco: Jossey-Bass, 1990.

Shuler, S.C. "Why High School Students Should Study the Arts." *Music Educators Journal* 83 (July 1996): 22-26.

Slavin, P. "The Information Age and the Civil Society: An Interview with Jeremy Rifkin." *Phi Delta Kappan* 77 (May 1996): 607-609.

Smith, R.A. "Trends and Issues in Policy-Making for Arts Education." In *Handbook of Research on Music Teaching and Learning*, edited by R. Colwell. New York: Schirmer Books, 1992.

Wirth, A.G. *Education and Work for the Year 2000.* San Francisco: Jossey-Bass, 1992.

Envisioning the Future of Education

BY TODD SILER

Todd Siler, Ph.D., author of Think Like a Genius *(Bantam, 1997), is the founder of Psi-Phi Communications, a company that specializes in developing innovative multimedia learning materials and processes for fostering integrative thinking in education, business, and the home.*

H.G. Wells, in his 1920 book, *The Outline of History*, wrote: "Human history becomes more and more a race between education and catastrophe." In this essay, I invite readers to learn three things, none of which should seem foreign. That is, you probably know them without realizing it. "That is what learning is," Doris Lessing reminds us. "You suddenly understand something you've understood all your life, but in a new way."

First, you'll learn why there is a crisis in education that is serious enough to threaten the growth and stability of our world, from our physical and mental wellness to our ecological well-being (Chorover 1994; Eisler 1987; Fuller 1969; Kaplan 1994). This is not alarmist rhetoric. Rather, it is a lifetime observation that resonates with other concerned educators and citizens. What does the expression "advancement of education" mean if our schools run efficiently but our societies do not? What does education mean, if a billion people live in abject poverty, if 450 million people are starving, if there are more than 10 million refugees worldwide, if there are 850 million illiterate adults, and if our physical environment and natural resources remain in constant jeopardy (Myers 1984)?

At the root of this crisis is a basic confusion about the meaning and practice of education (Ginott 1972; Casals 1978). Education has become less and less about fostering the learning process and more about the accumulation and management of disassociated information (Siler 1993). All too often we mistakenly measure education by acquired degrees instead of by levels of awareness and self-knowledge. Perhaps part of the problem lies in the measured cadence of formal education, which is more predictable and tightly structured than the process of learning. When we are learning, we are constantly changing the beat, changing the rhythm of our absorption and use of new information.

Every human being naturally engages in learning when their "need to know" is kindled by curiosity (Montessori 1969; Bruner 1962; Guilford 1967). Learning involves questioning, rethinking, and reframing perceptions, ideas, and personal knowledge (Root-Bernstein 1988). It is a transition phase, in which we move from the known to the unknown, exercising our ability to see creatively and think critically. It is neither an endpoint nor a series of ends with points. Learning is what happens *in between* the things we know or thought we knew. It is a connective, associative, and integrative process (James 1890; Poincaré 1924; Taylor 1959; Koestler 1964; Siler 1986).

For me, Robert Frost captured the essence of learning when he commented in an interview:

> All thought is a feat of association: having what's in front of you bring up something in your mind that you almost didn't know you knew. Putting this and that together. That click. (Plimpton 1965)

Education today is not clicking. It is squeaking like a rusty wheel, even with the sensitive lubricants of reform.

The most forward-thinking questions we should be asking ourselves now are: What do we need to learn to flourish as individuals and to "flow" as a society (Csikszentmihalyi 1990)? How can we best use our knowledge — connecting and integrating information — in more personally meaningful and productive ways?

What forms of knowledge are just plain unforgiving when abused, and how do we control them along with our destructive tendencies (Chorover 1979)?

How can schools teach common sense? What exactly is "common" about it: the sense of rational decision-making and behavior? Does it change as we mature?

How are information technologies and advanced multimedia systems changing the way we learn and apply our knowledge? How can the arts help develop these multimedia systems to enhance the learning process (Ambron 1988; Hicks 1993)? Once these network technologies and interactive learning systems are fully operational, will formal education institutions be necessary? Or will education by mid-21st century be so individually customized — "up close and personal" — that institutional teaching, as we know it, will no longer serve its purpose (Kay 1991)?

Finally, how can we best apply our teachings of traditional disciplinary knowledge in schools to everyday life? These are the kinds of open-ended questions I hear regularly but which often are left unresolved. Our responses and interpretations will determine the way in which education fosters learning — or hinders it.

The second thing you will learn in this article is why the arts and humanities — in conjunction with science and technology — are crucial for raising the public's awareness of the importance of learning. This primary awareness is a necessary catalyst for helping people work en masse as a society of minds intent on fulfilling our potential.

Both art and science are creative ways of understanding the world and representing what we understand. They show us how to search life for meaning; how to analyze our perceptions, experiences, and creations; how to communicate our personal and collective imaginings, while inspiring us to appreciate the depth and reach of our imaginations. Both are as basic to our mental life as oxygen and water are to our physical life. Both are entwined in our being, in the same way the two strands of genetic material are twisted into the famous double helix of DNA that carries our past and future in its strands. We could barely make sense of our world without these two unique sources and forms of knowledge. Each offers a multitude of possibilities for enriching our lives.

One of the most powerful and effective ways of breaking down the intellectual, social, economic, political, religious, and racial barriers that block communication is through the arts. By the arts, I mean all forms of symbol-making, visual thinking, and aesthetic exploration expressed in all media, from literature to computer animation to film to performance arts. By aesthetic exploration, I also mean to include the conceptualization and creative design process of science and mathematics. The pursuit of beauty and truth is relevant and essential to the arts *and* to the sciences, engineering, and technology.

At present, there is a great effort on the part of educators in the fields of science and mathematics to inform all citizens about today's and tomorrow's complex world. Two important projects and publications — *Benchmarks for Science Literacy, Project 2061* (1993) and *Science for All Americans* (1989), both by the American Association for the Advancement of Science — represent commendable long-term planning to develop "our understandings and ways of thinking [that] are essential for all citizens in a world shaped by science and technology." However, these efforts to advance our intellectual skills will not reach their maximum efficacy unless we develop our ability to think integratively through a program that unites art, science, technology, and society. Fulfilling this need involves showing how the arts can combine and integrate information in *all* learning programs at *all* levels of learning.

The field and influence of education urgently need to be expanded to include every citizen, not just some, not just an elite. One way of accomplishing this expansion is through the arts interacting with all forms of knowledge. With increasing social fragmentation, violence, and political strife worldwide, well-planned, thoughtful work needs to be done to rediscover our commonalities and to reflect on what it means to be human (Boyer and Levine 1981). Here, again, the arts and humanities have an invaluable contribution to make in the service of society. Without this discovery and reflection, there will be no true appreciation or tolerance for our different forms of knowledge, value systems, and worldviews. Moreover, our common sense will be lost, along with our collective sense of humanity.

One idea proposed here is to initiate a "new and improved" collaborative partnership between the arts and sciences — a partnership that is deeper than their present cooperative relationship (Siler 1990a). This is one of the first steps we need to move our world forward.

The connections between the arts and humanities, science, and technology have a long history, as well as common foundations (Koestler 1965). The interactions of these domains have helped transform the fields of knowledge and processes of exploration that have provided us with a deeper understanding of ourselves and our environment. They also have demonstrated over centuries that they can stimulate, enrich, and sustain our imagination, which, as Albert Einstein shrewdly pointed out, is more important than knowledge (Einstein 1933). Think about it: A person can have all the knowledge in the world and not have the imagination to do anything inventive with real consequence. Einstein spoke to this point when he said:

> The mere formulation of a problem is far more often essential than its solution, which may be merely a matter of mathematical or experimental skill. To raise new questions, new possibilities, to regard old problems from a new angle requires creative imagination and marks real advances in science. (Einstein 1956)

It also marks real advances in learning. Within the past 25 years the general public and educators alike have come to grasp the fact that there are many forms of intelligence (Guilford 1967; Gardner 1983; Goleman 1995). We now need to recognize and make use of the many forms of knowledge and educational practices that have evolved from the arts and humanities, science and mathematics, and other sources of disciplinary knowledge. Just as the arts and sciences represent two ways of creatively seeing and exploring the world, we need to examine other ways of gaining and representing knowledge.

The third thing you will learn here is how you can participate — and why you should participate — in shaping the course of education. What is in it for you? The answer is your future and your family's future, as well as a lifetime of personal growth. So far, this act of shaping education has been relegated to professional educators. There is an annoying assumption that this is *their* responsibility, not ours. The invitation to participate — or, more accurately, to collaborate — has not been extended to all citizens. In order to move this collaboration along, we need virtually everyone's support in developing the field of education. Meeting the challenge of development includes preparing our minds to recognize and use the many forms of knowledge. This work is comparable to preparing the ground for the cultivation of many different kinds of plants. It requires thinkers of all ages, backgrounds, cultures, rather than a "group think" and mass action by educators alone. We need to experience anew the truism that in the school of life, everyone is both a learner and a teacher. Everyone has something to contribute.

Where Is Education Heading and What Are Our Expectations?

Given the importance of learning in our lives and the gravity of its absence, why have we not placed education at the top of our national agenda? Why have the general public, legislators, and policy makers still not focused on the need to improve education as a means of improving society? Considering that education affects every aspect of civilization — from facilitating international cooperation to boosting the productivity of industry, from increasing the effectiveness of government to heightening the responsiveness of business and the economy — one would think that considerable energies would be invested in securing the future of education. Not so.

I mentioned this point not because I am trying to represent the dissatisfaction of legions of committed teachers, but because I am looking at the problems of education and how they affect our lives in the broadest sense. For me, the people who do not see these problems are part of the problem. Often, they are the same people who thrive in our over-compartmentalized and specialized world. They are so wrapped up or walled off in their little compartments that they do not see beyond those barriers. Nor do they care to see the social fragmentation and dysfunctions we continue to face. Call it denial. Call it sleepwalking. Call it anything, but let us deal with these problems.

I smile whenever I reflect on the American satirist Ambrose Bierce's definition of education: "That which discloses to the wise and disguises from the foolish their lack of understanding." Clearly, you can have a lot of knowledge about something but still have little true understanding.

If you made up your own broad survey of 50 people and asked each person, "What does *education* mean to you?" you would need to be prepared for some rather disconcerting statements. The responses resemble a jumble of jigsaw puzzles with no single puzzle having all the pieces.

Many concerned educators are not sanguine about where education is heading (Postman 1995; Kozol 1968, 1995). Never mind the role of arts and humanities, or culture, in education. Never mind the role of science and mathematics in education. They're concerned about the very *concept and practice* of education as it is understood — or confused — by the general public and educators alike.

The most basic questions remain exposed, like open wounds that won't heal: What is this thing called education, and how does it help foster our development as human beings (Csikszentmihalyi 1988)? How can it help improve the quality of life, especially the teaching of science (Carin and Sund 1980)? What does it mean to be educated today? What is entailed in educating minds

(Perkins 1992)? Why are so many educated people irresponsible? Why are they narrow-minded and intolerant of other people's ways of learning, living, and being? The 19th century French novelist Alexander Dumas echoed this frustration when he commented: "How is it that little children are so intelligent and men so stupid? It must be education that does it." I believe the confusion largely concerns the usefulness of the information and experiences gathered in schooling. Perhaps this is what Mark Twain had in mind when he remarked, "I have never let my schooling interfere with my education." Twain's vision of education was considerably broader than school and more personally meaningful.

For many people, the lexical definition of education — that is, imparting or acquiring knowledge and developing one's ability to reason, evaluate, and judge — no longer holds. It is something different now. It is something more (or less) than acquiring knowledge, depending on whom you ask. To progressive educators who keep their sensitive ears pressed to the ground and their fingers on the pulse of their students' interests, education is seen not only as the result of training, study, or experience, but also as a process of self-discovery and means of making discoveries (Thomson 1983; Root-Bernstein 1988; Hurwitz 1994). They see their course material as something to be explored and experienced, rather than memorized, explained, and then tucked away. They invite themselves and their students to question the material, rather than blindly accept it without reflection or experimentation. That is how knowledge is grown and cultivated. That is how we experience the "immense journey" and learn from our experiences (Eisley 1956).

By contrast, to those who look at education from the outside or from afar, it is seen as a degree-granting process, a means to an end. The product is the only thing valued, not the process and the quality of the experiences. These two things, which influence and enrich a person's life, often are overlooked or undervalued because they do not necessarily (or obviously) help the learner to secure a job. Perhaps we need to seriously reflect on the viewpoint of the American historian James Truslow Adams, who wrote, "There are obviously two educations. One should teach us how to make a living and the other how to live." As I see it, there also is a "third education" — the one that teaches us how to integrate the other two.

Examining Postmodern Education

Added to the general confusion about what education is or is not is the question of *postmodern* education, which revolves around the notion of modernism and the evolution of education.

Historian Will Durant wrote, "Sixty years ago, I knew everything; now I know nothing; education is a progressive discovery of our own ignorance." Perhaps postmodern education is the recognition of our ignorance, as we humbly build from there.

These days the term *postmodern* is used to preface almost everything, from postmodern architecture to postmodern zoology. I have yet to read a definition of this term that embodies what I think it means: the move beyond modern approaches to new ways of understanding the world and expressing what we understand; the divergence of ancient and modern values; and the birth of a more comprehensive and integrative means of communication. In this collective definition, we may discover what educator Jacques Barzun observed, "Teaching is not a lost art, but regard for it is a lost tradition." Perhaps postmodernity is really the loss of regard for our traditions and the values they instill. Perhaps it marks our loss of memory; we may have simply forgotten the *unconditional* conditions in which teaching and learning take place (Barzun 1991).

When I first heard the term *postmodern* years ago, it was used in the context of art and architecture alone. It evoked the word "postmortem," with reference to the time following death. I remember wondering whether we perhaps might conduct an autopsy on society. In that way we might figure out exactly what expired and what new sensibilities are emerging. This examination could help illuminate the emerging world civilization, and what our collective future looks like. It also might reveal how we envision the arts and humanities interacting with science, technology, and society. What are some of the consequences and benefits of these interactions. By researching and modeling these interactions, we will gain some insights into the range of roles and contributions the arts and humanities will make to the advancement of education. We also stand to gain fresh insights into creating new learning environments that nurture powerful, original thinkers (Onosko and Newmann 1994).

In examining our concepts of what education is and what constitutes its advancement, we need to ask ourselves, Are we interested in creating a just and humane society of thinkers (Bronowski 1956; Wasserman and Hutchinson 1978)? Is that what we mean by *advancement*, when we speak of creating an educated society (Williams 1972)? Or are we merely concerned with creating a society of people who can read and write but are "clueless" about the deeper meanings of and connections between the things they are reading?

Do we want to create a technologically sophisticated society that has little understanding of, regard for, and connection with the things it creates, uses, and abuses (Postman 1991)? Even though our society may be brilliant at applying its powers of invention and technological innovation, it is nevertheless inept at managing these powers. Furthermore, it accepts no responsibility for guiding its decisions and actions, maintaining a carefree attitude of "Let the [computer] chips fall where they may." In our supposedly *advanced* society, information is perceived as "neutral." This means there are no "positive" and "negative," "good" and "bad" value judgments attached to the use of information. The issues of ethical, moral, and conscionable behavior do not apply to society's use of information and technology.

I would like to believe that the creation of this technological society is less attractive to us than creating a society of minds and thinkers who understand the natural "attachments," or connections, that exist between the things we think, feel, do, and act on (Moravec 1988). However, the thing that worries me is that this long-term thinking about our future is not something that is developed in formal schooling. In fact, if I were to name one flaw of the education process, it is that it leaves us in the trenches of everyday problems, grappling with the reality of our immediate survival, without engaging us in an aerial perspective of our lives. Editor Norman Cousins said it best: "The main failure of education is that it has not prepared people to comprehend matters concerning human destiny." I tend to think that this is only one of many problems, none of which are insurmountable. For me, education fails the moment we can no longer learn on our own and continue learning. Helping children pose and explore their own questions about a subject or issue in which they are personally interested is crucial for moving young minds along the lifetime odyssey of learning.

The Crisis of a Disconnected, Fragmented Society

Few things in life are as frustrating and psychologically paralyzing as experiencing true disconnection between peoples, cultures, philosophies of life, and ideas. Imagine if every person you spoke to on the telephone hung up on you in mid-sentence, without warning or provocation — without reason or purpose, they simply hung up and never called back. Period. End of conversation. How could you ever communicate with anyone? If this dysfunctional pattern of behavior were repeated enough times, you would feel hopeless.

That's a disconnected society! Everyone speaks without listening; everyone's in his or her own world, and each world is detached from the next. There is no common world or sensibility, just as there is no common ground on which to stand. No one is willing to share anything — neither natural nor human resources, which includes understanding, love, and compassion — because the act of sharing is based on communication.

If you think this one-dimensional scenario is unrelated to the 10-dimensional reality of our hypercivilization, consider the implications of the books, scholarly journals, articles, television programs, movies, and other news that describe an anxiety-ridden, disconnected world. If we keep blindly heading along this path

253

through a jungle that we have created, then we may soon recognize ourselves in the description offered by author Jonathan Schell about "A Republic of Insects and Grass" in his haunting book, *The Fate of the Earth* (1982). Our future may have the "look" of Kafka's *Metamorphosis* and the "feel" of Sartre's *Nausea.*

It is hard to fathom a world in which we have more linking and connection-making occurring per second than in any other period in history (because of electronics and telecommunications), and yet we also inhabit a world filled with more chronic personal and global tensions than ever before. The tensions are created from what I call the "disconnected syndrome." We have become disconnected from ourselves and from one another. This disconnection has sparked social and political turmoil. And, if left unchecked, it will cause the sort of international dissonance and stress that yield nothing short of global pandemonium.

With these uncomfortable thoughts in mind, we need to ask ourselves, What significant contributions can the arts and humanities — united with the sciences and technology — offer our fragmented world? How can their union help draw people's involvement to that one area of human endeavor — education — which has proven to help people learn? And how can this concerted effort sustain people's involvement? How can it help engage our imaginations and powers of reasoning?

How the Arts and Humanities Bridge and Transform Worlds

Specifically, how can a new cultural renaissance help us to understand the interrelated concepts of schooling, learning, teaching, discovering, and the "getting of wisdom"? How will this renaissance, which represents a new synthesis of intellect, spirit, sensibility, and resources, point us toward a future that is as intriguing to contemplate as it is rewarding to experience (Kepes 1956; Siler 1990*b*)?

There are numerous examples of extraordinary art work and research that represent this emerging cultural renaissance. Fol-

254

lowing are examples of contemporary artists who demonstrate the possibilities of integrative and collaborative work, as they do more than simply cross and combine various fields of knowledge. This new work moves beyond interdisciplinary and cooperative work, which we tend to associate with the more traditional interactions between the arts and sciences.

Consider the conceptual, computer-generated models of the atom created by the sculptor and photographer Kenneth Snelson in his studies of "The Nature of Structure." These models were inspired by Snelson's 30-year quest to understand the basic structures of nature.

Consider the visionary work of Piotr Kowalski with computer technology and time, which is evident in his "Population Cube II" installation and the "Time Machine II" installation.

The explorations of the physicality of light and space by James Turrell are brought to life in his "Roden Crater" project in Flagstaff, Arizona. Turrell manages to make the physics of light touchable in curiously subtle but forceful ways that move beyond formal artistic and scientific studies of light, providing unique experiences of various light sources.

Consider Helen Mayer Harrison and Newton Harrison's large-scale environmental works, such as the "The Fifth Lagoon: On the Purification of the Flow of Waters." Also, consider conceptual painter Arakawa's experimental works, such as "The Mechanism of Meaning," "Constructing the Perceiver," and his experiential museum, titled "Site of Reversible Destiny," in Yoro Park, Gifu, Japan, which he designed and built with his lifelong collaborator, writer Madeline Gins.

The environmental constructions and installations by Mierle Laderman Ukeles recycle industrial refuse while providing remarkable commentaries on our perceptions and practices of recycling waste.

Tom Van Sant's "Eyes On Earth" Project and his GeoSphere Project with NASA integrate satellite technologies in uniquely aesthetic and scientific ways.

Consider the integrative thinking expressed in Stanley Kubrick's profoundly inspiring films, such as *2001: A Space Odyssey* and

255

2010, both based on the writing of Arthur C. Clark. Think about how the arts are integrated with science, engineering, and media technology in George Lucas' *Star Wars*, Gene Roddenberry's *Star Trek: The Next Generation*, Ridley Scott's *Blade Runner*, and Steven Spielberg's *Jurassic Park*, among many other films.

Consider Jacob Bronowski's book and television series, "The Ascent of Man"; Carl Sagan's "Cosmos" series; John Burkes' BBC productions and book, "Connections"; and the IMAX Theater productions on the Space Shuttle.

One distinguishing feature of most of these works is that they demonstrate an integrative vision of nature. Another feature is their superb use of metaphor, which swiftly connects various aspects of a system or phenomenon. The chemist, poet, and Nobel laureate Raold Hoffmann observed: "The images that scientists have as they do science are metaphorical. . . . The imaginative faculty are set in motion by mental metaphor. Metaphor shifts the discourse, not gradually, but with a vengeance. You see what no one had seen before."

From prehistoric times until today, the languages of the arts have taken every form imaginable and have evolved our senses and intellect. The media for making art are as diverse as they are inexhaustible: from rock carvings and earthworks to lasers and telecommunications; from the plucked rooster that the witty Greek "conceptual" artist Diogenes fashioned in response to Plato's statement ("Man is a featherless biped") to the bicycle wheel and chair that the French Dadaist Marcel Duchamp used to challenge the canons of modern art; from the first primal dance performed on this planet to the holograms, visual artifacts, and sounds of life on earth created for a Space Shuttle payload by the visionary artist Lowry Burgess in his expansive cosmic work, "The Quiet Axis."

The broad definition of the arts includes all pictures or representations of thought and the creative process. The pictures can be poetic or illustrative, scientific or mathematical, logical or lyrical in nature. They also can be motion pictures that play either as real films or as private mental images in the cinema of imagination. In this sense, a work of art does not have to take a concrete form, but can exist as a concept or experience alone.

Art also can be appreciated purely as an aesthetic experience, sort of "art of the moment," such as realizing the beauty of a sunset or drawing inspiration from an object of nature. Educator John Dewey spoke of art as both the experience and the expression of experience.

Painter Joseph Albers linked art to all aspects of design and design to all aspects of life. He wrote, "To design is to plan and to organize, to relate and to control. In short, it embraces all means opposing disorder and accident. Therefore it signifies a human need and qualifies man's thinking and doing."

In illuminating the creative process, author James Baldwin once remarked, "The purpose of art is to lay bare the questions that have been concealed by the answers." The purpose of science is to participate in this process as well. The broader the definition of the arts, the more accurately it captures the arts' infinite degrees of freedom, which are their essence and power.

The Arts as Beacons of Social and Moral Realities

Finally, how will our new vision of education guard us against the more dogmatic and dire forms of education that have numbed our imaginations in the past? One disjointed form I have in mind did *not* help us make sense of the otherwise senseless actions of people who do not think — educated people, knowledgeable people, people whom the psychologist Haim Ginott (1972) singled out when revisiting his past:

> Dear Teacher:
> I am a survivor of a concentration camp. My eyes saw what no man should witness:
> Gas chambers built by LEARNED engineers. Children poisoned by EDUCATED physicians. Infants killed by TRAINED nurses. Women and babies shot and burned by HIGH SCHOOL and COLLEGE graduates.
> So I am suspicious of education.
> My request is:

Help your students become human. Your efforts must never produce learned monsters, skilled psychopaths, educated Eichmanns.

Reading, writing, and arithmetic are important only if they serve to make our children more humane.

If one were to recall this emotional reflection by Ginott with one by the legendary cellist Pablo Casals (1978), one would have a sense of the limited thinking skills exercised in many schools. Casals' extraordinary blend of creativity and humanism shine in this passage:

Each second we live is a new and unique moment of the universe, a moment that never was before and will never be again. And what do we teach our children in school? We teach them that two and two makes four, and that Paris is the capital of France? When will we teach them what they are? You are a marvel. You are unique. In all of the world there is no other child exactly like you. In the millions of years that have passed there has never been another child like you. . . . You have the capacity for anything. Yes, you are a marvel. And when you grow up, can you then harm another who is, like you, a marvel? You must cherish one another. You must work — we all must work — to make this world worthy of its children.

The last line should be framed and kept fresh: "To make this world worthy of its children."

Improving Education, Designing the Ideal

In step with the impressive strives toward education reform (Gardner 1992; Torrance 1993) and progressive programs (Clark 1986; Passow 1989) — and in step with the commendable moves these days of bridging worlds through the Internet and advanced network technology — we need to develop more "visible" forums for discussing the future of education. The majority of existing forums have been separated into special interest groups. Few discuss interrelated interests. Also, though these forums supposedly have been open to the general public, only a small percentage of the public accepts the invitation. Keep in mind Congress' addresses on education are considerably different from the discussions taking place within and between school districts, individual schools, and classrooms. To my knowledge, there are even fewer discussions about the health and well-being of education in corporate boardrooms. Ironically, the life of corporations depends as much on the personnel operating the corporation as it does on the consumers of their products and services. And education — or more specifically, the ability to learn — is essential to the quality of personnel performance.

Improvement can begin only when we have a clear sense of what our common plans (goals and expectations) are for education. We must show, not simply tell, what these plans are, because so much is lost in the translation of the tellings and imaginings.

I invite readers now to respond (in a literally "constructive" way) to the three points I've raised in this essay.

One of the hands-on, inquiry-based exercises I conduct in my ArtScience Program Workshops for education institutions and corporations is worth sharing here (Siler 1996a). The exercise seems to get at the core of many of the issues and questions I have mentioned. Basically, it is an experiment in designing the ideal learning environment, giving visual form and definition to your ideas. The exercise asks you to envision the learning process, showing how this process is manifest in education today — or could be, in time. As you engage in this exercise, you are encouraged to examine and discover the effect of this process on your life. You also are directed to discover how the arts can foster learning and discovery while improving communication.

In this exercise, participants are free to use whatever materials they see fit for creating an environment that, they think, represents the very best aspects and thoughtful processes of learning. The symbolic models that participants have created in the past take on a wide range of shapes, dimensions, and agendas. I state at the outset that the more honest the participants are in describing the way they prefer to learn and what they would like to experience in their environment, the more likely that they will be able to glimpse the future of learning systems and educational practices.

Ultimately, that is the impetus behind the goal: to see and model the future of education and to prepare their minds for what they see ahead. This includes designing the educational systems with which we learn.

The process of building these multidimensional models can be as straightforward and simple as one chooses to make it. The procedure is fairly direct: Participants list and sketch the various attributes of their learning environment. In doing so, they address their most pressing concerns, such as the types and qualities of experiences they would imagine having there. They generally proceed by imagining environments in which they are the most comfortable and analyzing what factors make them feel comfortable there. Some choose to prioritize these comfort and health factors.

Following are some of the questions that I ask participants to consider when envisioning their ideal learning environments:

- What does "ideal" mean to you? What special features does this new learning environment have that makes it so ideal?
- What would your ideal learning environment look like? Where would it be? What natural and human-made things have the same attributes as these environments?
- What would you like to learn or teach there? How will this learning unfold? Will students and teachers instruct one another?
- How do you envision your ideal learning environment reaching and interacting with the local and world community?
- How would you integrate art, science, and technology in this environment? How would this environment benefit from this integration?

I have found that this visual and conceptual exercise is particularly useful in helping people discover and understand what they enjoy about the experience of learning. It also seems to heighten the learning experience. This exercise was inspired by Benjamin

Franklin's proposition in his *Poor Richard's Almanac*: "Think of three Things: whence you came, where you are going, and to whom you must account." Each of these three things can be interpreted in the context of education: Whence did education come, where is it going, and to whom must it account?

In working with educators to construct these ideal learning environments, I try to emphasize the importance of collaboration that moves beyond conventional brainstorming activity. Some exciting and unusual things happen in groups that do not happen individually, provided that the participants are comfortable working with each other. Of course, the chemistry of personalities can influence the outcomes and productivity of the exercise.

In presenting the directives, I request that the participants not focus on the aesthetics of their models — at least not initially. In this way they are not concerned with making their models "beautiful." Instead, they can concentrate on the various processes of learning that interest them and that they wish to integrate into programs in education. Their models' lasting beauty are their honesty and directness.

Although participants are engaging in both artistic and scientific inquiry during this model-building process, I do not introduce these terms or discuss how they are "making art" and "making science." Since many people are intimidated by these disciplines, I try to avoid naming them. Instead, we discuss the art, science, and technology issues only after the participants are comfortable with the process.

After the participants have completed their models, they learn how to "unpack" and analyze the symbols and meanings of the images, drawings, and objects they have created. Then they discuss the forms and contents. Participants respond to these types of questions about the model: What are some of the similarities between the images, or icons, and symbols you created? Are the shapes, forms, and media similar? How would these works be different if they were three-dimensional — the size of a room or bigger — and you could walk into or through them? How would these works be different if they were four-dimensional, that is, if

261

they have the dimension of time or motion to them? It may be helpful to make a list of all of these responses. Here I remind them that their physical models actually are five-dimensional; I point out that the fifth dimension is symbolism, which is represented by all forms of our symbolic languages.

The next thing I ask participants to do is explain why they selected the symbols, colors, shapes, and so on, that they did. Often I ask them also to note what other creations (human-made and natural objects) are similar to their creations and why. At other times I will ask them to observe how their models are both personal and universal in nature. In other words, though the drawings represent their own views of an ideal learning environment, many elements of their drawings also are applicable to the learning environments of others.

I ask them to try to come up with some actual inventions based on the models they created, as well as applications for their inventions. For example, if they represented their ideal learning environment as a game, then it may be a good idea to explain how they want to teach or learn things through their games. Similarly, if some of the more common images in their models are computers, televisions, telephones, faxes, and other media of communication, then they are asked to try to cast whatever it is they have chosen to learn in their ideal environment in terms of these media. Thus I encourage them to invent a learning activity that incorporates these media.

Participants tend to rethink their notions of education and learning over the course of this experience. For the first time, many of them realize that there is indeed a significant difference between the two. Most conclude that learning is a continuous process that engages all of our modes of thought. Education is not. Learning always has a future. Education may not. The best way to make education a learning process — or to revitalize it — is to first define for yourself what learning means to you, identifying when and how it occurs.

This model-building activity helps people gain insights into their creative process and ways of learning. It also increases a person's understanding of how one's learning process is similar to that of others. Most participants use their model and experiences to critique current learning environments and systems.

The Future of Postmodern Education

The clues to the future of postmodern education are in the 5-D models we make and our interpretations of them. The 19th century English philosopher John Stuart Mill provided other clues when he wrote:

> The end of education is not to *teach*, but to fit the mind for learning from its own consciousness and observation. . . . As the memory is trained by remembering, so is the reasoning power by reasoning; the imaginative by imagining; the analytical by analyzing; the inventive by finding out. Let the education of the mind consist in calling out and exercising these faculties: never trouble yourself about giving knowledge — train the *mind* — keep it supplied with materials, and knowledge will come of itself. (Mill 1832)

In examining our models of ideal learning environments, we might want to modify Mill's observation. One's memory is "trained" not only by remembering. It also is trained and developed by imagining, analyzing, investigating, and exercising all faculties in ways that continually refresh one's perspectives on life.

Our models may move our imaginations well beyond the limited experiences in classrooms, schools, and other formal settings in which we were taught, and in which learning is supposedly taking place. In fact, they may contrast sharply with the settings that have come to represent the learning environments of education institutions.

As past models indicate, everyday life and its lessons are some of the best teachers. It is the nonclassroom environments, such as zoos, art and science museums, cultural centers — or even television programs, films, and plays — that seem to vigorously stimulate the learning process. Even tragedy may have a place and value in one's environment. Ralph Waldo Emerson's observation rings true: "Bad times have a scientific value. . . . We learn geology the morning after the earthquake." Somehow these *natural* sources and realities must become part of the traditional teaching and learning environments wherever and whenever possible.

If we move in the direction in which the education process includes learning about a wide range of forms of knowledge and their applications, then education potentially has a radiant future. Moreover, the curricular content presented in school will have a relevance, meaning, and usefulness that will last a lifetime — especially as it is integrated with everyday life.

However, if we move in the opposite direction — further fragmenting, compartmentalizing, and "segregating" our disciplinary knowledge — then education will suffer greatly. Consequently, we will continue to separate this knowledge from our life experiences. We will not learn from our tragedies and bad times. Instead of growing from a "field" to an ocean filled with diverse life forms, education will become a desert — one polluted by the excesses of technological innovation with misguided applications.

Historian Arnold Toynbee wrote, "Human affairs do not become intelligible until they are seen as a whole" (1975). When one explores Toynbee's statement in the context of education, one begins to wonder whether education becomes "intelligible" until it is seen as a whole. The whole includes every facet of our individual and collective lives.

How do our models of ideal learning environments reflect the whole world and the relationship of the parts to the whole? How are our models similar to one another in terms of the vision they convey? How can we work together to invent the future of education using our ideal learning environments as a means of communication? What are some of the possibilities and challenges?

In engaging in this exercise myself, I find that there is one model in particular that has influenced my vision of education. It is the NASA Space Center model, give or take a few serious modifications. In launching a space shuttle, there are hundreds of highly specialized divisions coordinating and managing this

264

endeavor. Instead of keeping these specialized divisions apart from one another, in my model I pose the possibility of having an equal number of generalists who would be responsible for linking and integrating all of these specializations. In other words, increased specialization would not result in increased fragmentation. A common language and system of communication would prevail at all times, which would be like the glue holding all the communications together. In my model, there would be no barriers between each domain of knowledge and specialized division. Their walls would behave like semipermeable membranes, rather than rigid structures (Siler 1996*b*).

When I began to draw my plans and articulate them, I realized I was describing an orchestra and one of its melodious products, a symphony. I also realized that part of the reason that many people have trouble initiating their models and delving into the discovery process is that they do not have a general model or idea in mind that they can incorporate into their drawings, respond to, or spring from. On this point, I disagree with the painter Paul Klee's notion that "all true creation is born from nothing." There always are unseen forces of influence at work. The subconscious mind seems to naturally absorb — and create from — everything.

The models produced by this exercise teach us at least two things: 1) A connected world is healthier, more responsible, and ecologically sound, whereas a disconnected, fragmented world is dysfunctional and violent; and 2) as demonstrated by this model-building process, the arts and humanities are particularly helpful in depicting and illuminating ways in which we can integrate and share our knowledge, ideas, and experiences. Both the process and the 5-D models reveal how we might best maximize our abilities to share and transform our knowledge and ideas.

Twentieth century educational programs have produced generations of "semiconscious" people whose reflections on their personal development often are as limited as their reflections on the development of humankind and the environment. How many years of being bombarded by frightening facts on health, education, and social and ecological issues will it take to alert us to the alarming reality that many of the key pieces are missing from the puzzle of learning? This fact must be articulated more clearly and debated in our education institutions. What seems to be missing is the understanding that education — in the broadest sense — is about becoming aware through learning. It is not just about learning many subjects and disciplines; it is about learning how to synthesize, evaluate, share, and communicate knowledge and experiences. Fortunately, there are many programs under way that are sensitive to this issue of whole versus partial learning. And many are exploring the idea of teaching thinking skills in versatile ways (Nickerson et al. 1985; Niehaus 1994).

Over the years my concept of education has evolved into one of inclusion rather than exclusion. Instead of filtering out subjects and issues that may be deemed irrelevant to some other subject, I have begun to question the issue of relevancy based on how we frame our perceptions. I began to see things "out of context" or, rather, I tried to put things back in their original, broadest context. I wanted to discover the "infinite contexts" of information. In fact, nothing is "taken out of context" if the context in which we understand things is ever-changing or includes "everything." For example, I was determined to understand how something that is seen in one context as "art" can be interpreted in another context as "science." Consider, for example, Leonardo da Vinci's artistic and scientific renderings of human anatomy and physiology, or the neuroanatomist Santiago Ramon y Cajal's exquisite drawing of nerve cells. The idea of differentiating perceptions, information, and frames of reference often seemed confusing. I saw all compartmentalized teaching as creating intellectual deficits and mental blindness.

To my way of thinking, any increase in the number of specialists needs to be countered by an increase in the number of generalists. My life plan is to become a generalist who specializes in integrating various specialties. This has meant becoming a specialist trained in generalizing and theorizing. Naturally, this direction leads me to consider the possibilities of educating one's vision (Kepes 1965) and sense of unity and exploring E.M. Forster's assertion, "Only connect." Connect one's own mind to other minds. Connect one's creative energies with others' energies. Connect worldviews, regardless of differences. And, equally important, explore one's reflections on the meaning and significance of these connections.

At the Gihon Foundation's 1996 Council on Ideas, I and a small group of colleagues (which included Apple Computer visionary Alan Kay, anthropologist Mary Catherine Bateson, and the deputy national editor of the *Washington Post*, Roberto Suro) concluded that the overarching global issue today is learning. The position statement we drafted out of that gathering reads:

> Humankind is still in grade school. We don't yet know all that we need to know to flourish. But we already know enough to destroy ourselves. Every major threat we are now facing — from world population explosion to environmental pollution to violence — is linked to the problems of learning. The 1996 Council on Ideas believes that the solutions begin with the lifelong human capacity to enjoy and share the process of learning. Learning must become a means to bridge social fragmentation. Finally we need to take responsibility for the way we act on our learning.
>
> 1. Learning and education are not the same. All too often educational institutions, while trying to transmit information and skills, extinguish curiosity and the delight in learning. Learning is too important to be left to educational institutions alone.
>
> 2. To facilitate learning we must break down the barriers of compartmentalization and specialization.
>
> 3. Learning requires much more than incorporating information. It involves a continuing process of connecting information and applying it in new contexts. This includes a search for meaning and coherence.
>
> 4. The unequal distribution of learning reinforces social fragmentation and violence. Shared learning is one basic element of community.
>
> 5. Openness to learning does not entail the abandonment of traditional teachings but the ability to add, expand, compare, and integrate information. It does entail the willingness

to set aside prejudice and to think critically. We are not what we know but what we are willing to learn. We respect others not for what they know but for what they are willing to learn.

"Much learning is not understanding," wrote the fifth century Greek philosopher Heraclitus. For postmodern education to be effective and truly meaningful, it must help us learn to see and understand ourselves. This involves seeing our knowledge from many perspectives, using it in many contexts, and sharing what we have learned.

References

Ambron, S. "New Visions of Reality: Multimedia and Education." In *Interactive Multimedia: Visions of Multimedia for Developers, Educators, and Information Providers*, edited by S. Ambron and K. Hooper. Redmond, Wash.: Microsoft Press, 1988.

American Association for the Advancement of Science (AAAS). *Benchmarks for Science Literacy: Project 2061*. New York: Oxford University Press, 1993.

American Association for the Advancement of Science (AAAS). *Science for All Americans*. Washington, D.C., 1989.

Barzun, Jacques. *Begin Here: The Forgotten Conditions of Teaching and Learning*. Chicago: University of Chicago Press, 1991.

Boyer, Ernest, and Levine, Art. *Quest for Common Learning: The Aims of General Education*. Washington, D.C.: Carnegie Foundation for the Advancement of Teaching, 1981.

Bronowski, Jacob. *Science and Human Values*. New York: Harper & Row, 1956.

Bruner, Jerome S. "The Conditions of Creativity." In *Contemporary Approaches to Creative Thinking*, edited by H.E. Gruber, G. Terrell, and M. Wertheimer. New York: Atherton Press, 1962.

Carin, A.A., and Sund, R.B. *Teaching Science Through Discovery*. 4th ed. Columbus, Ohio: Merrill, 1980.

Casals, Pablo, as told to Albert E. Kahn. *Joys and Sorrows: Reflections*. New York: Simon and Schuster, 1978.

Chorover, Stephan L. *From Genesis to Genocide: The Meaning of Human Nature and the Power of Behavior Control*. Cambridge, Mass.: MIT Press, 1979.

Chorover, Stephan L. *Homework: An Environmental Literacy Primer*. Cambridge, Mass.: Collaborative Learning Systems, 1994.

Clark, B. *Optimizing Learning: The Integrative Education Model in the Classroom*. Columbus, Ohio: Merrill, 1986.

Csikszentmihalyi, Mihaly. "Society, Culture, and Person: A Systems View of Creativity." In *The Nature of Creativity: Contemporary Psychological Perspectives*, edited by R.J. Sternberg. New York: Cambridge University Press, 1988.

Csikszentmihalyi, Mihaly. *Flow: The Psychology of Optimal Experience*. New York: HarperCollins, 1990.

Einstein, Albert. *Essays in Science*. New York: Philosophical Library, 1933.

Einstein, Albert. "A Message to Intellectuals." In *Out of My Later Years*. Secaucus, N.J.: Citadel Press, 1956.

Eisler, Riane. *The Chalice and the Blade*. New York: Harper & Row, 1987.

Eisley, Loren. *The Immense Journey*. New York: Vintage, 1956.

Fuller, R. Buckminster. *Utopia or Oblivion: The Prospects for Humanity*. New York: Bantam, 1969.

Gardner, Howard. *Frames of Mind: The Theory of Multiple Intelligences*. New York: Basic Books, 1983.

Gardner, Howard. "Assessment in Context: The Alternative to Standardized Testing." In *Changing Assessments: Alternative Views of Aptitude, Achievement, Instruction*, edited by B.R. Gifford and G. O'Connor. Norwell, Mass.: Kluwer Academic, 1992.

Ginott, Haim. *Teacher and Child*. New York: Macmillan, 1972.

Goleman, Daniel. *Emotional Intelligence*. New York: Bantam, 1995.

Guilford, J.P. *The Nature of Human Intelligence*. New York: McGraw-Hill, 1967.

Hicks, John. "Technology and Aesthetic Education: A Crucial Synthesis." *Art Education* 46 (November 1993): 42-47.

Hurwitz, Al. *Asthetische Erziehung in der USA* (Art Education in the United States of America). Berlin: Hochschule der Kunste, 1994.

James, William. *Principles of Psychology*. 2 vols. New York: Dover, 1890.

Kaplan, Robert D. "The Coming Anarchy." *Atlantic Monthly* (February 1994): 44-76.

Kay, Alan. "Computers, Networks, and Education." *Scientific American* 265 (September 1991): 138.

Kepes, Gyorgy. *The New Landscape in the Arts and Sciences.* Chicago: Paul Theobald, 1956.

Kepes, Gyorgy. *The Education of Vision.* Chicago: Paul Theobald, 1965.

Koestler, Arthur. *The Act of Creation: The Art of Discovery and the Discoveries of Art.* London: Hutchinson, 1964.

Koestler, Arthur. *Insight and Outlook; An Inquiry into the Common Foundations of Science, Art, and Social Ethics.* Lincoln: University of Nebraska Press, 1965.

Kozol, Jonathan. *Death at an Early Age.* New York: Bantam, 1968.

Kozol, Jonathan. "Knocking On Heaven's Door." *Teachers Magazine* (October 1995): 29-35.

Mill, John Stuart. "On Genius." *Monthly Repository* (1832).

Montessori, Maria. *The Absorbent Mind.* Translated by Claude A. Claremont. New York: Holt, Rinehart and Winston, 1969.

Moravec, Hans. *Mind Children: The Future of Robot and Human Intelligence.* Cambridge, Mass.: Harvard University Press, 1988.

Myers, Norman, ed. *Gaia: An Atlas of Planet Management.* Garden City, N.Y.: Doubleday, Anchor Press, 1984.

Nickerson, R.; Perkins, D.N.; and Smith, E. *The Teaching of Thinking.* Hillsdale, N.J.: Lawrence Erlbaum Associates, 1985.

Niehaus, Judy H. "Learning by Framing: Increasing Understanding by Showing Students What They Already Know." *Journal of College Science Teaching* 24 (November 1994).

Oddleifson, Eric. *The Visual Artist as Artscientist: The Ghost in the Machine Made Manifest, the Arts as Legitimate Sources of Truth.* Keynote address, Wisconsin Art Education Association, Center for Arts in the Basic Curriculum, 19 March 1994.

Onosko, J.J., and Newmann, F.M. "Creating More Thoughtful Learning Environments." In *Creating Powerful Thinkers in Teachers and Students: Diverse Perspectives,* edited by J.N. Mangieri and C.C. Block. Fort Worth, Texas: Harcourt, Brace College Publishers, 1994.

Passow, Harry A. "Designing a Global Curriculum." *Gifted Child Today* 12, no. 3 (1989): 24-26.

Perkins, D.N. *Smart Schools: From Training Memories to Educating Minds.* New York: Free Press, 1992.

Plimpton, George, ed. *Writers at Work: Second Series.* New York: Viking, 1965.

Poincaré, Jules Henri. "Mathematical Creation." In *The Foundations of Science,* translated by G.B. Halstead. New York: Science Press, 1924.

270

Postman, Neil. *Technology: The Surrender of Culture to Technology.* New York: Alfred A. Knopf, 1991.

Postman, Neil. *The End of Education: Redefining the Value of School.* New York: Alfred A. Knopf, 1995.

Root-Bernstein, Robert S. "Visual Thinking: The Art of Imagining Reality." *Transactions of the American Philosophical Society* 75 (1985): 50-67.

Root-Bernstein, Robert S. "Setting the Stage for Discovery." *The Sciences* 28 (May-June 1988): 26-35.

Schell, Jonathan. *The Fate of the Earth.* New York: Avon, 1982.

Siler, Todd. "Architectonics of Thought: A Symbolic Model of Neuro-psychological Processes." Doctoral dissertation, Massachusetts Institute of Technology, 1986.

Siler, Todd. *Breaking the Mind Barrier: The Artscience of Neurocosmology.* New York: Simon and Schuster, 1990. a

Siler, Todd. "Nurturing Renaissance Thinkers: One Direction in Gifted Education." in *Education of the Gifted in the 21st Century: Applying New Ideas and Innovative Approaches to Gifted Education.* Proceedings of the Towbes Conference, Santa Barbara, California, 18-21 July 1990. b

Siler, Todd. *Cerebralism: Creating a New Millennium of Minds, Bodies and Civilizations.* New York: Ronald Feldman Fine Arts, 1993.

Siler, Todd. *Freeing Your Mind: The ArtScience Program.* Englewood, Colo.: ArtScience, 1996. a

Siler, Todd. "The ArtScience Program: Connecting Realms of Knowledge & Experience." In *1996 "Make Space for Space" Resource Guide.* Colorado Space Education Initiative (CSEI): Using Space Education to Meet Standards, The Next Millennium — Looking to the Classroom of the Future, sponsored by Ball Aerospace, the Colorado Department of Education, Lockheed Martin, and the National Aeronautics and Space Administration, 1996. b

Taylor, C.W. "The Nature of the Creative Process," in *Creativity: An Evaluation of the Creative Process*, edited by P. Smith. New York: Hastings House, 1959.

Thomson, Keith. "The Sense of Discovery and Vice Versa." *American Scientist* 71 (September-October 1983): 522-24.

Torrance, E.P. *Thinking in the Classroom: Resources for Teachers. Vol. 2: Experiences that Enhance Thoughtful Learning.* Victoria: British

271

Columbia Ministry of Education and Ministry for Multiculturalism and Human Rights, 1993.

Toynbee, Arnold J. "Vision of God's Creation." *Time*, 3 November 1975, p. 49.

Wasserman, Miriam, and Hutchinson, Linda. *Teaching Human Dignity.* Minneapolis: Education Exploration Center, 1978.

Williams, F.E. *A Total Creativity Program for Individualizing and Humanizing the Learning Process*. Englewood Cliffs, N.J.: Educational Technology, 1972.